D1246425

The Upper Room

Disciplines

1997

Lee : Doris .

Thanks for your
service in a great
year at First.

love!
Dan

The Upper Room
Disciplines
1997

Coordinating Editor
Glenda Webb

Copy Editors
Kathryn M. Armistead
E. Michael Fleenor
Janet R. Knight
Cathy Cole Wright

Proofreader
Carl Gilliam

Editorial Secretary
Betty Estes

The Upper Room Disciplines 1997

© 1996 by The Upper Room. All rights reserved.

No part of this book may be used or reproduced in any manner whatsoever without permission except in the case of brief quotations embodied in critical articles or reviews. For information write: Upper Room Books, P.O. Box 189, Nashville, TN 37202-0189

Cover photo © Frances Dorris
Cover design: Jim Bateman
Interior design, typesetting, and layout: Nancy Cole

Revised Common Lectionary copyright © 1992 by the Consultation on Common Texts (CCT). Used with permission.

Scripture quotations not otherwise identified are from the New Revised Standard Version of the Bible, © 1989 by the Division of Christian Education of the National Council of the Churches of Christ in the USA. Used by permission. All rights reserved.

Scripture quotations designated RSV are from the Revised Standard Version of the Bible, copyrighted 1946, 1952, and © 1971 by the Division of Christian Education, National Council of the Churches of Christ in the USA. Used by permission.

Scripture quotations designated TEV are from the *Good News Bible*, The Bible in Today's English Version - Old Testament: Copyright © American Bible Society 1976; New Testament: Copyright © American Bible Society 1966, 1971, 1976.

Scripture quotations designated NIV are from the *Holy Bible, New International Version*. Copyright © 1973, 1978, 1984 International Bible Society. Used by permission of Zondervan Bible Publishers.

Page 385 constitutes an extension of this copyright page.

ISBN: 0-8358-0747-9
Printed in the United States of America

CONTENTS

Foreword 11
Carolyn Stahl Bohler

January 1–5, 1997 13
Back to Basics
Justo L. González

January 6–12, 1997 18
Water, Wind, and Spirit
Linda J. Johnson

January 13–19, 1997 25
Echoes of Love
Larry J. Peacock

January 20–26, 1997 32
Responding from the Heart
Ron James

January 27–February 2, 1997 39
God's Work of Restoration
Sally Dyck

February 3–9, 1997 46
To Know God Truly
David Maldonado, Jr.

February 10–16, 1997 53
Signs of Life
Paul Barton

February 17–23, 1997 60
Our God—An Ever-Present Help
D. S. Dharmapalan

February 24–March 2, 1997 67
God's Initiative
Thomas R. Hawkins

March 3–9, 1997 74
From Death to Eternal Life
Jerry L. McGlone

March 10–16, 1997 81
The Shaping of a New Heart
Elizabeth Nordquist

March 17–23, 1997 88
Praise and Passion
Mary Lou Santillán Baert

March 24–30, 1997 95
Holy Week
M. Garlinda Burton

March 31–April 6, 1997 102
That You May Believe
Willis H. Moore

April 7–13, 1997 109
God in Us
Pedro A. Sandín-Fremaint

April 14–20, 1997 116
By What Power?
James A. Harnish

April 21–27, 1997 123
God's Great Love for Us
Richard H. Schmidt

April 28–May 4, 1997 130
Living Victoriously
Chan-Hie Kim

May 5–11, 1997 137
Following Instructions
Linda Worthington

May 12–18, 1997 144
The Holy Spirit Today
J. Ellsworth Kalas

May 19–25, 1997 151
We Experience the Trinity
John O. Gooch

May 26–June 1, 1997 158
Responding to God
Trudy Flenniken

June 2–8, 1997 165
The Bible's Wisdom on Leadership
Grant Hagiya

June 9–15, 1997 172
God Always Has a Plan
A. Safiyah Fosua

June 16–22, 1997 179
Courage in the Face of Opposition
Robert V. Dodd

June 23–29, 1997 186
In Giving, We Receive
Robert K. Smyth

June 30–July 6, 1997 193
Encounter Power
Mamie Ko

July 7–13, 1997 200
Choices
Mary A. Avram

July 14–20, 1997 207
God's New Household
David Lowes Watson

July 21–27, 1997 214
Empty or Full?
Trudy M. Archambeau

July 28–August 3, 1997 221
Rags to Riches
Alec Gilmore

August 4–10, 1997 228
Offering up My Relationships
Gerrit Dawson

August 11–17, 1997 235
Living Wisely
Catherine Gunsalus González

August 18–24, 1997 242
A Refuge for the Redeemed
Kenneth L. Waters, Sr.

August 25–31, 1997 249
The Internals of Faith
Will H. Willimon

September 1–7, 1997 256
Faith Enacted
John Indermark

September 8–14, 1997 264
God's Wisdom
Wightman Weese

September 15–21, 1997 271
Models of Goodness
Raymond K. DeHainaut

September 22–28, 1997 278
Tools of the Trade
Susan Ives Spieth

September 29–October 5, 1997 285
Living with Integrity
Sister Barbara Jean, SHN

October 6–12, 1997 292
When God Seems Far Away
Richard Bowyer

October 13–19, 1997 299
Dependence, Obedience, and Freedom
Larry R. Kalajainen

October 20–26, 1997 306
The Loving Mercies of Our Lord
Arturio Mariscal

October 27–November 2, 1997 313
The Saints—Past, Present, and Future
Betsy Schwarzentraub

November 3–9, 1997 320
Give to Really Live
Charles B. Simmons

November 10–16, 1997 327
In Covenant with God
Hugo Luciano López

November 17–23, 1997 334
Being God's Kingdom
Charles A. Waugaman

November 24–30, 1997 341
Staying on the Path
Yolanda Pupo-Ortíz

December 1–7, 1997 348
Forerunners of God's Reign
John D. Copenhaver, Jr.

December 8–14, 1997 355
Awaken to God's Presence with Joy
Judith Freeman Clark

December 15–21, 1997 362
Expecting the Unexpected
M. Robert Mulholland

December 22–28, 1997 369
Wearing the Clothes of Christ
Phyllis Tyler-Wayman

December 29–31, 1997 376
The Fullness of the Word
Cindy Schnasa Jacobsen and David Schnasa Jacobsen

The Revised Common Lectionary 1997 379
(*Disciplines* Edition)

FOREWORD

Some of our prayers fall with the tears that we shed into our pillows at night. Some of our prayers embed themselves in our wide-eyed wonder when we witness beauty—in nature or art.

Some of our prayers are repetitious affirmations in the midst of a difficult task. Sometimes we pray by holding in mind focused images of hopeful outcomes: completed peace accords, successful surgical procedures, the healing of communities, wisdom for families that face conflict.

We express many of our prayers communally during worship through the liturgy, the prayers, and the comingling of silent yearnings with thoughts of God.

The "prayers" in *Disciplines 1997* begin with scripture, the biblical readings of the ecumenical lectionary texts throughout the year. Reading these passages, reflections, and prayers is like "praying the scripture" or the process of "devotional exegesis."

We take the passages seriously on their own terms as much as possible, even within their own contexts. Yet we do not stay there. We attend also to our own context and worldviews in order to grasp divine wisdom for how these passages (or the themes that they address) can offer guidance, consolation, or challenge for us today. The fact that we meditate upon these thoughts with thousands of others around the world enhances our sense of community and purpose. We share with contemporaries while praying out of an ancient tradition.

Something about the discipline of praying daily, regularly, adds to these devotions. We are intentionally aligning ourselves daily with the desire to follow God's intent. We root the chaos around us in order. We center our days.

Prayer is an activity, conscious communication with God. Its value depends upon the intent, purpose, mood, and goal of the prayer. We can enlist our imagination to bring the passages to life

11

or keep a diary of feelings and thoughts. Especially if we are not self-conscious—and alone—we can read some of these biblical passages and prayers, then act out or dance the meanings.

Prayer is private, interpersonal, and public. We can find a solitary moment or, with a partner, share our readings. We can seek silence to read or listen to music simultaneously. (It's even possible to practice *Disciplines 1997* while waiting for soccer games to begin.) Make *Disciplines 1997* yours. Avoid putting this practice on your "to do" list, something to feel guilty about not doing. It can be a grace-filled discipline.

—CAROLYN STAHL BOHLER

Emma Sanborn Tousant Professor
of Pastoral Theology and Counseling
United Theological Seminary

January 1–5, 1997   **Justo L. González**✤
Wednesday, January 1   Read Revelation 21:1-6*a*.

New Year's Day

Few occasions remind us of the passing of time as strongly as New Year's Day. Our soon-forgotten resolutions of last year have passed as have the good times, which are now memories. Thus, the new year, which is a time of rejoicing in new beginnings, often is also a time of sadness and nostalgia when we remember times past, people who are no longer with us, hope laid aside or even forgotten. For most of us, the passing of all things is a reason for sadness.

For the writer of Revelation, the passing of all things also gives reason to rejoice. Even after the passing of this heaven and this earth, God has promised a new heaven and a new earth. These will not be fleeting like the present heaven and earth. They will not be places of weeping and struggle where nothing is ever complete.

As we look at the past and begin to think about the new year opening before us, let us remember the longer future, the final end of all things and all of life. Here lies our ultimate hope—that God will wipe away every tear from our eyes. "Death will be no more; mourning and crying and pain will be no more."

As we begin a new year, we look to the future with hope and expectation. Let us look with hope to the future beyond all futures. Let us look with a hope that no one can take from us—that God will even wipe every tear from our eyes!

Prayer: **Teach me, Lord, to trust in the future you have promised that my life may be filled with joy and hope. Amen.**

✤Retired clergy, Río Grande Annual Conference of The United Methodist Church; resides in Decatur, Georgia.

13

Thursday, January 2   Read John 1:10-18.

Our text yesterday spoke of a future hope in which we can live in the present, knowing that God's promises will be fulfilled. Today's reading brings our hope and joy much closer. It speaks not only of a future hope but also of a hope already fulfilled: "The Word became flesh and lived among us, and we have seen his glory." In a sense, we no longer have to wait until the day when "a new heaven and a new earth" will come down from heaven. The Creator of heaven and earth, through whom "all things were made," has come to be one of us. We await God's future with hope and joy because in Jesus and in our fellowship with him we have come to know God's purposes, and we have experienced them to be purposes of love and joy.

We are beginning a new year. We have made resolutions, many of which we will not keep. Eventually we will feel guilty because we have abandoned our best resolutions. Many of us may have become so despondent over our inability to keep past resolutions that this year we did not even make any. Yet this week's lections remind us that we need not allow our past failures to enslave us. God offers the possibility of a new beginning. This is the meaning of forgiveness.

Today's reading reminds us of something else that is equally important: When we make a new beginning, we do not do so alone. We are not just starting over; we are starting now in the company of the New Beginning, Jesus Christ. We dare to live in hope; we dare to decide to renew our lives because we are not alone. In Jesus Christ, the Word made flesh, there is a new beginning and the power for *us* to begin anew!

Prayer: **Thank you, dear God, that as we begin a new year we know that we shall not have to traverse the days and nights alone. We thank you that in Jesus Christ you stand with us in this and all our new beginnings. In his name we pray. Amen.**

14

Friday, January 3   Read Psalm 147:12-20.

We are able to make new beginnings thanks to God's forgiveness, God's promise, and God's presence with us in Jesus Christ. Today's psalm begins and ends with a call to praise. But between that beginning and that end, the subject of every sentence is God. Read the psalm again. It does not call us to do anything more than to praise. It says little about "Jerusalem" or "Zion"—the people of God who were the original singers of the psalm, but it says much about God.

This psalm serves as an important reminder. Often we are so concerned about doing what is right, about being forgiven, about growing in spirituality, and about being saved that we place ourselves—not God—at the center of our faith. Our questions revolve around ourselves: What must I do to please God? How can I be forgiven for my sin? What must I do to be saved?

All these matters are important, but God is infinitely more important. When we meet and come to know God, the proper response is one of awe and praise. At that point, we are no longer the subject of most of our sentences; instead God is the subject and the center of our concern and our praise. This is the true content of praise.

Suggestion for meditation: **As I go through the hours of today, I will look for all the reasons I have to praise God. And praise!**

Prayer: **I praise you, O God, for life and for the freshness of this new year and of this new day. Praise to you for all your bounty we see. And praise to you for what I do not see but know is there. Praise! Praise! Praise! Amen.**

Saturday, January 4   Read Ephesians 1:3-10.

God's plan is "for the fullness of time, to gather up all things in him [Christ], things in heaven and things on earth."

As I was growing up in Havana, Cuba, I was walking across a cemetery one evening. For the first time I noticed a theme in many of the monuments covering the tombs: a broken obelisk—the top missing—with a heavy cloth draped over it. These monuments referred to lives that had ended abruptly, full of unfulfilled promise, leaving survivors with the mystery of what might have been.

I was in a particularly meditative mood that evening, and as I looked at those monuments and read the inscriptions under them it occurred to me that those obelisks represent much of our lives. There are so many things left unfinished! Unfinished are many of last year's resolutions. Unfinished are many projects we undertook, many relationships we entered, many efforts that for a while seemed important but now have been forgotten.

Yet this text tells us that God's eternal and mysterious plan is somehow to bring *all things* to completion in Jesus Christ, to gather them all up in him. (A more literal translation would be "to make Christ the head or completion of all things.")

In Christ there are no unfinished obelisks; no meaningless, uncompleted loose ends. We do not quite understand how this will be, but we trust. And we know that in him all that is unfulfilled will find fulfillment, all in our lives that is incomplete will find completion! And in this knowledge we rejoice!

Prayer: **I thank you, God, that you have given me a glimpse of your eternal purpose to bring together all things in Christ, so that in him all things—even my incomplete life, find completion. Let it be so! Amen.**

Sunday, January 5   Read Ephesians 1:3-14.

Today's reading is the longest sentence in the Bible. The New Revised Standard Version divides it into five sentences, as do other English translations, because in modern English we have difficulties with such long sentences. However, in the original Greek it is a single sentence—from verse 3 to verse 14!

This passage is also an enormously inclusive sentence. Read it slowly and carefully. Notice that it includes things that took place "before the foundation of the world," as well as things that will take place in the final consummation of all things.

Much of this is difficult to understand, even impossible to understand! We can only form a vague idea of what the words "before the foundation of the world" mean. That is why the word *mystery* stands at the center of the sentence. It is a mystery that has been revealed but still remains mysterious, for we cannot understand its full implication.

Two things, however, we can understand. The first is that this long sentence clearly tells us that all things, from beginning to end, are in the hands of God—of the God whose love we have known in Jesus Christ. Even though we may not understand it all, we have no reason to fear, for we are certain that it is all in the hands of the One who loves us.

The second is that this sentence begins and ends with a word of praise. Even though we may not understand all of it, we certainly can understand that the vast scope of God's grace and God's overarching power over all of creation and all of history is a motive for praise. Thus, with the writer of the epistle, we can exclaim, "Blessed be the God and Father of our Lord Jesus Christ"!

Prayer: **Blessed be you, my God, Father of my Lord Jesus Christ, who has blessed me with God's love, which reaches beyond all ages! Amen.**

January 6–12, 1997   **Linda J. Johnson✤**
Monday, January 6   Read Isaiah 60:1-6;
                              Ephesians 3:1-12; Matthew 2:1-12.

Epiphany, observed on January 6, begins the liturgical season that celebrates God's manifestation in Jesus and explores who Jesus is. Who is this child, born to an unmarried mother and an adopted father, announced by angels and visited by nobility?

After Jesus' birth, wise men from the East came to Jerusalem looking for him. They went to the palace since they were expecting to find him among royalty. What they found was a king who knew nothing of this new baby king and who was frightened by the very thought, especially when his scribes verified the prophecy that a king, the Messiah, would be born in Bethlehem (see Mic. 5:2). Leaving Herod, the wise men followed the star until it stopped over the place where the child was, and "they were overwhelmed with joy."

Already the meaning of God's manifestation in Jesus is being made known. The Magi were Gentiles, and they came to the light of Christ soon after his birth. Lest we forget, we too are Gentiles. We were once the strange outsiders, aliens to the covenant of promise. Can we imagine what it would feel like to be left out of God's promise? If so, then perhaps we can gain empathy toward those we now consider outsiders. Perhaps we also can rekindle the joy of the Magi in now being participants in God's manifestation in Jesus.

Suggestion for meditation: **Give thanks to God for being included.**

✤Minister of Development, Miriam's Promise: Pregnancy, Parenting, and Adoption Services, an agency of the Tennessee Annual Conference of The United Methodist Church; Nashville, Tennessee.

Tuesday, January 7   Read Genesis 1:1-5.

Imagine a dark, watery chaos; the waters surging, threatening, rebellious. The earth is a void, formless. Picture a wind breathed from God, sweeping over the surface of the water. See God's breath blowing the chaotic waters back to make a space that is dry and safe for life. Hear God's voice say, "Let there be light."

To bring order out of chaos, shape out of formlessness, God used wind. We may interpret the Hebrew term *ruah* to mean either wind or spirit. It is God's life-force blowing a new world into being. It is the same spirit that blew the church into being at Pentecost, that gives new life in baptism.

Made in the image of God, we know something of God's work in creation. When expecting a new baby, parents begin to make things ready. From painting the nursery to buying diapers, we prepare for the advent of a new life.

On the first day of creation, God began to ready things for a life-friendly world. If we consider the genius of the life cycle, the interdependence of all nature; if we reflect on the teeming life in an inch of earth; if we've ever witnessed the miracle of birth or the dignity of death—then we surely are awed by God's glorious creation. In our age of discovering new planets and dropping old ones, may we realize that the mystery of God far exceeds our imagination.

Prayer: **Creator God, blow your breath of calm and order across the chaos of my life. Speak light into my darkness. Recreate me in your image and give me a new beginning. Amen.**

Wednesday, January 8   Read Psalm 29.

Read Psalm 29 aloud with expression; give your imagination full rein. The ancient Israelites probably used this psalm in worship as part of the fall festival—a new year's celebration and a time to anticipate the rains of autumn.

The liturgy begins with a call to worship, a call to members of the heavenly council to give glory to the Lord. We often find the term *glory* in priestly literature when speaking of a theophany, or appearance, of God. This appearance occurs within the life of the people.

The body of the psalm describes the manner in which God appears. The powerful God of glory appears over the mighty waters. The voice of the Lord creates such a storm that mighty trees are broken and mountains appear to skip around. Oaks whirl, and the forest is stripped bare.

In Genesis God calmed the turbulent waters and pushed them back to make room for life. In this psalm God appears in the storm, churning the water, bending the oaks, shaking the land with divine thunder. Still, the purpose is life. God brings life-sustaining rain to the land.

It is one thing to ask God to stand by us when the storms of life are raging. It is another to see God *in* the storm. It is a powerful image to think of the people gathered in the Temple. While the wind howls and the thunder roars, the people cry, "Glory!" The storm may be frightening; but when we view the storm through the eyes of faith, we see the larger picture. The storm brings the rain that promotes growth.

Prayer: **God of glory, storm into the barren places of my life and bring refreshing rain. Amen.**

Thursday, January 9   Read Acts 19:1-7.

Paul found unusual disciples in Ephesus. Their baptism was at the hands of John, a baptism of repentance. Paul had to fill in the missing pages of their book of faith, telling them that John baptized with the baptism of repentance to prepare the way for faith in Jesus.

After Paul proclaimed Jesus, the Ephesians received baptism in Jesus' name. Then Paul laid his hands on them, and they received the Holy Spirit. The Spirit gave them power to prophesy and speak in tongues.

The Christians in the church at Ephesus were already believers. They had fulfilled their understanding of the requirements of faith, but their understanding stopped short of the critical nature of God's work in Christ. Their understanding lacked both knowledge and experience of the Spirit.

Today many persons long for something called spirituality. Within the church, people long for a faith that is more vital, more alive. Outside the church, people search for answers to their spiritual questions, spiritual food for their spiritual hunger. The believers at Ephesus received from Paul the Word proclaimed and the sacrament of baptism; but they received from God the gift of the Spirit, which gave them a new depth of worship and a new power of discipleship.

In what ways does our understanding of faith's power stop short? In what areas have we assumed that we know all there is to know? Where have we settled for a mediocre life of faith, missing out on the possibilities of spiritual power? What in our lives evidences our readiness to move to a deeper spirituality, a more active discipleship?

Prayer: **God of power, blow new life into my faith. Fill me with your Spirit. Keep me from stopping short of your possibilities in me. Amen.**

21

Friday, January 10   Read Mark 1:4-11.

From the beginning of his narrative, Mark gets right to the point: "The beginning of the good news of Jesus Christ, the Son of God." With no angels or shepherds or kings to set the stage, Mark launches Jesus into public life as an adult. His first act is to be baptized by John the Baptizer, that woolly wild man from the wilderness who preached a baptism of repentance.

When Jesus comes out of the baptismal waters, he sees the heavens rip apart and the Spirit drifting dovelike upon him. The heavenly voice declares Jesus as "my Son, the Beloved."

The Spirit, God's life-force that ordered creation out of chaos, now creates something new. The heavens' splitting, the Spirit's descending, the voice's declaration: all signs of the beginning of a new age. God is doing something new in Jesus. The heavenly voice declares it. The disciples and the early church knew it; they had to give up the old to be part of the new.

Often the times don't feel like a new age. Politicians still argue according to party lines instead of for the good of the people. Too many children are denied the innocence of a childhood protected and free. War and terrorism have not ended. It might be tempting to give in to despair and cynicism if not for baptism. In baptism we see God's grace at work. We celebrate God's cleansing and renewing power. The primal waters of chaos have been rolled back. The cleansing water of baptism promises new life in a new age.

Prayer: **God of creation, give me baptism faith to live the new life of the Spirit in the midst of this weary old world. Give me strength to let go of the old ways as I walk ever more boldly in the new ways of Christ. Amen.**

Saturday, January 11   Read Mark 1:4-11.

When John baptized Jesus, the voice of God named Jesus beloved Son. God the Creator claimed a parent-child relationship with Jesus. The relationship between parent and child is the most intimate and permanent kind of relationship we know of in our human realm. One feature of this relationship is that the child receives more than she or he gives. Ideally the child receives unconditional love, the kind of love that accepts, forgives, endures. Parent love should provide the security that allows a child to flourish amid the challenges of growing up. None of us received perfect love as children; we have not provided perfect love as parents, but it is our aim.

At Jesus' baptism, God lays claim on Jesus as the beloved Son, the one to witness to the world what God is like and what God intends for us. The parable of the loving father (Luke 15:11-32) reveals the kind of relationship God has established with us. Before the son reaches home to beg for forgiveness, the father runs to meet him, rejoicing in his return, ready to celebrate.

In Christ, God runs to meet us, reaching out to us. In baptism God adopts us as daughters and sons. God claims us as God's children and promises a grace that will surround us all our days. That grace offers the assurance that we are loved and cared for, never forgotten, always forgiven, never alone.

Prayer: **God of Grace, I may be a grown-up now with children and grandchildren of my own, but I never outgrow my need to be loved. Help me remember your love anew. Amen.**

Sunday, January 12   Read Acts 19:1-7; Mark 1:4-11.

As the pastor of Walnut Grove United Methodist Church, one of my monthly responsibilities was to interview people for the "Mystery Person" column in our newsletter. To do so was a joy because I got to know people better; besides, I heard some great stories.

One day in October I interviewed an eighty-year-old woman named Mary. Mary told me many stories of her life on the farm in Tennessee, including the story of her baptism. She described the beautiful weather that day, the dress she wore, the shoes and the bonnet. She told me who was there and about all the good food they ate after church. Then she told me about how they passed her around until everybody got to hold her. It was a great day, she said. She would never forget it.

I felt a little confused. "You remember your baptism?" I asked. She nodded. "And you were a baby?" I asked. She nodded. "You must have been told the story of your baptism so often that you think you remember it," I suggested. "No," she said. "I remember it as though it were yesterday. It was a wonderful day. They passed me around until everybody got to hold me. Everybody wanted to hold me. They stood around in a big group smiling at me. I'll never forget the day I was baptized." And she smiled a warm secret smile, the memory of her baptism sustaining her still.

"Remember your baptism and be thankful."*

Prayer: **Gracious God, keep me in the ever-present memory of my baptism that I may live with the assurance of your Spirit in my life, that I may trust your forgiving grace, and that I may never forget that I am a beloved member of your family. Amen.**

---

*From the ritual reaffirmation of the Baptismal Covenant, *The United Methodist Hymnal* (Nashville: The United Methodist Publishing House, 1989), 37.

January 13–19, 1997   **Larry J. Peacock**✣
Monday, January 13   Read Psalm 139:13-18.

A wise spiritual director told me to lay aside all the books I had brought to read on a week-long retreat and begin by reading and praying Psalm 139. It was a wise word to me—and a good one for us this week. God's love for us permeates verses 1-18. God searches us and examines us. God knows us and forms us even while each of us is in our mother's womb. This week's scripture echoes this awesome and incomprehensible love of God.

Begin with praise. There are external and objective reasons to praise the Creator of the universe, but the poet is wonderfully personal in this psalm. The psalmist reflects on being created, formed, knit together in the womb by God. Such awareness elicits praise. "A wonder am I" (v. 14, JB). All of me is created to be wonderful. We are God's delight, the apple of God's eye (Psalm 17:8). Indeed, everything that God has created is wonderful. We are all "fearfully and wonderfully made" and connected to the source of creation. The appropriate posture is one of praise.

God touches not only the beginning of life but all the days of one's life. The hint of predestination in the thought that our days are written already in God's book is more likely the psalmist's reflection that all one's days have been and are under the scrutiny and care of an amazing God. So the psalmist concludes with reverential wonder at the greatness of God, who though personal and loving is still beyond grasp and comprehension.

Suggestion for meditation: **In a period of silent prayer repeat either, "I am God's delight" or "A wonder am I." End your prayer time with a word of praise and gratitude for God who created you and continues to form you.**

✣Copastor, Malibu United Methodist Church, Malibu, California; author, retreat leader, and publisher.

Tuesday, January 14   Read 1 Corinthians 6:12-20.

"Do you not know that your bodies are members of Christ?" Thus Paul addresses a group of believers who seem to have forgotten that they are "fearfully and wonderfully made" by the loving touch of the Creator. This group in the Corinthian fellowship was pushing Paul's theme of freedom in Christ beyond its intentions. They were separating the body from the spirit, and by elevating the spiritual they claimed it did not matter so much what the body did. By their devious reasoning, how much one ate and who one slept with were no major concern to the wider community. After all, they argued, "All things are lawful."

Paul calls the minority back to wholeness. Our bodies, minds, and spirits are connected within the human personality and linked to the body of Christ. Our Monday behaviors and Saturday night flings are connected to our Sunday prayers. Our body, mind, and spirit are part of the gift of God and under the rule of the risen Christ. The body is not merely physical; it is the temple of God. God delighted in making us with bodies—bodies that run and dance, make love and enjoy good food, skip and jump, hug and laugh. So Paul advises us to glorify God by taking care of our bodies, shunning sexual immorality, and honoring the precious gift of our relationships.

Prayer: **Loving God, we see the pain of broken relationships, we read the reports of sexual abuse even in the church family, and we know the temptations that abound. Keep us in your loving embrace so that our thoughts may be pure, our eyes may see you in all and in each, and our hearts may be filled with your joy. Loving God, help us to glorify you in our thoughts, words, and deeds. Amen.**

Wednesday, January 15   Read Psalm 139:1-6.

I climbed the hill behind the retreat center and found an isolated spot to sit and pray. The high desert country was quiet, except for a few birds and a few flies that buzzed. There in the silence, in the depths of my being, I heard God call my name. I felt known and loved. God had listened to the complaints that I had just reeled off and now called my name, assured me of love, chided me gently, and encouraged me to go back and continue the ministry to which I had been called.

Like the psalmist, I discovered that it is an awesome and somewhat frightening thing to be known by God. God's complete knowledge staggers the psalmist—God knows our rising, sitting, and lying down; God knows the words before we speak them; God even knows the thoughts we harbor. Such knowledge is both comforting and discomforting to the psalmist and is often so to us. God's hand is always there to guide us and hold us (vv. 5, 10). Such knowledge is wonderful.

Yet sometimes we do not wish all our thoughts known, all our deeds seen, all our words heard. It is like being hemmed in, behind and before. Even if we wished to hide our error and sin, God searches for us (vv. 1, 7). But thank God that the One who searches us, who knows us inside and out, is also the One who loves us with a love that goes to the depths of our despair, to the farthest corners of our darkness, to the silent places of our hiding, and to the pinnacles of our joy.

Such knowledge is wonderful beyond compare. Even as we are known, faults and all, so are we loved. We are known by name and loved by the Holy One, who formed us in the beginning. So again we take our place in worship and take the posture of praise.

Prayer: **Tender Friend, you know me and love me. Place your hand upon me and let me feel your blessing throughout this day. Bless my rising to activity, my sitting with others, and my lying down to rest in peace. And let my life be a blessing to others. Amen.**

Thursday, January 16   Read John 1:43-51.

Nathanael would fit right into much of contemporary North American society. His first words are skeptical, "Can anything good come out of Nazareth?" He echoes the doubts of many U. S. citizens. Can Washington, D.C. produce significant change? Can politicians keep their hands clean? Can any leader lead us in compassion for the homeless and justice for the poor and oppressed?

Philip takes a skeptical yet searching Nathanael to see Jesus. Jesus knows Nathanael like God knew the psalmist. Jesus sees through the cynicism and sees one without deceit or guile. Here is one like the trickster Jacob of Hebrew Scriptures, who is capable of seeing the truth.

Such knowledge of himself is astounding to Nathanael. "Where did you get to know me?" he asks. Again Jesus refers to the Hebrew Scriptures and knows that when Nathanael was sitting under the fig tree he was meditating on peace and the One who was to bring the reign of peace (Mic. 4:4). Nathanael is amazed that Jesus could see the depths of his heart, know the longing in his prayer. Yet he catches the messianic hints in Jesus' words and sees in Jesus the One who is promised, the One who will transform all people. He confesses his faith, and Jesus tells him that he shall see even more, shall see into the heights of heaven.

To be known and loved is a transforming experience. It calls us from skepticism to belief, from caution to action, from despair to hope. Jesus knows us, loves us, calls us, and leads us to the realms beyond.

Suggestion for meditation: **Imagine yourself sitting under a tree deep in prayer, when Jesus comes, calls you by name, and asks to sit with you. Open your heart to him.**

Friday, January 17   Read 1 Samuel 3:1-10.

God's call comes to each of us. It may come as a sudden experience like Paul's on the road to Damascus or as a persistent beckoning like the four calls to Samuel. God often speaks in the language of everyday events. Our conversations with others, the walk to the mailbox, a night rich with dreams, even the seemingly chance encounter may hold a clue to God's call. God works in and through many events.

Sometimes God calls us to do something we feel inclined toward. Other times God invites us to walk out in faith, trusting in God's empowerment. Usually a call carries a summons to be of service to others. Always a call involves listening and obeying.

But listening is not always easy. Evidently the art of listening to God was neglected in Eli and Samuel's time. Seldom was the word of God heard. They were out of practice, so Samuel did not know that it was God calling the first three times. Finally, Eli reached back into his memory and remembered that God used to call. His two sons had forgotten how to listen, but maybe not this young boy Samuel. Perhaps he would hear again the voice of God and bring a message back to the people. Thus the word of God that Samuel heard "came to all Israel" (1 Sam. 4:1).

We need to recover the art of listening. "If we go on listening, we feel God pulling us, drawing us into another current, a larger, deeper, stronger one than our usual little force."*

God calls each of us. God is continually drawing us into the deeper current.

Suggestion for meditation: **Remember a time you felt God's presence, heard God's call. Give thanks. End your prayer time by repeating, "Speak, Holy God, your servant is listening." Take a few moments to listen in silence.**

---

*Ann Ulanov and Barry Ulanov, *Primary Speech* (Atlanta: John Know Press, 1982), 9.

Saturday, January 18   Read John 1:43-51.

Follow me. Two words, simple and direct, spoken by Jesus, which have the power to change the course of a person's life and even alter the course of human history. *Follow me.* A Saint Francis leaves the comfortable life and becomes a fool for Christ, befriending the poor, loving all creatures and creations. *Follow me.* A Mother Teresa sees the face of Christ in the dying of India and discovers a shift in her vocation that has captivated the world. *Follow me.* A Martin Luther King, Jr., hears a new call in the action of a Rosa Parks, who refuses to sit in the back of the bus, and thus becomes a drum major for justice and a prophet to the nation.

Follow me. According to the scripture, from this call Philip becomes a disciple and evangelist—for God's call usually involves ministry on behalf of the loving God, in service to all God's creation. Philip searches for Nathanael and tells him, "We have found him about whom Moses . . . and also the prophets wrote." Philip carries the good news of Jesus Christ to Samaria (Acts 8:5) and opens the word to the Ethiopian eunuch (Acts 8:26-40). *Follow me.* Philip's own world is changed forever. He is a follower, a listener, a disciple. And the people that he meets are affected forever because he's a channel of God's love, a minister of the word, a teller of the good news.

In the days of Samuel, "The word of the LORD was rare" (1 Sam. 3:1); but now in Jesus Christ, the word of God is alive and active. It searches for us, finds us, and calls us again and again to "follow me."

Suggestion for mediation: **Philip tells Nathanael, "Come and see." Imagine in your mind's eye that a friend is taking you to Jesus. See Jesus waiting for you, beckoning you to come and sit awhile. Tell Jesus you want to follow him. Ask for his guidance. Listen for his response. Let him give you a blessing before you go. Thank Jesus. Thank your friend.**

30

Sunday, January 19   Read 1 Samuel 3:1-10.

Priestly tasks and prophetic calls are woven in this passage. Eli is preparing Samuel for priestly duties. No doubt he is instructing him in the performance of the rituals and the offering of appropriate sacrifices. Samuel learns to care for the ark, to keep the lamps lighted, and to counsel the community of faith. He sleeps near the ark; thus, he is constantly in the presence of God. We would say he is being formed, shaped, trained for God's service.

Yet the prophetic word weaves its way into this priestly path. The remark that visions were not widespread at the time lets us know that prophets have been rare. Whereas priests were usually born into or given to the priestly role, prophets were usually called in dreams or visions. Though Samuel was preparing to be a priest, he is called to the prophetic office. His first word from God is against his mentor, the priest Eli. Such is often the hard task of the prophet.

All week we have considered the echoes of love—the confirmation and fuller development in the New Testament of various themes from the Hebrew Scriptures. We return now on this holy day to the ways we have been formed in love and for love. Though we are not all priests, we can live out a priestly care for others and a reverence for things that are holy. Though we are not all prophets, we can speak on behalf of the poor, work with the forgotten, and challenge the principalities and powers. Though we are not Samuel, we can keep close to God through worship, prayer, scripture study, and service. With open hearts and sensitive spirits, we can be ready when God calls us by name.

Prayer: **Holy God, on this day of worship keep me near, hold me in your tender embrace, and open my ears and heart to receive your word. Amen.**

31

RESPONDING FROM THE HEART

January 20–26, 1997   **Ron James***
Monday, January 20   Read Jonah 3:1-5.

Jonah didn't respond well the first time God called. He didn't like the Ninevites one bit, so he sailed from Joppa in the opposite direction, resisting the divine mandate. Was he in for a surprise! When a storm came roaring in, he advised the crew to throw him overboard to save the ship. They didn't hesitate, and the next thing he knew he was in the belly of the great fish.

As always, our human extremity becomes God's opportunity. When life brings us into darkness and distress, to the door of death, we see things differently. No wonder the psalmist wrote, "Out of the depths I cry to you, O LORD" (130:1). When the fish spit Jonah out upon the beach, or when you and I are delivered from whatever chaos has engulfed us, our response to God changes forever. Then we understand the psalmist's experience of God as rock and salvation!

Now at God's second call, Jonah, in ready response, put on his walkin' shoes to make tracks for Nineveh. Spirit chastened, soul deepened, he trod the length and breadth of that great Gentile city proclaiming the redemptive word of God. Because the messenger felt the fire in his bones, "The people of Nineveh believed God," and the city was saved.

Prayer: **Teach me your truth in the dark places of my life, God, my rock. Amen.**

---

*Retired Presbyterian minister and author who lives in western Colorado.

Tuesday, January 21   Read Psalm 62:5-12.

The ringing affirmation with which this passage begins leaves us with no doubt about the writer's spiritual ground. For the psalmist, God is like the substratum of the world, the immovable rock on which ultimate reality rests. Should everything else shake, this remains firm.

Here we have the age-old conviction of the person of faith: that an invisible world underlies the visible; that the supportive breath of the Creator forms, informs, and indwells the tangible, the material, the sensate. No matter how deep the darkness, we are never alone for it is God's world. These opening verses make their timeless appeal and embrace the reader with their emotive power: "For God alone my soul waits in silence. . . . He alone is my rock." They elicit a response that rises up from the heart like a clear artesian spring.

The psalmist's poetry conveys the real-life trouble of the time, perhaps political struggles in places of national leadership. As always, some use public office for personal gain; while for others, the primary concern is social distinction. The latter is a delusion, and both receive just recompense from God, so we are informed. Though these storms may roll across the politics of the time, beneath that raging water lies the psalmist's rock foundation.

And what a rock for us as well, to know that beneath our own times of turmoil lies the great reality of God, affirmed by the psalm: "Power belongs to God, and steadfast love belongs to you, O LORD." And we respond, "O God, my rock!"

Prayer: **Lord, you are my peace and joy. Amen.**

Wednesday, January 22   Read 1 Corinthians 7:29-31.

Here we have a passage about focus. How does the Christian balance or focus life energies between this world and the world to come, between the secular and the sacred? How is one to respond to the demands of each? What is fascinating here is the extent to which Paul's passionate but mistaken view that the *parousia*, the second coming of Christ, is imminent distorts the passage. Were this not so, the text's advice is most difficult. (His view does seem to moderate in later epistles.) Surely it is neither the Christian duty of husbands to behave as though they had no wives, nor is it normal or acceptable to act as if mourning and rejoicing were irrelevant to this human journey. Indeed, they are critically important.

Most of us do not regard Christianity as basically world-denying. It has an abundance of pain and darkness, but we accept God's pronouncement about the creation in Genesis, "It [is] very good!" Jesus heartily affirmed human life. Its mystery, beauty, and grandeur are beyond description.

How, then, are we to treat these verses? Perhaps we simply need to read Paul's heart. In and around his words is the clear implication, "Do not treat this world as if it were the only reality." It is beautiful, but we are just passing through. Do not let the temporal obscure the eternal, give the body more significance than the spirit. How are we to respond? There is only one place of final rest and trust—in the embrace of God.

Prayer: **Your touch has left beauty and mystery everywhere, Creator God. Touch my life as well. Amen.**

Thursday, January 23   Read Mark 1:14-15.

The call of Christ. Customarily that phrase means the call of Christ *to us*: to our awakening, conversion, discipleship, service, eternal life. But our text focuses on Jesus' response to his own call from God. He is our brother in this as well. His call, of course, is the reason he "came to Galilee, proclaiming the good news of God." Confirmed as Son of God in his baptism, tested in the refining fires of the wilderness temptation, Jesus now announces the beginning of his public ministry. At the threshold of the work God has set before him, this is his moment—a crystal moment— to which he brings passionate intention. "The time is fulfilled"!

Perhaps we do not perceive the gemlike quality of these verses. They are clarion in tone and brilliantly clear, a message no Jew could fail to understand. Jesus' whole message comes in a single flashing sentence, imperative in tone, joyful in quality. That which the prophets had foretold, always in the indefinable future, is now present, at the doors, rising in Israel's life like a new dawn: the sovereign presence of God, the kingdom. Its emissary is Jesus.

I can remember my own response to the call of God: the moments of awakening, consciousness of the Presence, a growing desire to share my discovery, and that first parish after years of preparation. What expectation! Remember your own response to the call of God and the ministry to which you set your hand by the grace of God.

Prayer: **Keep me sensitive, God of my heart, to your sovereign call. Amen.**

Friday, January 24   Read Mark 1:16-20.

Morning on Galilee: sun up now over the eastern heights, breeze rippling across bright water, waves catching and refracting light, air fresh from the cool of the night now past and the moist fragrance of the inland sea; fishermen, long garments caught up between their legs and cinched at the waist, casting sun-drenched nets. Bearded and bronzed from long hours in the sun, muscles rippling with the weight of the nets, the fishermen did as their fathers had done for generations—at least until today.

For there along the shore comes a young man in the prime of life, bearded like them, moving with graceful and confident stride, drinking in the beauty of the morning. They, half watching his approach in the midst of their work, expect he is on his way to Capernaum; but no, his tack is more toward them. It is only then, when they pause to study his appearance, that they recognize one whom they have seen before, seen recently, seen among the crowds listening to the Baptizer, John. Indeed, that whole region of Galilee is not soon to forget the baptism of this man, this Jesus of Nazareth, or the esteem and reverence in which John holds him.

There is a power in these stories of the calling of the disciples and their ready response, of the circle of the twelve Jesus built around him, of the magnetic appeal of his person. We who call ourselves by his name, who stand beneath the mantle of his love like Peter and Andrew, James and John, are forever changed.

Prayer: **Teach me to follow you, Lord Jesus. Amen.**

Saturday, January 25   Read Jonah 3:4-5, 10.

How remarkable that Nineveh is a notable, indeed a notorious, Gentile city—the capital of Assyria. The prophet Nahum cries, "Ah! City of bloodshed, utterly deceitful, full of booty—no end to the plunder!" (Nahum 3:1). The Assyrians were fierce warriors, often cutting off the hands and feet of their captives, raising up mounds of human heads. They were hated and feared by Israel, despised for their worship of the goddess Ishtar. The sacred writings of the Hebrews declared that Yahweh was God of all the nations and all the world, but this declaration couldn't withstand the horrors of war against Assyria.

Yet here is God, calling Jonah to preach repentance to so wicked a city, declaring a forty-day grace period before destruction. Jonah, perhaps reluctantly, obeys the command of God. As a result of his preaching, the entire city repents, from the king to the common citizen. Then God "changed his mind," and did not destroy the city. Sounds a lot like Jeremiah, "But if that nation . . . turns from its evil, I will change my mind about the disaster that I intended to bring on it" (Jer. 18:8).

Here is the everlasting mercy of God—broader than the measure of our minds—for national and personal enemies, unbelievers, the callous and the coarse and the different. They, and we, need but respond to the gracious, self-giving God of all the world.

Prayer: **Just and loving God, forgive me for thinking *I* am in and *they* are out, for your mercy embraces all. Amen.**

Sunday, January 26   Read Psalm 62:8.

If the psalms are nothing else, they are passionate! And how fine an example we read here in the psalmist's exhortation, "Pour out your heart before him." Feel the ardor of the statement, the flow of vitality, the emotive depth. The problem for most of us who call ourselves Christian is not too much passion but too little. We are afraid of the world lest somehow our physical side will overwhelm the spiritual, so we steer a course close to shore rather than into the wind and open sea. Perhaps what we ought to fear is that the spiritual will overwhelm the physical, leaving us pale, airy, and insubstantial. Whether one shuts down the physical side of life or the spiritual side of life, it results in loss of vitality. We are body and soul, earth and sky! That is how God made us.

Revelation 3:15-16 accuses the Laodicean church of being neither hot nor cold but lukewarm—as great a fault in religion as in love. How easy it is to cultivate the middle course, to risk nothing, fearfully adjusting the self downward to mediocrity.

If King David was "a man after God's own heart" (1 Sam. 13:14), it was not because he was cautious but because he was passionate. And what are we to say of Jesus—that daring, intense, and joyful man who lived with equal depth at a dinner party as on a healing mission? "Pour out your heart before God," in whose creative energy we live and move and have our being.

Prayer: **God of life, instill life in my divided heart. Amen.**

GOD'S WORK OF RESTORATION

January 27–February 2, 1997   **Sally Dyck**✤
Monday, January 27   Read Deuteronomy 18:15-20.

Leonardo da Vinci worked for over two years on his masterpiece *The Last Supper*. It was an act of faith as much as a work of art. He revolutionized portrayals of the Lord's Supper because he put Judas on the same side of the table as the other disciples. Prior to this time, artists depicted Judas as isolated in some way from Jesus and the other disciples; usually on the opposite side of the table as a sign of his alienation from Jesus and the others. Da Vinci's interpretation, based on the scriptures, scandalized people. They were uncomfortable with its statement of fellowship around the Lord's table.

For centuries viewers have been moved by the power of this painting. I know a woman who was converted to Christianity as a teenager. She was taken to the museums in Europe by her parents; and after viewing the works of art that told the story of Christ's life, death, and resurrection, she committed herself to Christ.

Few would consider Leonardo da Vinci to be a prophet, yet he has communicated the word of God through his artistic gifts to a large population over the centuries. In our work and faith, we too are called to communicate the good news.

Prayer: **Let the works of my life and faith communicate your love and grace to the world around me. Amen.**

✤Pastor, Church of the Redeemer (United Methodist), Cleveland Heights, Ohio.

Tuesday, January 28   Read Deuteronomy 18:9-20.

Our church needed to make a controversial and potentially divisive decision. Church members discussed the issue for months. Through the process we learned something about good communication. It is essential in order for us to be the church at work.

Finally it was time to make the decision. As people entered the room, they recorded their names on a large sheet of newsprint if they wanted to speak. We went without interruption from one speaker to the next. Because each speaker was allotted only two minutes, most people came well prepared. As each person spoke, he or she held a white ceramic dove, a symbol of peace. Between the words of each speaker, we allowed fifteen to thirty seconds of silence for those present to meditate on what had been said.

People felt that they had been listened to rather than consumed by the energy of someone with a stronger voice or greater influence. After thirty-seven people had spoken, the person who closed the meeting that day said, "I believe this has been our finest hour!"

Deuteronomy 18:20 says that if we speak in the name of another god, we will surely die. I believe this is still true in our congregations! If we speak in the name of the gods that we accept in our society—the gods of violence, force, domination, hatred, and self-centeredness—our churches and our faith risk dying. Speaking in a manner reflective of the God of love and grace will bring life and healing into the most difficult and controversial situations.

Prayer: **O God, let our speech reflect your grace and love. Amen.**

Wednesday, January 29   Read Psalm 111.

Leonardo da Vinci's masterpiece of art, *The Last Supper*, has experienced disasters and neglect over the centuries. Completed in the late 1490s, by 1517 the paint had begun to flake off due to the effects of nature. In 1556 the painting was described as "a muddle of blots." War and pollution brought serious damage in our century.

The masterpiece has been restored six times. The last cleaning and restoration took three years. Each small area was viewed through a microscope; and once-obscured objects, like a lemon slice on a pewter plate, began to appear beneath the layers of paint, dirt, wax, glue, and oil that had accumulated over the years. Brighter colors appeared and the painting's original beauty began to shine through again.

How great was this work of art, and yet it still needed restoration! How great is God's work in our soul and yet it too needs restoration from time to time! Restoring our soul is a joint effort between God and us. God's redemption brings grace to our sin and neglect.

Psalm 111 offers some pointers on joining God in this restorative process. *Remembering* what God has done for us in the past sounds so simple, and yet we often live as if there were no yesterday in God's care for us! *Giving thanks* with our whole heart brings the "brighter colors" of our lives to the fore and helps us see God in ways that have become obscured by our dulled perspectives on life.

Prayer: **O God, restore my soul through your grace. Remove all that obscures true wisdom and graciousness. Amen.**

Thursday, January 30   Read Mark 1:21-28.

I was midsentence in midsermon when a visitor stood up and began to yell at me that women should be silent in the church. All of us in the sanctuary were taken aback by her outburst. I invited the person to talk to me about her concern after the service, but she left before it was over.

Interestingly, this visitor was not someone from a nearby street filled with prostitutes. She was not from the pornographic theater across the street from our church. She was not from the bar down the other way. She was from another church, sent to straighten us out on our theology!

The basis of the sermon she interrupted that morning was the scripture from Mark about a man gripped by an unclean spirit. He confronted Jesus not in a place of ill-repute but *in the synagogue*. Perhaps the man gripped by an unclean spirit was a high-ranking member of the synagogue, and Jesus' ways were too new and different for him!

As Christians we are all much like that visitor, threatened by others' ways of living out the faith. We need to look for the *fruit* of how others live out their faith. Likewise, when the way we live out our faith differs from others, it is not necessarily the *world* that may get upset. People within our own faith community may challenge our thoughts and practices. God calls us from time to time to follow the prompting of the Spirit in ways that are new and surprising, even to ourselves!

Prayer: **O God, forgive me when I fail to respond lovingly to those around me who experience you in new and different ways. Help me risk being faithful to your calling even when it is different and new to others and maybe even to myself! Amen.**

Friday, January 31   Read 1 Corinthians 8:1-13.

A group of women meet for Bible study once a week. We read one book of the Bible after another. Our reading for the week dealt with the issue raised in Revelation 2: People were not to eat meat offered to idols under any circumstances. Prior to reading Revelation, we had read First Corinthians; we remembered the passage about eating meat in 1 Corinthians 8. Paul wrote that since idols were nothing anyway, eating meat offered to them was meaningless. He cautioned people against offending others who were sensitive to such practices due to their own religious pasts and experiences.

The women wondered about this "contradiction" in scripture. Someone asked, "What did Jesus say about eating meat offered to idols?" Someone else replied, "Nothing!" and went on to point out that Jesus ate with all kinds of people and did not seem too concerned about offending the Pharisees when he did!

Discernment is necessary in order to know when and how to live out the will of God. Rather than requiring us to adhere to strict formulas, the scriptures and our faith require us to delve deeply into each situation, listen to the Spirit as well as the scripture, and keep compassion and justice in our hearts. Having come to understand that, we moved on to discuss other issues that are far more controversial to us today than whether or not we eat meat offered to idols!

Prayer: **O God, give me a mind to understand you, a heart open to your Spirit, and a grasp of your unique calling in my age of history. Amen.**

Saturday, February 1   Read 1 Corinthians 8:1-13.

Paul spoke about a community issue that often created division among people. The community was comprised of persons from various backgrounds, and for some the eating of meat offered to idols was not a problem while for others it was the height of unacceptable behavior. Paul wanted to build Christian community through love.

A leader of a workshop told the group that the Golden Rule ("Do to others as you would have them do to you," Matt. 7:12) is sometimes inadequate because it assumes that everyone wants the same thing, likes to be treated the same way, thinks and acts the same way. The leader said that people need to take the Golden Rule a step further when dealing with our diverse society, communities, workplaces, and churches.

The leader suggested the Platinum Rule, which is "Treat others as we know they want to be treated." This interpretation of Jesus' teaching has helped me focus on *agape* love: treating others as they would want to be treated and deserve to be treated in God's sight—not treating them based on my own preferences.

Understood this way, the Golden Rule speaks to this passage on eating meat offered to idols. Paul makes it clear that the issue is not whether or not it is right or wrong to eat meat offered to idols but how we treat others. The greatest training and rule is to love one another.

Prayer: **O God, help me listen and be aware of the diversity of needs around me and teach me to love others. Amen.**

Sunday, February 2   Read Mark 1:21-28.

Leonardo da Vinci's *The Last Supper* has been reproduced into almost every known medium*—beautiful tapestries, black velvet paintings, cross-stitched hangings, and amateur caricatures. I once saw a plastic-covered placemat of the masterpiece. I was irritated at first and then somewhat amused that such a work of art could be reduced to such a common object.

In many ways the plastic-covered placemat actually provides a message about our faith and the meaning of the Lord's Supper. Imagine eating spaghetti over this plastic-covered placemat, the drippings of sauce and chunks of meat or vegetables splattering across the face of Jesus and the disciples. Yet it only takes a cloth to wipe it and make it clean again.

God has created each one of us as a masterpiece of the soul, made in God's image and restored and redeemed by God's grace. We dribble our lives away and miss the mark and make a mess on a regular basis. God's grace wipes our souls clean, making us whole again.

After Jesus healed the man gripped by an unclean spirit, everyone was astonished and amazed at his teaching; and Jesus' fame spread throughout the land. Perhaps people realized at some level that, as amazing as the physical healing was, grace—and the restoration of the soul that it brings—is God's most amazing gift. May our lives give witness to God's grace so that others may know and believe!

Prayer: **O God, wipe away my sin and redeem me. Let my life show the power of your amazing grace through the change that comes within me! Amen.**

---

*Ernest Pellegrini's wood-carved reproduction of da Vinci's work hangs in the chapel at The Upper Room in Nashville.

TO KNOW GOD TRULY

February 3–9, 1997   **David Maldonado, Jr.✤**
Monday, February 3   Read Mark 9:2-9.

How do we know God? How do we know God *truly*? How can we tell that what we are witnessing, hearing, or experiencing is of God? It is easy to deceive ourselves into believing what we want to believe or to believe what others want us to believe. We might even be afraid to accept that what is before us could be God. The question of faith is the question of knowing God.

The disciples, along with many other people, witnessed the life and work of Jesus firsthand. They observed Jesus as he fed the hungry, healed the sick, and proclaimed the kingdom of God. Some of those eyewitnesses saw political interests; others heard blasphemies; others saw the Christ. Each was deciding who Jesus was on the basis of his or her own experience, social position, and perspective. But what about the disciples? How did they know who Jesus truly was?

The story of the transfiguration is the story of God's revelation of Jesus' identity: Jesus is the son of God. Most of us will probably never experience such spectacular disclosures, but that does not mean that God does not speak to us in many other ways. In the transfiguration, God addresses our questions of faith. It is the story of our own transformation to a life of knowing God truly.

Prayer: **God, I seek to know you truly. Grant that I might be transformed before your eyes. Amen.**

✤Professor of Church and Society at Perkins School of Theology, Dallas, Texas.

Tuesday, February 4   Read 2 Kings 2:1-8.

Elisha knew Elijah as a servant of God. He had witnessed Elijah's mighty deeds and heard his powerful words. They were the very words and deeds of God. Elisha was convinced that Elijah was of God. To know Elijah truly was to know him as a man of God. Such understanding called for a profound commitment and devotion, and Elisha was devoted to Elijah.

As Elijah responded to God's call to move on to Bethel, Jericho, and across the Jordan, he instructed Elisha to stay. However, Elisha could not stay behind. His devotion to Elijah was such that he could not let go of the one he had come to know as a servant of God. "As the Lord lives, and as you yourself live, I will not leave you." Such words remind us that Elisha was not confusing Elijah with God, but Elisha saw God's spirit in Elijah.

Why would Elisha insist on staying with Elijah? Maybe Elisha came to love Elijah because of what he had done for God, and he wanted to serve Elijah's needs as his ministry was coming to an end. Maybe Elisha saw God's spirit in Elijah and wanted to know God more fully. Whatever the reasons for insisting to stay, the devotion was clear and strong. In spite of distracting remarks by others, Elisha stayed with Elijah all the way across the Jordan.

Prayer: **God, I know Jesus as your son. Grant that I might be faithful to you through him in the journey you have chosen for me. Amen.**

Wednesday, February 5   Read 2 Kings 2:9-12.

Elijah had noticed Elisha's devotion and determination to stay with him to the very end. Although others had discouraged him, Elisha stayed with Elijah on the journey to Bethel, Jericho, and across the Jordan. Elijah knew that he was approaching the end of his life and work. However, Elijah did not know exactly what awaited him, nor did Elisha. Yet Elisha remained firm in his commitment to stay with him. This commitment impressed Elijah; and in response to Elisha's faithfulness, Elijah asked what he might do for Elisha.

Imagine Elisha's feelings when Elijah said, "Tell me what I may do for you." Elisha knew Elijah and the fantastic things that he could do; this was a tempting offer. But Elisha knew Elijah first and foremost as a servant of God. Elisha did not ask for personal power or material things. Rather, Elisha asked for a share of Elijah's spirit. As a prophet of God, the spirit that led and empowered him was God's spirit. Elisha desired to receive a share of that spirit.

Elijah recognized the nature of Elisha's request. It was not a small request. God's spirit is not something obtained simply by asking for it. There was still something Elisha must do. He must remain faithful to the very end. Elisha must keep his eyes on Elijah. Elisha was faithful and became a prophet himself.

To know God is to desire God's spirit. God desires us to have and to share in the Spirit. However, it involves total commitment and faithfulness.

Prayer: **God, grant me your spirit. Amen.**

Thursday, February 6   Read Psalm 50:1-6.

To know God, to know God truly, is to know oneself. The more we seek to know God and seek intimacy with God, the more we encounter ourselves and the more we seek self-understanding. To ask the question Who is God? is to ask Who am I? There is no way to avoid ourselves in our seeking God; when we find God, we finally find ourselves.

The psalmist knew God. To him God was the mighty One who shone forth in a mighty light and perfection. God is the light that penetrates and enlightens all. Nothing is hidden. To know God is to stand before God in total disclosure and honesty. It is to stand in the fullness of God's light and finally to see ourselves. The faithful do not fear or hide from God's judgment. According to the psalmist, God comes and calls the faithful that God may judge them.

Standing before God is to stand in God's light. Thus, those who seek to know God seek God's light and judgment. They seek God's grace for they have come to know God and themselves truly.

Prayer: **God, I stand before you in the confidence that you know me totally and that there is nothing I can or would want to hide from you. You enter my life as the rising of the sun and enlighten my world. Do not keep silent, but speak to me that I might know you more fully. I pray in the name of Christ who came that I might see and hear you. Amen.**

Friday, February 7   Read 2 Corinthians 4:3-4.

To know God truly is to stand in the confidence of faith that is ours through God's grace and mercy. This confidence does not rely on our own abilities or the assurances of others. It does not depend on the success of our witness or how convincing we think we might be or not be. Knowing God truly comes from standing before God and God's truth.

Paul raises the issue of why everyone does not know God. It would seem that all persons would desire such a relationship with God, particularly when that relationship is readily available. Why do people not know God? What blinds or prohibits them from truly knowing God? It is as if something blocks God's light in people's lives.

According to Paul this lack of knowing is not because God refuses to shine upon them or because God does not seek them. They are blinded in their own minds. They are blinded by the "gods of this world." Our own sinfulness and selfishness blind us and keep us from recognizing and seeing God fully. Only we can remove the blinds that prevent our seeing the splendor of God's grace.

Prayer: **God, grant that I might have the strength to remove my blinds of sinfulness and selfishness that I may truly see you and know you. Help me to step out of the darkness of disbelief and into the fullness of your light. I pray in the name of him through whom your light has shone. Amen.**

Saturday, February 8   Read 2 Corinthians 4:5-6.

To know God truly is to be illumined by the light of God's grace through Jesus Christ. It is through Christ that we know God fully. Not to know God is like being in darkness and chaos, in a void or emptiness. To know God is like stepping into a light that only God can radiate—a light that shines within us, a spiritual light that opens our eyes and allows us to see ourselves and to see God's presence in our lives. Such is the fullness of the knowledge that God provides.

However, knowing God is a gift. It comes from God's act of grace through Christ. It is God's light that shines within us; it is not a light that we generate. Thus, knowing God is not something that produces self-importance, self-righteousness, or self-pride. On the contrary, knowing God leads to a life of service to others.

To know God is to know others as God's children whom God loves as dearly as God loves us. We see others as neighbor—as sister or brother. The light we receive from God is not to be held and hidden. It is God's light, and all who receive God's light join in sharing it with the world. God's light shines within us. It illumines our inner life, nourishing and strengthening us inwardly. But it is also God's light that radiates through us to the neighbor, the stranger, and the outcast.

Prayer: **God, shine your light upon me that I may know you truly and give me the fullness of your Spirit that I might shine your light in this world for the sake of others. In the name of Jesus who came as the light of the world that I might know you. Amen.**

51

Sunday, February 9   Read Mark 9:2-9.

To know God is an awesome experience. Our awareness of divine presence bears witness to God's self-disclosure, for God is making the divine presence known to us. For many of us, that disclosure can be an overwhelming experience.

Mark's story of the transfiguration tells about the revelatory transformation of Jesus before Peter, James, and John. These disciples had witnessed Jesus' ministry over a period of time. They were under some stress already because of what people were saying about him. Their immediate response to such an awesome event as Jesus' transfiguration was fear and confusion. Their first reaction (to build three dwellings—one for each of the three persons revealed to them) was an expected human response to the incredible event they had observed.

God's purpose was not to find somebody to build dwellings or temples for Jesus, Moses, and Elijah. God did not need another temple. God's purpose was to reveal that Jesus was the Son, the Beloved. God needed to make known who Jesus was. Could it be that in spite of all they had seen and heard themselves, they still had not truly believed or known Jesus' divine identity? Could it be that we do not see God's presence and spirit around us? Could it be that we are so busy building temples that we fail to see God?

To know God truly involves responsibility. "This is my Son, the Beloved; listen to him!" The transfiguration was not only for the purpose of knowing Jesus' true identity; it involved the mandate to listen to him. To know God truly is to listen to God.

Prayer: **God, I pray that I might know you and hear you. Amen.**

February 10–16, 1997   **Paul Barton**✤
Monday, February 10   Read Genesis 9:8-17.

On hot summer afternoons, the smog hangs thick over the city sky. News bulletins warn us not to venture outside because of the health threat posed by the polluted air. Smog is a sign of the times for most cities; the filthy sky is a daily reminder of the inability of humanity to live in harmony with creation.

When rainclouds wash away the polluted air, it restores the sky to its original, beautiful state. Sometimes a rainbow sparkles through the clouds, reminding us that God continually desires to restore creation to its original and beautiful condition. The rainbow is a sign of comfort for, no matter how polluted the sky becomes, its appearance after the rain elicits a sense of cleansing and renewal. The rainbow serves as a sign of God's restoration of creation.

The passage states that God placed the rainbow in the clouds to remind *God* never again to use water to destroy creation. If God needs signs to remember the need for faithfulness, how much more do we! The rainbow also serves as a sign of life to us, reminding us that God can make the sun shine through the dark clouds and restore life to its original beauty.

Prayer: **God of beauty and life, help me to live in such a way that I may contribute to the preservation of your creation. Amen.**

✤United Methodist clergy in the Río Grande Annual Conference and a Ph.D. student in church history at Southern Methodist University; Dallas, Texas.

Tuesday, February 11   Read Psalm 25:1-10.

"According to your steadfast love, remember me."

A friend experiences a series of difficulties that causes him to question whether God has remembered him. He passes through years of unemployment and suffers the frustration of unfulfilled dreams. Now his father has called him to live nearby as his father endures a terminal illness.

My friend feels as if God has forgotten him, turned God's back on him. What sign of life can I provide for my friend? What sign of life can remind him that God is present even when he does not feel this is so? A letter, a phone call, a visit? Just as God used the dove to bring a sign to Noah that he would soon see an end to his drifting, God can use us to bring a word that God's promises will be fulfilled. God can use us as agents of hope for others. When life has become unbearable for friends and family who feel as if God has abandoned them, we can become a rainbow to let them know that healing is possible, that their suffering has an end.

Like the dove and the rainbow, God can use us to remind others that God's love is steadfast; God's love endures even when our faith does not. Our witness to others who are suffering can become a message of promise and hope.

Prayer: **Lord, your rainbow reminds me of your steadfast love and your promises. Let your Spirit shine in me that I may be a living reminder of your love and signs of life. Amen.**

Ash Wednesday

Wednesday, February 12   Read Isaiah 58:1-12.

On Ash Wednesday, the Jaguars, Cadillacs, Mercedes-Benzes, and other new cars fill the church's parking lot. The wealthy return to worship in the middle of a poor barrio. Because of previous violent incidents, some of the church members will not come to church at night. It is always possible that they or their cars will be assaulted. The bars on the windows are signs of the destructive forces in the neighborhood that constantly threaten the church.

Erroneous ideas inside the church can cause more damage than violent forces outside. Some persons believe that coming to worship is a sufficient sacrifice to God. The point for Isaiah is that worship alone is not sufficient to God. Isaiah declares that the concern we show our neighbor is the clearest sign of our love for God.

Isaiah calls us to seek a new relationship with God through caring for the poor and the neglected. Some practice fasting during Lent, others give up certain things—all with the hope that such denial will result in a deeper relationship with God. My wish is that such inward and personal sacrifice will be accompanied with external, sacrificial giving. While self-denial is certainly a beneficial spiritual practice, almsgiving and caring for the needy also means of drawing us closer to God.

Suggestion for meditation: **The needy pass my church doors every day. In what ways does my church serve as a sign of hope to those who walk by? How does my church offer hope, respect, and hospitality to the needy?**

Thursday, February 13   Read Psalm 25.

The psalmist asks God to pardon his offenses because they are an obstacle to his experiencing God's steadfast love. Just as the opened dam allows the river to flow to its destiny in the ocean, so does forgiveness allow us to flow into the ocean of God's love. Forgiveness reunites us with God.

Forgiveness also reunites us with others. The forgiveness we seek and receive from God challenges us to forgive those from whom we are alienated. As the Lord's Prayer reminds us, restoration with God implies forgiveness of those who have hurt us. Our healing requires the need to forgive as well as to be forgiven. Lent, as a time of restoration, challenges us to forgive so that we may be reconciled to God.

The communion table is a place and sign of forgiveness and reconciliation. During a youth retreat, two adults offended each other. During worship they served Communion to each other. As they shared the signs of Christ's body and blood, they were moved to ask for forgiveness for their behavior. As signs of forgiveness, tne body and blood of Christ challenge us to seek forgiveness from God and offer forgiveness to others.

Prayer: **God, grant me humility to ask for forgiveness for my sins and strength to forgive those who have done evil against me. May this forgiveness be a sign of restoration that you offer all humanity. Amen.**

Friday, February 14   Read 1 Peter 3:18-22.

The author of First Peter views the waters that caused the great flood, not as a destructive force but as an agent of salvation. The point for the author is not that the water destroyed a rebellious people, but that it preserved a righteous remnant. For this writer, the flood prefigures baptism because it serves as a means of restoring the loving relationship between God and human beings. The covenant that God made with Noah after the flood is recapitulated in baptism as a covenant of eternal union with God through Christ.

Our baby daughter will be baptized in a few months. She will be too young to understand the meaning of this ritual, but her parents and those present will understand it as a sign of new life in Jesus Christ and as an initiation into a covenantal relationship with God. The baptismal water will be seen, not as a means of destruction, but as an earthly symbol of God's grace.

Baptismal water is viewed as a sign of promise also. The covenant and promise that God made with Noah and the covenant given in Jesus Christ will be made once again for Elisa Marina and celebrated by the whole congregation. Baptism, as a ritual of covenant and promise, is a sign of hope. Elisa Marina and her parents will have a hope that for the remainder of their days God will be present to give strength, comfort, wisdom, and renewal.

Prayer: **God, let the baptismal waters be a sign that leads me, draws me, and calls me back to you, so I can remember your promise of grace. Amen.**

Saturday, February 15   Read Mark 1:9-15.

Throughout the centuries, Christians have practiced self-denial during Lent in order to prepare for the celebration of Easter. Today's passage reminds us that Jesus also prepared himself through self-denial to proclaim the gospel with power and authority. It is no coincidence that Jesus began his preaching and teaching career with such boldness following his struggle in the wilderness. In the desert, Satan tempted him to forsake his calling and to pursue other less worthy goals, using his power for personal gain.

In the wilderness alone, Jesus faced himself, his fears, and his temptations. Alone he faced the doubts and fears about what lay ahead. And alone he examined his relationship with his Father. Yet God did not abandon Jesus to his temptations but sent angels to minister to him.

One year I went camping by myself in Big Bend National Park. I got lost during a hike, and I suddenly became very supplicant before God: "God, do not let me die alone in the desert!" I could endure the solitude but not the possibility that I might not find my way back. So I sat down and asked God to guide me home.

Self-denial and trials in the wilderness are not ends in themselves. Jesus' trials in the desert gave him strength to endure even greater hardships later. The practice of self-denial during Lent can serve as a time of testing for us also, so that we might celebrate the Easter faith with conviction and endure the consequences of sharing the gospel with boldness.

Prayer: **God, may your Spirit strengthen me when I find myself enduring the hardships of the desert. Amen.**

Sunday, February 16   Read Mark 1:9-15.

This passage marks Jesus' transformation from one who receives from God at his baptism to one who is ministered to during a time of trial and finally to one who boldly proclaims the good news. Lent is a period of the Christian year that invites us to relive this process of transformation: from receiving from God to offering ourselves to God, from repentance to forgiveness, from temptation and trials to bold action. As we follow Jesus' journey from Galilee to Jerusalem, we move through Lent so that we too may proclaim Jesus' words for the world: "The time is fulfilled, and the kingdom of God has come near; repent, and believe in the good news."

The Spirit is at work in this process of transformation. The Spirit descended upon Jesus in the form of a dove, then drove him into the wilderness. Certainly the Spirit dwelled within Jesus as he proclaimed the good news of the kingdom. The Lenten journey is a journey led by the movements of the Spirit.

The signs we see along the Lenten journey point to the presence of God in our midst. The signs of water, dove, baptism, and wilderness point to a sacred reality that we can experience in the present. Yet other signs in the world point to the presence of God beyond the church: the beauty of creation, the poor in our midst. These signs lead us to experience God's transforming presence more deeply and prepare us to experience the fullness of the Resurrection message at Easter.

Prayer: **Lord, as I move along the Lenten journey, transform me into a living sign of your Spirit. Amen.**

OUR GOD—AN EVER-PRESENT HELP

February 17–23, 1997   **D. S. Dharmapalan**✤
Monday, February 17   Read Genesis 17:1-7, 15-16.

The promise keeper

Today's scripture deals with a threefold covenant God made with Abram: (1) the promise of the land of Canaan, (2) the promise of progeny, and (3) the promise to be his God and the God of all his descendants. The important thing to remember here is that the God of the Bible, while dealing with humans on a human level (the Incarnation being the ultimate), is portrayed also as One who keeps promises. Often our experiences with people fall into the area of broken promises.

Many years ago, a ministerial candidate would call on me at the parsonage on a weekly basis. My older daughter, barely three years old, thought he came to play with her; and when I happened to delay, she got him to play with her. On one such occasion, she told him, "Uncle Sathie, wait here and I'll bring my toys." The young man promised he would. But when she returned with her toys, he was gone. To this day, even as an adult, she remembers that broken promise.

This is where God is different. Abram and countless women and men after him have experienced the fulfillment of God's promises. God's promises are the same for you and me, if only we believe.

Prayer: Dear God, fill my day with your rich promises that I may learn to trust in your goodness night and day. Through Jesus Christ our Lord. Amen.

✤Pastor, First United Methodist Church, Milford, Massachusetts.

Tuesday, February 18   Read Psalm 22:23-24.

The companion on life's path

Psalm 22 is classified as a "prophetic psalm" since it makes reference to some of the sufferings of Christ—especially his feeling of being "abandoned" by the very people he came to save. Notwithstanding the fact that Jesus, the son of God, felt "abandoned," the psalmist echoes an unparalleled confidence in God: God "did not despise or abhor the affliction of the afflicted."

Often we feel lost in life's maze and in our own devices. By reading this psalm, we can experience an explosion of confidence in the fact that God's companionship is ever sure to the one who believes.

One time I was taking a walk with my three-year-old grandson. As usual, he would hold on to my middle finger while walking alongside of me. Every now and then he would trip over some rough spot on the road and even fall to the ground. One time he looked up to me and said, "Papa, you hold my hand, then I won't fall." So I did. My holding his hand did not prevent his tripping over rough spots, but he never hit the ground.

The presence of God in our lives is more assured when we allow God to hold our hand. That does not mean we will never trip over life's rough spots, but it does mean that God will never let us fall.

Prayer: **Precious Lord, take my hand, lead me on that I may not stumble. Held by your mighty power, I know that I can live in confidence and safety. Amen.**

Wednesday, February 19　　　　　　　Read Psalm 22:25-31.

Our God—worthy of praise

Most Christians take time to pray. Invariably we find ourselves praying for our own immediate needs. However, this psalm takes us to a higher level of prayer—a level where our prayers and the "vows" we make not only satisfy our needs but also go beyond to the point that even the "poor shall eat and be satisfied." In other words, true worship assures that everyone's needs are "satisfied." Think about it. That certainly is a different way of looking at prayer.

I have often wondered why, when everything else in life has the future in mind—namely our work, our family, our finances, our prosperity—why our prayers are so much for the moment. Remember Jesus' prayer in the garden of Gethsemane. "Father," he prayed, "remove this cup from me; yet, not what I want, but what you want" (Mark 14:36). While it was a prayer for self-deliverance, Jesus did not take his eyes off his mission and the future of the human race. He accepted the "cup" for the sake of the world he came to save. He knew he was at a point of no return. Imagine where we might be if God had removed that "cup" from Jesus.

May this be our prayer for this Lent: "Lord, let your will be done in my life, according to what you want. Amen."

Suggestion for meditation: You may want to take a moment to reflect on the nature and the character of your prayer, the prayers of your family, and even the prayers you offer in congregational worship to consider the changes you might make in your "talk" with God.

Thursday, February 20   Read Romans 4:13-16.

The faithful one

Rules are essential to life, and laws give stability to human society. As far back as 3,000 years before Christ, the Hebrews were endowed with laws (*torah*) to create a stable society. However, Paul says that in our relationship with God we need something more than Law—we need faith. A skilled craftsman, Paul points to Abraham as the father of faith to explain what he means. Paul says that God declared righteousness long before God instituted the Law. Therefore, being "righteous" has little to do with the Law. In no way is Paul trying to disregard the Law; instead he is giving greater validity to faith.

Once I had to retrieve a tennis ball that was drifting out on a lake. The closer I swam to the ball, the further it drifted because of the ripples I was creating on the water. At one stage, I felt a cramp in one of my legs and decided to abandon my attempt. I decided to put into practice every rule I learned about swimming to get me back to the shore, only to find myself in deeper water. Just then I heard a voice inside me saying, "Just let go and float. Put your faith in the water." And that's what I did, and that's what got me to shore.

Paul is saying that rules and laws are good, but they are no substitutes for faith. These are days when some of us will strive to follow some rule of conduct, to practice some discipline in observance of Lent. It may help us see that our rules can get in the way, pushing faith into a back seat.

Prayer: **"My faith looks up to thee, thou Lamb of Calvary." Enable me to trust you so that your strength might undergird me during life's turbulence. Amen.**

Friday, February 21   Read Romans 4:17-25.

Our confidence

Abraham was certain of the object of his faith, namely God. Therefore, his faith is exemplary not because of its strength or the lack of it, but because of its object—God. By faith, Abraham knew that God "gives life to the dead" and "calls into existence the things that do not exist."

We must understand that the people who lived during Abraham's time believed perhaps as fervently as he did. However, the object of their faith was limited—limited by the lack of knowledge of the One they worshiped.

Each winter here in New England tragedies are reported because persons fall into frigid waters while trying to walk on thin ice. Unfortunately their strong, yet misplaced, faith in the thin ice results in death; whereas, those with a weak faith on thick ice survive.

Lent is the season that calls us once again to recognize the object of our faith—the God who, says Paul, "raised Jesus our Lord from the dead." Paul promotes Abraham as the prototype who refuses to be intimidated by circumstances, walking with faith on "thick ice."

Prayer: **Dear God of Abraham, Isaac, and Jacob, instill in me a faith that is focused on you, that I may always stand on solid ground. Amen.**

Saturday, February 22   Read Mark 8:31-33.

The Savior

Most teenagers resist discipline and order. One day recently, our son was musing over his mother's discipline during his teenage years, and he had this to say: "If Mother's demand for discipline and good behavior weren't that important, God would have hatched us from eggs." How true. We were not "hatched" from eggs but created in the very image of God, to live a life of faith and order.

In today's passage, Peter seems to have a problem with the question of Jesus' life and death. Only a few days before, this very same Peter had publicly declared that Jesus is the "Messiah, the Son of the living God" (Matt. 16:16). Now he is ambivalent about Christ's power.

Some of us Christians tend to act as though we were "hatched" from eggs, without direction or discipline in our faith. We don't quite understand how, in God's reign, a saving Christ can be a suffering servant as well. The paradox of accepting Christ both as the Messiah and as the Lamb of God is the crux of our faith, but many a Christian—just like Peter—have difficulty accepting both. That is why so many Christians are more comfortable with Christmas than with Good Friday or even Easter.

We need to ask ourselves whether we, like Peter, confess Christ as the Messiah but are ambivalent about the mission of our Lord.

Prayer: **Dear Lord, saved by your suffering, death, and resurrection, may I confess you publicly both as the suffering servant and as the Lord of my life, so that the world may see you as the only hope. Amen.**

Sunday, February 23   Read Mark 8:34-38.

Guardian of our souls

   When my youngest daughter was about four years old, often she would sit beside my desk and play with her toys while I worked. One day I asked her to get me a book from the shelf while I continued with my work. For a moment I forgot all about the book. But when I remembered, I turned in her direction to discover that the floor near me was piled with books. My little girl had not only brought the book I wanted, she had emptied the whole shelf.

   I believe that when God deals with us God not only gives us what we ask but much more. That is why God decided to send Jesus into this world.

   What then is our response to God's overwhelming generosity? Today's reading lays before us the cost of discipleship, the appropriate response. Jesus calls us to give in response to God's giving—to give our lives.

   Just as God in Jesus "emptied the whole shelf" on our behalf, so our response requires a total emptying of ourselves. Only through loss do we gain.

Prayer: Dear God, may I continually empty myself in response to your giving. Amen.

GOD'S INITIATIVE

February 24–March 2, 1997   **Thomas R. Hawkins**✤
Monday, February 24   Read 1 Corinthians 1:18-25.

Our society is obsessed with self-improvement. Bookstores are crammed with "how-to" titles that describe ways we can change our lives by practicing seven self-evident laws or by adopting ten successful habits.

We often bring this same outlook to the spiritual life. We reduce our growth in grace to our own efforts at self-improvement. We feel that if we adopt some spiritual technique during Lent, we will feel more loved by God when Easter arrives.

Paul sharply rebukes this tendency. The cross contradicts our attempts to manage our own spiritual growth. We are saved by God's grace, not by our efforts. The initiative is God's, not our own.

This is why the cross is a stumbling block to those who think they can reach God through their own ability to understand spiritual truths and a folly to those who want to prove their salvation by demonstrations of spiritual power.

As we move through Lent, growth in grace demands less of our efforts and more of a capacity to open ourselves lovingly to the One who first loved us.

Prayer: **Loving God, my longing for you is only an echo of your longing for me. Help me to let go of my need to take charge of my own growth. Empower me to trust in your grace. Amen.**

✤Dean of doctoral programs; Associate Professor of Ministry, McCormick Theological Seminary, Chicago, Illinois.

Tuesday, February 25   Read Exodus 20:1-17.

I once worshiped in an old New England church where the Ten Commandments were printed in large letters on the wall behind the pulpit. The people who built this church practiced a religion characterized more by legalism than by grace. They believed in a God who rewarded the obedient and punished sinners. Some people still view the Ten Commandments in this way: God will love us only if we obey God's laws.

A different picture emerges when we put the Ten Commandments back into their narrative context. God has liberated a mixed company of refugees and slaves from Egyptian oppression. Camping around the mountain of God, they who were once no people now become God's people. In response to God's salvation, Israel chooses to live by God's commandments.

Obedience is a response to, not a precondition for, God's grace. We do not earn salvation by following God's commandments. We take these commandments upon ourselves as a joyous response to God's reaching out and embracing us.

As we meditate on the Ten Commandments, we need to make sure that we do not use them to justify how we are earning God's grace. Similarly, "giving up" something for Lent or engaging in extraordinary acts of Lenten devotion are valid only when they are responses to God's grace rather than a way to earn it.

Above all else, Lent is a time to remember how God takes the initiative in Jesus Christ to save us. We turn first to the cross of Christ and only afterward to our lives, choices, and actions.

Prayer: **Gracious God, may I keep your commandments not under threat of divine punishment but as a joyous response to your amazing grace. Amen.**

Wednesday, February 26   Read Psalm 19:7-10.

A friend tells about his grandfather's first experience in a small Jewish school in eastern Europe. The rabbi smeared honey on the slate tablets on which the students wrote their daily Torah lesson. He then told his students to taste their tablets. As my friend's grandfather licked the honey from his tablet, he tasted the sweetness of God's law.

The psalmist also extols the sweetness of God's law. God's commandments are "sweeter also than honey, and the drippings of the honeycomb." They are not a burden. They are instead a gift, a source of grace and peace that revives the soul. They make wise the simple. They fill the heart with joy, guiding us to know God's will and way. They enlighten our eyes, showing us the path of life and giving us a new perspective on ourselves and our world.

The psalmist sees obedience to God's law as a joyous response to a gracious God who has liberated Israel from bondage and made covenant to be its God. God's commandments are not a burden to be grimly shouldered in order to earn God's acceptance. They are a response to God's prior action.

As we observe this Lenten season, how do we approach our religious obligations? Are they a joyous response to God's salvation or a subtle attempt to manipulate God into accepting us? Does our devotional life fill us with joy, or does it burden us with one more thing to do? Does it open our eyes to see the world differently, or does it limit our vision to our own feelings, moods, and thoughts?

Suggestion for meditation: **How can obedience to God's commandments transform the bitter experiences of my life into ones that are sweeter than honey?**

Thursday, February 27   Read Psalm 19:1-6, 11-14.

The psalmist's thoughts move from the outermost reaches of creation—the sun and the stars—to the deepest recesses of the human heart. Like the noonday sun that illumines everything, God's law exposes our innermost lives. God's law leaves nothing hidden in the shadows. It calls into question all human standards of adequacy that settle for whatever may appear "good enough" either to ourselves or to onlookers.

Knowing this moves the psalmist to a critical self-examination. The focus is on both extremes: sins that are so much in the shadows that we never catch a glimpse of them—"Clear me from hidden faults"—as well as those of which we are all too aware—"Keep back thy servant also from presumptuous sins" (RSV). As Paul knew, it is very easy to confuse God's ways with our own. We can presumptuously confuse our will with God's will. We can unknowingly substitute our wisdom for God's wisdom, particularly when God's wisdom looks like foolishness to the world.

Lent offers an opportunity for us to engage in the same critical self-examination that the psalmist undertakes. If we open ourselves to God, the bright light of God's grace may illumine the shadowy recesses of the human heart and heal our hidden faults. If we keep our focus on the cross, we may discover the grace to acknowledge how we sin presumptuously, confusing the foolishness of the world with the wisdom of God.

Prayer: **Creator God, you fill the whole universe and yet live within my heart. Grant me your Holy Spirit that what I know (the words of my mouth) and what I do not know (the secret meditations of my heart) may be acceptable in your sight. Amen.**

Friday, February 28   Read Exodus 20:1-17.

The coach at a nearby university always begins the first practice by holding up a football and telling his players, "This is a football." After the laughter dies down, he makes his point: Good players never outgrow their need to review the basics, no matter how advanced, sophisticated, or successful they are.

The Ten Commandments are God's basic instructions. We never outgrow our need to review these commandments, no matter how religiously sophisticated, spiritually mature, or institutionally successful we are. These commandments express the matters about which God cares most deeply.

One way to read and to keep the Ten Commandments is to see everything as an elaboration of the first commandment. "I am the LORD your God. . . . You shall have no other gods before me." We keep the Sabbath because we are not to make a god of our work. We refuse to murder because those who extinguish another life have taken it upon themselves to play god, making life-and-death decisions about another's fate. We do not allow money or possessions to become gods that dominate our lives.

Lent is a time to review the Christian life's basic instructions. Is God at the center of our lives? Has something else become a god that controls and dominates our daily existence?

Suggestion for meditation: **While false gods always control, the God who brought Israel out of bondage invites me into true freedom. Where am I tempted to make something a god that controls me? How do I experience God's freedom in that same area of my life?**

Saturday, March 1   Read John 2:13-17.

Here is no gentle Jesus, meek and mild. Here is an angry Messiah who turns over tables and makes a whip from cords. The cleansing of the Temple reminds us that Jesus comes as a savior to those who need grace but as a judge to those who erect barriers between God and humankind.

Some congregations use this text to explain why they will not have a church supper or sponsor a bazaar. But the cleansing of the Temple refers to more than selling books in the narthex.

Herod's Temple was divided into several courts. Jewish worshipers had access to the inner courts; Gentile seekers could enter only the outermost court, the Court of the Gentiles. The Court of the Gentiles was the same place where money was changed and sacrificial animals sold. The only place a Gentile seeker could pray was loud, noisy, chaotic—hardly a quiet place of prayer. Sincere seekers after God were being shut out of the very place where they should receive welcome.

Jesus' cleansing of the Temple stands as a challenge to present-day congregations that create barriers, shutting out the seekers after God who need their welcome.

Lent is not a time for individual reflection and repentance alone. It is also a time to look at our corporate sinfulness, at how we create barriers to the people God wants us to welcome. How easily can the physically challenged enter our building? In what ways does our language or worship exclude some people? How do our habits of worship create a hospitable space that welcomes outside seekers?

Suggestion for meditation: **How can my congregation welcome the stranger? How do the members create hospitable space for sincere seekers who are on the fringes of the congregation?**

Sunday, March 2   Read John 2:18-22.

Change the order of worship, and some families withdraw their financial support. Move the pulpit or replace the altar, and a few members angrily leave the church. We often are tempted to control the structures of religious life so that they prop up our own self-esteem or justify our own self-worth. We forget that the power to bring us near to God does not lie in our own resources but in God's infinite grace.

"Destroy this temple, and in three days I will raise it up," Jesus says. His listeners respond, "This temple has been under construction forty-six years, and will you raise it up in three days?"

The Temple, built as a meeting place of the holy and the human, has become a human achievement, a sign of human accomplishment, power, and control. It took us forty-six years to build this Temple through our own ingenuity and resources. How dare you claim that a power so much greater than our own can rebuild it in just three days?

Like Jesus' listeners, we want to be in charge of our relationship with God, managing it for our own well-being. How have we absolutized Lenten customs originally meant to bring us closer to God so that they are now a proud tower of defense against God? How have we absolutized our present church life so that we dare not allow it to be challenged by new forms of worship and prayer?

Prayer: **Merciful God, keep me from treating the means you have given me to meet you as my own creation. Let me be open to the new ways you reveal yourself to me. Amen.**

73

March 3–9, 1997   **Jerry L. McGlone**✤
Monday, March 3   Read Numbers 21:4-6.

A very bad day

The people of Israel were having it rough. They had been wandering around that wilderness for a long time. They had been walking a long way, but they were not one step closer to that promised land where the milk and honey flowed. They were weary and worn, hungry and thirsty, homeless and impatient, and they feared that circumstances would never improve.

To make matters worse, as soon as they gave vent to their frustrations and fears, the Lord punished them by sending serpents into their camp—serpents whose fiery bites wounded, maimed, and killed. Today's scripture puts them in the middle of a very bad day.

Have you ever had a terrible, horrible, very bad day—a day when you sensed the serpents slithering in the underbrush, a day stolen by depression and hurts, a day ruined by pain and fear? Have you ever had a day when nothing went right, when everyone came grabbing at you, when you didn't get a moment's peace? Have you ever had a day when all the news was bad?

What did you do? How did you make it through? Jesus met Simon on a bad day (see Luke 5:1-10). Jesus told Simon to move out of the shallows into the deep waters. Maybe making it through to better days requires us to move out into the deep waters of faith and trust.

***Prayer:* Lord, strengthen my faith that I may trust in your goodness even on a very bad day. Amen.**

✤Pastor, Payne Avenue Christian Church (Disciples of Christ); North Tonawanda, New York.

Tuesday, March 4   Read Numbers 21:7-9.

A look of faith

What a strange tale! The cure for a snakebite is to look at a bronze snake! The Israelites realized that this torment from the snakes came as a result of their sin. They asked Moses to intercede with God to take away the result of their sin.

But the Lord did not do what they wanted; the Lord did something different. The result of their sin stayed with the people, but the Lord gave them a way to be healed.

Our sin has consequences. Sometimes other people are hurt; sometimes problems become more difficult; sometimes troubles are compounded. In turning to God we discover some truths that may surprise us. God does not wipe out the consequences of sin or erase the hurts we caused or solve the problems we began. God *does* provide the tools we need to help heal the hurts.

We all come to this place in life wounded in some way, carrying the result of our sins, bearing the burden of past actions. If we have any feelings, if we have invested any of our self in another, if we have tasted life, we will be wounded.

When we are wounded by life, Jesus calls us to go out and bind up someone else's wounds. Jesus calls us to move through our hurts to become a "wounded healer."[*] Jesus calls us to make a contribution to this life, a contribution that brings joy and acceptance somewhere, beauty and forgiveness somewhere, life and hope somewhere.

Prayer: **Dear Lord, teach me to accept the consequences of my actions and my sins. Show me how to become a wounded healer. Amen.**

---

[*]The term *wounded healer* is best known from the book *Wounded Healer* by Henri J. M. Nouwen (Garden City, NY: Doubleday, 1972).

Wednesday, March 5   Read Psalm 107:1-3, 17-22.

A cry to the Lord

The psalmist writes from a worldview that saw a causative relationship between sinfulness and sickness. Consulting a physician would not make a man well. Exercise and good nutrition would not bring a woman healing. The only hope for the one who was ill was to restore the broken relationship with the Lord.

Most of us have outgrown the notion that all suffering and illness come as punishment for sin. Yet we may still suspect a connection. When we are disappointed, diseased, or depressed; when we feel deluded, deserted, or denuded; we may well ask, "Why am I being punished?" or "What did I do to deserve this?"

Our experience tells us that sin does not stand alone. A sinful act begins a string of events that cannot be undone. Sin causes much suffering: It dashes dreams, it ruins relationships, it deepens despair. Through it all, the psalmist reminds us of the ray of hope. Hope comes through the steadfast love of the Lord.

When we are drowning in a sea of sinfulness, wandering in a wilderness of despondency, cut off from everything that is good, our only hope *is* to cry to the Lord. Do we have enough faith to cry to the Lord in our trouble? Can we stand with the psalmist, knowing the Lord will save us and will send the holy Word to heal us, that the Lord will deliver us from destruction?

God will not relieve us of the responsibility for our sin or treat us like spoiled children. God will not restore what we have ruined or rebuild what we have destroyed. But God *will* give us faith to rebuild.

Prayer: Dear Lord, I cry to you in my time of trouble, for your steadfast love is my only hope. Come to me. Forgive my sin and strengthen my faith. Amen.

Thursday, March 6   Read Ephesians 2:1-7.

From broken to whole

This world is falling apart. Where there should be harmony and peace, there is discord and war. What should be beautiful and sweet has turned ugly and bitter. What should be whole has been broken. Why is there so much brokenness in this world—broken relationships, broken promises, broken trusts, broken confidences?

The author of Ephesians answers this question: Sin is the cause. The power of evil is at work in the world, ruining relationships, leading people astray. Evil performs its deadly work in us. It dares us to be disobedient, stirring our desires and inflaming our passions. Sin breaks our connectedness with God; it cuts us off from God's holiness and condemns us to death. We are "by nature children of wrath," conflicting emotions battle within us and pull us in different directions.

Yes, this world may be falling apart, but God desires wholeness for each of us. God wants *you* to be whole. The message that shines through this scripture is one of healing and unity. Although we neither deserve nor earn it, God is rich in mercy toward us. Even though we are dead through sin, God makes us alive through Christ.

Something—some wonderful something—happened that takes what was broken and makes it whole. That something is the Resurrection. The Christian church is a resurrection society, a family of believers who once were dead but now live.

The church, as imperfect as it is, remains the place where one finds this new life. It is a place for mending, for healing, for making whole. Are you a breaker or a mender, a hurter or a healer?

Prayer: **Dear Lord, thank you for taking the torn shreds of my broken life and making me whole. Amen.**

Friday, March 7   Read Ephesians 2:8-10.

The gift of grace

The question is asked, On which should the Christian depend—grace or works? Will grace bring us the gift of eternal life, or will we depend on our good works to purchase our admission ticket into heaven?

Thinking we can make it alone will be our undoing. Today's scripture passage is clear: We are saved by grace. Salvation is not of our own doing; it is not the result of our good works.

On the contrary, our works—by themselves—will condemn us. We have not fulfilled the Law. We do not obey the Sermon on the Mount. Even though our public actions may appear pure, we have not cleansed our minds of impure thoughts. Although we give to charity, we do not give enough. The closer we come into God's presence, the more we recognize our own sinfulness. Our conscience will never give us a passing final grade.

Neither you nor I can work our way into heaven; we have to depend upon God's gift of grace. Forgiveness is a gift. Resurrection is a gift. Eternal life is a gift.

Once we believe in the gift and have faith in God's grace for our lives, we will come to understand that God wants us to do good works. We are not fully "practicing" Christians unless we fill our lives with good works. It is by grace that we live, but it is through works that we show where our hearts belong. Jesus said, "Thus you will know them by their fruits" (Matt. 7:20).

Prayer: **Dear Lord, thank you for your mercy and grace. Show me what I can do in obedience to you this day and then give me the strength to do it. Amen.**

Saturday, March 8   Read John 3:14-15.

Look up in faith

Today's scripture takes us back to where the week's scripture readings began, back to the wilderness with Moses and the people of Israel, back to the biting snakes, back to the bronze serpent.

This time Jesus is continuing his clandestine discussion with Nicodemus, who asked, "How can anyone be born after having grown old?" (John 3:4). What Nicodemus wanted to know was how to enter the kingdom of God. Jesus told Nicodemus that just as healing and life came to the snakebitten Israelites when they looked up and saw that serpent of bronze hanging from a pole, so too will life be given to those who look up with the eyes of faith and see the Son of Man.

Whether in the wilderness with Moses and the snakes, with Nicodemus and Jesus in the darkness, or in the world today, a student of scripture can see three parallels. First, death is caused by sin. For the Israelites death came through the bite of the serpents, but the serpents came as a result of the people's sin. Our sinful nature separates us from God, and that separation spells death for our souls.

Second, to conquer death, God lifts up a savior. God told Moses to lift up a bronze serpent on a pole. That night with Nicodemus, humankind learned that God would lift up the Son of Man.

Third, we must lift up our eyes in faith. The Israelites believed healing would come when they looked up to that serpent of bronze. We must have faith that when we look up to Christ, we will receive eternal life because Christ on the cross has overcome death on our behalf already.

Prayer: Dear Lord, I thank you for sending Jesus so that I might look toward him with eyes of faith. Amen.

Sunday, March 9   Read John 3:16-21.

The gospel in miniature

Occasionally a funeral director will give me a call, asking if I will perform a funeral service for a family without a minister. It happens more frequently than it should.

On one such occasion, I went to the home to meet with some of the family members. A woman had died; she was survived by her husband, several children, and their families. During our time of talking together, as I tried to find out something about this woman, her husband started crying. "Tell me the truth," he said between sobs. "Will my wife be allowed into heaven? Even though we never went to church, does God still love her?"

The best answer I could give was to recite John 3:16.

If we want a condensed version of the scriptures, if we want a gospel in miniature, if we want only one verse to pin our hopes on, we could not pick a better verse than this. While it does not disclose all the information available in the scriptures, it tells three great themes of the Bible.

"For God so loved the world" is the key that can unlock the mysteries of faith. God loves us. God loves even the unlovable and the unlovely, the lonely and the lost, the rejected and those who have given up. God loves unconditionally.

"He gave his only Son": God's love comes to us as a gift. This gift to the world is God's own presence in Jesus Christ. We are not alone; God is always with us.

"Whoever believes in him may not perish but may have eternal life." God promises that if we believe, we will have everlasting life.

Prayer: Dear Lord, thank you for giving me the promise of your love and your presence and the hope of everlasting life. Amen.

THE SHAPING OF A NEW HEART

March 10–16, 1997   **Elizabeth Nordquist**✤
Monday, March 10   Read Jeremiah 31:31-33.

The promise of a new heart

The season of Lent invites us to focus on the condition of our hearts. We have many options when our physical hearts deteriorate—repair, bypass surgery, transplants, medication. However, God is interested in our whole person, our whole being, expressed in Hebrew Scriptures as our heart.

It does not take long on our Lenten journey to discover that we cannot repair some parts of our "heart"—we need a new heart altogether. In God's mercy, God promises us a new heart. The prophet Jeremiah first made the promise to a people in trouble, a people separated from their first love and loyalty to God by their behaviors of indifference, callousness, and loving other seducers. Yet God still loves those people called by God's name and wants to make it possible for humans—individually and as a community—to reciprocate that love. God promises a new covenant so that those who have lost their way of loving will have a new heart. This new heart brings with it the capacity to have God's own communication, the law, written on it.

Suggestion for meditation: When and how has God made a part of my heart new? What part still needs to feel God's touch?

✤Associate pastor, St. Peter's by the Sea Presbyterian Church PC (USA); Rancho Palos Verdes, California.

Tuesday, March 11   Read Jeremiah 31:34.

What the heart knows

We have many ways of knowing: our senses, our intellect, our powers of reasoning. However, as we open ourselves to the new heart that God promises, we find that God has created our new hearts to know God. Jeremiah's listeners had many sources of information about God in their heritage: their history, the patriarchs, the songs they sang, and the prophets. They valued learning about God; yet all their information had not given them power to remain faithful to the God who was faithful to them. In their old weakened hearts, they seemed to have no capacity to know God in a compelling way.

Jeremiah reveals that God not only offers us a new heart, but that heart has a capacity for knowing the God who created and redeemed it. The new heart can know God's compassionate forgiveness no matter what its formal learning, its social status, its previous record of brokenness.

Lent calls us to examine our use of this new heart that God has given us. We begin by asking ourselves if we have acquired information about God only through Bible study, theological books, attentiveness to sermons. If head knowledge is the only knowledge of God we have, we may need a new heart—one that can teach us in relationship about the God who knows our name, who knows the number of hairs on our head.

Suggestion for meditation: **Jesus invites me to take his yoke and learn of him (Matt. 11:29). What can I learn about God from listening with my heart?**

Wednesday, March 12   Read Psalm 51:10-12.

Asking for God's new heart

Most of us believe that we can replace something old with something new, and life goes on; we will keep on ticking without missing a beat. Not so with a physiological heart; not so with the heart God gives. Heart transformation is a process; it begins with our recognition of need.

The Bible attributes Psalm 51 to King David of Israel after he was confronted with the implications of his acquisition of Bathsheba as his sexual partner, then wife and queen (2 Sam. 11-12). No one seemed to know God as David did. Yet when the prophet Nathan confronted David with the sequence of greedy choices and unprincipled manipulations he had committed, David had to acknowledge that what he had known heretofore was not enough. He needed a new heart!

So he asked for one. David sensed that the clean heart for which he asked was full of God's presence, the Spirit: "Put a new and right spirit within me. Do not take your holy spirit from me . . . sustain me with a willing spirit." In Hebrew the word for *spirit* is the same word for breath. David requests the organ that will give him a new life and the breath to live that life.

When I face a behavior or attitude of mine that I know is dehumanizing, dishonest, or death-dealing to another person, I know that more information about things will not bring wholeness; I must have a new heart about this matter, one that is fueled by the power of the Holy Spirit. God will not force it on me; I must ask, "Create in me a clean heart, O God."

Suggestion for meditation: **In what part of my life do I need a Spirit-driven new heart?**

Thursday, March 13   Read Psalm 51:1-12.

Letting God shape our heart

As I have been writing these passages, a beloved family in my parish has been living through the complexities of heart surgery. The diagnosis: Any chance of new life required surgery. The patient agreed to the procedure and decided to open himself up literally to the new possibility. However, in the days following, we have learned that the promise of a new heart and the acceptance of surgery is only the beginning of the process that can lead to a new way of living.

In this psalm, David acknowledges that this new heart he has requested will require much getting used to. To be ready for the new heart he must take inventory of his entire system. The spiritual practice of self-examination allows the knowing Spirit to illumine all the aspects of our being. This discipline shows us the ways in which we delight God and are faithful to that love. It also shows us the ways we have failed to be and to do the things that God has created us to be and to do.

David knows first that he has sinned against God. He has lied to himself, which has led to action that has crushed his integrity, honor, and faithfulness. He asks for mercy, cleansing, teaching, purging, and for restoration and joy. All of these gifts will take getting used to and will require a new way of being. Getting a new heart takes time.

Suggestion for meditation: **Am I willing to allow the new shape of the Spirit to take its form in me in God's good time?**

Friday, March 14   Read Hebrews 5:5-10.

Jesus, our model of the heart of God

The days of Jesus' struggle in the wilderness offer us a model for Lent. What we see in the Gospel accounts of Jesus' temptation is that Jesus had to struggle with living from the heart of God just as we do. It was a vocation that he lived out with difficulty. Jesus wept as he prayed and wrestled with God. Following the Spirit's lead can be painful.

It is sometimes easy to romanticize Jesus, to feel that our struggles of the heart were not part of his journey. The Gospels portray some of his struggles; some we know only by implication. How difficult was it to leave his mother and her intentions for him in order to do the thing to which the heart of God led him? How painful was it to live as a homeless one, dependent on the kindness of strangers rather than settle down to a more stable life? How did Jesus continually tolerate the uneven pace of the disciples whom he loved but who were frequently slow to follow his lead? And how did he ever come to grips with the horror of Jerusalem looming ahead of him as it became clear what was going to be required of him?

The author of Hebrews only tells us that through his struggle came salvation for all of us. This is Mystery! and a core of truthfulness we can affirm. If we know that Jesus is a companion on the way of shaping the new heart we receive from God, the way may be bearable.

Suggestion for meditation: **How can I invite Jesus to be present with me as I struggle to accept God's heart?**

85

Saturday, March 15   Read John 12:20-26.

Holding our hearts lightly

Once we get a new heart in place, we like to hang on to it, to stay in this new state of adjustment and accomplishment. Jesus interrupted this longing for stability with a further demand for the new heart: We receive new life to lose it.

Surely this is not fair; surely this does not even make sense to God. But Jesus is clear at this point—if we are to have this new life, we need to give it away. Having a new heart is not an end in itself; God gives a new heart so that we may glorify God and give life to others.

This may be the crux, the cross, of what separates Christian spirituality from other spiritualities that are finding their way into the popular media markets. Christian spirituality is about asking for and receiving a new heart for God's intended rule of the universe, not for making ourselves more comfortable and feeling better. God gives the new heart so we may multiply the grace we have been given in our new hearts, enabling others to see the goodness, greatness, and compassion of God.

Therefore, we get our new hearts to let go of them as a product, an end in themselves; we let them be reabsorbed into the ground of human need and longing for God where they become the organic catalysts for the flowering of hope and love in other people.

Suggestion for meditation: **I imagine my new heart falling into the ground. What fruit might spring from the gift of my heart?**

Sunday, March 16   Read John 12:27-33.

Where our hearts take us

The journey into our hearts at Lent is an unpredictable one. We cannot know where the Spirit will take us. Jesus had the same experience. His soul was troubled.

However, through this troubling of the soul came a more powerful call. When Jesus heard the voice from heaven affirm his direction, he followed where that voice led. The voice was more important than the practicalities, more compelling than the questions, more reasonable than the rational, more powerful than the pain. He would go where his heart, the heart of God, would take him—to the cross. Although he knew he would be going to his death, he experienced the freedom of walking in the light.

God offers us a new heart in order for us to be loved and loving representatives of God in the world. Our new hearts will lead us to bring light to a world in deep darkness. I am deeply touched when I see bearers of the light of God: the truthteller in a dangerous place, the nurturer of body and soul in the wilderness, the courageous standard-bearer in a hostile assembly. All these are ones who have let God give them and shape in them a new heart.

During Lent we can ask God to let us see and feel the shape of our hearts and then to replace it with a new one. It is a process, a journey that takes time, intention, and risk. Yet as we continue on that journey, it brings us to the right place for us, the place that glorifies God, the place that liberates the other; and we come home to God's heart.

Suggestion for meditation: **Am I walking freely in the light toward God's heart?**

March 17–23, 1997   **Mary Lou Santillán Baert**✤
Monday, March 17   Read Psalm 118:1-2, 19-29.

This royal psalm of thanksgiving begins by extolling the goodness of the Lord. The psalmist was in distress, surrounded by oppressive forces. Salvation came when he was rescued by "the right hand of the LORD" (vv. 15-16). The psalmist is not alone; those around him join in his praise and thanksgiving. They witness in amazement what mighty work the Lord has done for this one who has suffered greatly and has been rescued.

The psalmist knows from personal experience that God's goodness and love endure forever. This ordeal has made the psalmist aware that the Lord is on his side, that the Lord has never deserted him, that the Lord's mercy is everlasting, that the Lord will rescue him from his distress and not let him die.

The psalmist can now tell others about God's mighty acts. The salvation experienced is so important and so powerful that the psalmist links it to the salvation of the whole community, which has joined him in this litany of praise and thanksgiving.

How many times has the Lord rescued us from distress, illness, death, oppression? How many times have we joyfully witnessed to "the right hand of the LORD"? What have we done with the new life, the new opportunity, the new chance at life that God offers us out of sheer grace in a moment of great need? How many times have we cried out to someone to open the gates of the church that we and the company of believers might enter with praise and thanksgiving for the gift of salvation?

Prayer: **Almighty and loving God, grant me vision to see your powerful hand at work in my life. Amen.**

✤United Methodist clergy member of the Río Grande Conference, living in Dallas, Texas.

Tuesday, March 18   Read Mark 11:1-11.

The time for the Passover celebration is drawing near. Jesus sends two of his disciples into Bethpage to fetch a colt upon which he will ride into Jerusalem. Many pilgrims have assembled just outside the city of Jerusalem. They gather leafy branches from the fields, which the Gospel of John identifies as palms. Loud hosannas ring out as the people remove their garments and lay them in the path that Jesus will travel into the city of David. They cry out, "Blessed is the coming kingdom of our ancestor David!" No one seemed to recognize who Jesus really was. Did they understand the "save us" they raised with their voices? Do we know what we are saying when we too sing our hosannas?

Earlier Jesus and his disciples had been in Jericho. As they left that city, blind Bartimaeus, sitting on the roadside shouted out to Jesus when he heard that Jesus was approaching. "Jesus, son of David," he exclaimed. He sensed the presence of the living God in Jesus.

Outside of Jerusalem people were emotional and excited as they followed Jesus; but in reading the Gospel of Mark, it seems that Jesus entered the city and the Temple alone. What did the city of Jerusalem represent to the crowd? Was it the majestic, triumphant, glorious city where God dwelled? Or was it the city of death, violence, and disorder? Was it indeed the city that "kills the prophets and stones those [messengers] who are sent to it" (Matt. 23:37)?

And what about our cities? What does it mean to follow the Christ all the way into the city? Would we follow him even into the inner city?

Suggestion for meditation: **What does it mean for God to enter my city? In what ways could it mean the end of old structures and an opportunity to meet God in new and fresh ways?**

Wednesday, March 19   Read Isaiah 50:4-9*a*.

I would never choose to suffer voluntarily, especially since I have experienced needless pain and abuse simply because of who I am—a Mexican American.

Therefore, two words for a time were not very popular in my vocabulary: *sufriente*, suffering and *siervo*, servant. Suffering seemed so unfair, so useless, so crippling. And being a servant seemed so menial, so humiliating, so lowly.

In this the third of the Servant songs, the prophet Isaiah portrays the Suffering Servant as one whom God has blessed with gifts and graces. The servant has submitted his will and entrusted his life completely to God and thus has not been confounded. God has given him a tongue that brings comfort to the weary. God has also enabled him to be a good listener and has strengthened him to turn his back when others try to strike him.

The Suffering Servant is so confident of God and so trusts the power of God's love that he does not ask, "Why is this happening to me?" Rather, he lays down his life that others may live. He fulfills his calling through suffering and by doing so in silence; unlike Job, who cursed the day he was born or like most of us who meet suffering with complaints, swearing, bitterness, and "why me?"

What can we do with our suffering? How can God make it a blessing for us and for others?

To suffer is no disgrace for the servant, for trust is in the Lord, who brings vindication. When I discovered and finally understood how God could transform my suffering and servant experiences into gifts, joy overwhelmed me and I blessed God.

Prayer: **Show me, O merciful God, how to release my pain into your love that it may bless others. Amen.**

Thursday, March 20   Read Psalm 31:9-16

This long lament graphically expresses the intense feelings, frustrations, and confidence in God of one who felt mortally threatened. The psalmist leaves nothing unsaid. He has experienced pain, brokenness, and loneliness because of his physical condition.

The psalmist cries out in distress. His strength fails; his eyes burn with so much crying. His physical apearance is such that he is a "horror to his neighbors." Even those who see him on the street turn away from him and flee. He feels forsaken and forgotten. "I have passed out of mind like one who is dead." Physically, mentally, socially, emotionally, and spiritually the psalmist is a broken individual.

But then his confidence returns as he remembers the goodness and faithfulness of the Lord. The psalmist comes to the realization that God can be trusted, even with his life. Thus he declares, "You are my God." The Lord is in control even though seeming to be silent and powerless. Salvation comes as the psalmist encounters God through a personal relationship with God. Thus, the psalmist is able to offer his praise and thanksgiving to the God who responds and meets his need. The psalmist knows now that salvation has been available all along and that it has become a reality in his life. Once he had been on the brink of despair, but the Lord heard his cry. His adversaries and their taunts are powerless at last.

The psalmist bursts forth in a song of thanksgiving as he recounts his personal experience and bears witness to God's faithfulness. It is a moving picture of one who self-surrenders to God, trusts God completely, and witnesses to the God who saves.

Prayer: **Faithful God, help me to trust you with my life in sickness and in health, in fullness and in emptiness. Amen.**

Friday, March 21   Read Philippians 2:5-11.

What is success? Is your idea the same as that depicted by television commercials, billboards, newspaper and magazine advertisements, and famous personalities? The printed ads and the TV and radio commercials tell us that if we are to be "with it," we must use particular products, be seen in certain circles, engage in special activities, associate with the "right" people, and much more.

Yet in today's Bible passage, the paradigm of success is modeled by the one who took a towel and a basin and washed his disciples' feet, by the one who emptied himself and took the form of a slave, by the one who lay down his life in order to offer life to all, even to his enemies.

If Paul, in writing to the church at Philippi, is quoting an early Christian hymn, was this the church's understanding of Christian discipleship? Was this the lifestyle the church advocated for all believers? Was this how the early church grasped the meaning of the life, personhood, and work of Jesus Christ?

The Gospels portray Jesus as the great worker of miracles, wonders, and signs. He gives sight to the blind, makes the lame walk, feeds the hungry, frees those possessed by demons, cleanses the lepers, rebukes the winds and the sea, and raises the dead. But in this epistle Paul's deep amazement arises from Jesus' humility, his lowliness, his powerlessness, and his obedience and suffering even unto death, not Jesus' power and charisma.

How tragic that some even commit murder so that they or their children may become "número uno"—success at any price.

Are you wasting your time trying to save your life in order to be "with it"? What prevents you from considering servanthood as your lifestyle now and as long as you live?

Prayer: **Spirit of God, descend upon my life that I may joyfully and willingly empty myself and take the form of a servant. Amen.**

Saturday, March 22   Read Mark 14:1-71.

The plot thickens! The religious leaders move quickly to trap Jesus and to do away with him once and for all. They choose not to understand or accept him. He is a troublemaker, a Sabbath breaker, a friend of harlots and publicans. The central figure of Mark's Gospel has been Jesus and all that he did, but now the evangelist focuses not so much on what Jesus did as on what was done to him.

An unnamed woman enters the house of Simon the leper in Bethany, where Jesus is a guest. She breaks open an alabaster jar of ointment and pours it over Jesus' head. Judas Iscariot takes steps to betray Jesus. Two disciples make the necessary preparations for the celebration of Passover. As they eat this last supper together, the twelve are surprised to learn that one of them is a betrayer. In Gethsemane Peter, James, and John fall asleep while Jesus struggles to accept God's will. Then Judas comes, not with a sword in hand, but with a friendly kiss. Jesus is arrested and convicted. Peter denies Jesus and afterwards cries bitterly.

What a long day and night it must have been for Jesus! And how lonely he must have felt with death but a few hours away. His disciples and friends, except for Judas, did not necessarily turn against him; they just fled the scene and disappeared.

We often feel we are strong in our faith, that we would never betray Jesus or deny our faith. We are so confident, so sure of ourselves. So were the disciples, some even boasting that they would die for him. It was not an outsider who betrayed Jesus but an insider, one who had lived with him, eaten with him, been in mission with him, prayed with him, listened to him, loved him, participated in the covenant meal with him.

Prayer: **Forgiving God, grant that I may leave your table to go and sin no more. Amen.**

Sunday, March 23   Read Mark 15:1-47.

Jesus stands before Pilate with no one to defend him. The questioning begins. "Are you the king of the Jews?" The Roman ruler wants to know. The only response he gets is, "You say so." Pilate tries again and is amazed that Jesus will not defend himself, even when the chief priests continue to harass him. Pilate tries again to question him, but Jesus will answer no more questions. Jesus is not a pretender to anybody's throne; he is king because God has made him Lord.

Pilate cannot deal with silence, so he turns to the crowd. Jesus' own people, the Jews, had already rejected him and now the Gentiles, Rome, and the crowd reject him. The crowd clamors for blood, and Pilate offers them an innocent victim. He who is condemned to die is the only calm and confident one in the crowd. Jesus seems like the weak one, the powerless one, the humiliated one. All fail to see that he is the real monarch, the true ruler, the rightful sovereign. Jesus had power even though he seemed weak; his authority was undergirded by love.

Pilate pronounces the sentence. Mocking soldiers lead Jesus away to be crucified. The inscription on the cross reads, "The King of the Jews."

The question for us becomes then, "Who is Jesus indeed?" Whose answer do we use? The preacher's, our parents', a teacher's, a friend's—or our own, born out of our personal relationship with him?

Such a death on the cross moves a centurion to confess what Jesus' followers should have proclaimed, "Truly, this man was God's son!" The silent presence of the women also witnessed to their love and faith. Jesus died and was buried, but that is not the end of the story. To be continued . . .

Prayer: **O Lord God, instill in me the desire not only to love your kingdom but to witness to the living Christ and to bear the cross. Amen.**

March 24–30, 1997   **M. Garlinda Burton**♣
Monday, March 24   Read Isaiah 42:1-9.

"Only the strong survive." That was my father's reply every time one of us kids cried over a skinned knee or shrank away from discipline under his belt or ran from a fight at school. Even as children, we—especially my brothers—were berated for showing weakness in the form of tears or fear. My father had grown up under the domination of a father who battered his wife and children; and he, in turn, never learned—and, therefore, found it hard to demonstrate—tenderness. So his answer to almost every childhood pain was, "Don't cry. Grow up. Only the strong survive."

What a relief to find that God sent Jesus Christ not to berate or chastise or destroy the weak ones but to champion and protect them. The prophet Isaiah heralds the coming of One who would be "a light to the nations," establishing justice for all. "A bruised reed he will not break, and a dimly burning wick he will not quench," Isaiah writes. Rather, those who are bruised, bowed down, and careworn are enfolded in the everlasting arms. That is good news.

How wonderful to belong to One who understands our weaknesses and loves us anyway! It's a love worth passing on.

Prayer: **Brilliant Morning Star, you know all about my struggles, yet your love for me is patient, strong, endless. Teach me to be strong and patient when others around me need a hand to hold. Amen.**

♣Editor, *Interpreter*, a United Methodist magazine for laity and clergy; member, Hobson United Methodist Church, Nashville, Tennessee.

Tuesday, March 26   Read John 12:20-36.

A church in my city has an old-time gospel choir. Its director is a self-taught musician who teaches his multigenerational choir songs that I have never seen in any hymnbook.

One of my favorite songs goes, "Work while it's day, 'fore the night come in," a driving admonition to get about the business of serving God while we still have time. The song, of course, is based on John 12:35-36: "Walk while you have the light, so that the darkness may not overtake you."

As a youth, I couldn't understand the urgency this song implied. Time was all I seemed to have, marking a thousand forevers between Christmases, summer vacations, and birthday celebrations. I thought I would never reach the age where I would be racing a clock to get my life in order.

However, now that I am middle-aged, I find that days race by, and twenty-four hours seems an insufficient allotment for working, caring for my family, writing in my journal, doing volunteer work, and socializing, much less for evaluating and reordering my total life and work in order to be all Christ has called me to be. I'm in good company, according to my reading of the Easter story. Even Jesus' disciples were found lacking when their time with the earthly Savior was running out.

Still, God never promised that we would achieve perfection on earth or that we would enjoy a leisure hour while praising the Savior "all the day long." Rather, we are simply encouraged to "work while it's day" and to take pleasure in the striving as well as in the occasional achievement of our goals. Instead of lamenting the lack of sufficient time, we should give thanks that we are, according to God's grace, allowed to offer our service during our earthly walk. Work while it's day? Lord, yes!

Prayer: **Thank you, loving God, for the privilege of working. Amen.**

Wednesday, March 27   Read Isaiah 50:4-9*a*;
                                                              John 13:21-32.

In the third Servant Song recorded by Isaiah, the one who serves faithfully faces a hostile audience bravely, offering his cheek to those who would pull his beard. The Israelites rebuke and scorn the Servant, who humbly accepts their abuse, confident that God will vindicate all the faithful.

The bravest woman I have ever heard of was one who went to work as a youth minister in a local congregation where division and disagreement had brought the church's outreach ministries to a standstill. Within a year, the woman managed to help turn some things around but not without incurring the hostility of many members who criticized her as an interloper. One man in particular was so full of rage and bitterness that he had refused to speak to the woman from the moment she joined the staff.

One night at a board meeting, during which the leaders of the church had paused for prayer, the woman did an amazing thing. She moved from her seat to face the angry man. She knelt at his feet and stretched out her hands and said, "I know that you are angry at me. I don't know what I've done; I only know that I need your forgiveness. For whatever I have done, please forgive me, for the sake of Christ who loves us both."

The man's defenses shattered at that moment, he wept, and the other leaders wept. They decided to devote the next few meetings to talking through their pain and differences. In a few months, the church was bustling with new activity and new life.

The Servant found power in offering a cheek to those who would bruise it. What blessings might be in store for us if we humble ourselves for God's sake?

Prayer: **Thou fount of every blessing, teach me patience and forgiveness as you continually forgive my shortcomings and heal me with your balm of love. Amen.**

Maundy Thursday

Thursday, March 28   Read Exodus 12:1-4;
                                                          Psalm 116:1-7, 12-19.

She was homeless; she was dirty. She hadn't begged or pleaded with me or tried to block me as I walked into the restaurant. She had simply said, "I haven't eaten in three days." I had some extra money, so I bought two sandwiches instead of one and handed one to her as I walked to my car.

She thanked me, took her package to the curb, and sat down. After unwrapping her food she paused a moment, bowed her head, tore the sandwich in half and ate one half. The other portion she wrapped up and stuck in her pocket.

She noticed me watching her curiously and turned back to me, shouting, "Thanks again!"

I replied, "I thought you were hungry. Saving the rest for later?"

"Nope, for Rodney. He lives over by me, but he can't walk around and ask for food. I promised the Lord if I got anything to eat today, I'd share it with Rodney. I could eat the whole thing, but God didn't leave me hungry; now I gotta do my part."

Most Sundays, before I write out my check for the collection plate, I first estimate how much I'll need for bills, lunches out, the movies, and just walking-around money for the week. God will get what's left over, maybe. I've never had to decide between being hungry or half hungry.

The psalmist asks, "What shall I return to the LORD?" In gratitude for God's ultimate sacrifice—that Christ died for us—we give according to what we've been given. And our offering next Sunday will double—at least.

Prayer: **Selfless God, help me say thanks in tangible ways, so that my brothers and sisters will know that your kingdom has come near them. Amen.**

Good Friday

Friday, March 29   Read Isaiah 52:13-52;
                                                    Psalm 22; John 18:1–19:2.

In Frances Hodgson Burnett's classic children's novel *The Little Princess*, the heiress and boarding school favorite Sarah Crewe is left penniless and at the mercies of a cruel, mercenary headmistress, Miss Minchin. When found at last, Sarah has been reduced to living in a garret and dressing in rags, frequently deprived of her meals and beaten by the other servants.

At her rescue, Sarah is told that her father has not lost his fortune—that it was all a mistake—and that she has always been an heiress and a princess, even when she was cold and hungry and wretched.

Even as Jesus was beaten, dragged to Calvary, and hung between two thieves, he was the First and the Last, the Bright and Morning Star, the Savior of all humanity. Even as Jesus hung on the cross and the Roman soldiers mocked him, he was the Son of God glorified in heaven. That which human beings scorned was no less the Mighty God because he was despised by those who did not know him.

We fail; we flounder. We are a people—even a church—that lose our way. We are children of God who neglect our duties and who discount our blessings. Or if we live according to Christ's teaching, we face ridicule, criticism, and abuse.

Thanks be to God that is not the last word. God has not called us to succeed according to earthly standards in everything that we undertake. We simply are to be faithful, to remember that God is our rock and our salvation whether we triumph or fail utterly. God will always claim us as children of the promise.

Prayer: **Thank you, God of Easter, that a Sunday of glory awaits the Good Fridays in our lives. Amen.**

Holy Saturday

Saturday, March 30   Read John 19:38-42;
                                                          1 Peter 4:1-8.

Are there any people whom we scrutinize and criticize more
than those who publicly repent of raucous, hedonistic, free-
wheeling, or self-destructive lifestyles? For example, think of
overweight celebrities who lose 100 pounds, or those who swear
off drugs after a bad episode. Some of us are like vultures, waiting
for them to fail—watching to see if their waistlines bulge again,
scanning the papers for news of an arrest or a drug bust. Instead of
encouraging them and praying for their reformation, many people
are cynical in the face of their repentance and gleeful if they fall.

Peter knew the pressure of public transformation. The Gentiles
of the church of Asia Minor were suffering extreme persecution
from those who were trying to tempt them back into a life of sin
and excess—those who were skeptical of so-called new life in
Jesus Christ. And many of the new converts found it hard not to
give themselves over to peer pressure, not to reclaim lives of
"revels, carousing, and lawless idolatry."

The advice of the writer of First Peter? Cling to one another.
Seek out people who are walking the same walk, struggling
against the same temptations; people who will love you,
encourage you, and forgive your missteps even as God forgives
us. In other words, find a community of faith that will nurture and
care for you.

That's sound advice for God's people in any age. All kinds of
persecution and temptation exist, but God has given us a Holy
Comforter and one another for the journey. We are never alone.

Suggestion for meditation: **Name the people in your life who
have been with you at times when you were discouraged or
downhearted. Thank God for each one of them.**

Easter Sunday

Sunday, March 31   Read 1 Corinthians 15:1-11;
                                                        John 20:1-18.

In a world fraught with rigid standards and labels, it is easy for me to think, *I am too short, I am too dark, I have a perpetual "bad hair day," I'm too heavy, my face is too round, I'm too outspoken.* On the worst days, all those negative images bear down on me; and I can hardly face myself in the mirror.

But on those best days, those days when Easter runs through my veins, warm as my mother's hug; and I feel the Resurrection down to my toes, I celebrate Paul's words: "By the grace of God I am what I am!"

What I wouldn't give to have been there that "great, gettin' up morning," with the first women to encounter the newly risen Christ! Dejected and lost for the past three days, God suddenly fulfilled their hopes and God's promises beyond human imagination! Christ risen was shaking up the world and turning everything on its ear. Death was no longer the last word. Women, second-class citizens, were now telling the world the good news. Earthly powers no longer held the ultimate fate of humankind in their hands. The last would be first forever. And overweight girls with bad hair days are reconciled and made new and beautiful, thanks be to God.

Easter proclamation: **Easter people, raise your voices! Look in the mirror and love what you see! Look in the faces of one another and love what you see! By the grace of God and through the triumphant resurrection of Jesus Christ, we are what we are! Thanks be to God!**

101

March 31–April 6, 1997   **Willis H. Moore**✤
Monday, March 31   Read Acts 4:32-35.

"Now the whole group of those who believed were of one heart and soul" (TEV). The scripture passage jumps right out at you. Luke concisely sums up this group of early Christians: The power of the Holy Spirit bore vivid evidence in their lives. The phrase *of one heart and soul* rings in my ears. With complete trust in Christ as their savior, they could focus upon the needs of others.

"But it was easy for the disciples," I protest when confronted with my responsibility to embrace the spirit of "one heart and soul." "After all," I rationalize, "they experienced the risen Lord firsthand." Yet we too know the glow that follows a high moment in the presence of Jesus. Maybe you are experiencing it now. Yesterday was Easter, and the joyful music and drama that characterizes the celebration of the risen Lord lingers.

But today is Monday. Tiresome frustrations return to pester us. "Those disciples lived in a simpler time," you grumble. Let these words soak in: *those who believed.* Despite the times, belief makes the difference in the evidence of the Spirit's working in persons' lives. Luke's confidence rests in the assurance that persons who trust Christ will live forever with God. That assurance makes an eternal difference.

Suggestion for meditation: **Visualize a Christian group of which you are a part. Read the scripture passage reflecting on how your group might experience "one heart and soul." Pray, asking Jesus to make it so.**

✤United Methodist clergy, member of the South Georgia Conference; Associate Director, Conference Council on Ministries.

Tuesday, April 1   Read Acts 4:32-35.

The early disciples encountered the Resurrection in ways that transformed their living. Their single focus was Christ, and that focus resulted in a community in which "there was not a needy person among them."

Notice the disciples' deep sense of community: "No one claimed private ownership of any possessions." We also struggle with the possessions' issue.

Did your first reading of this passage trouble you as it did me? It is the possessions thing, I think. Mutually shared possessions with everyone's feeling a sense of profound joy and community is not a common experience. Few human beings are able to accomplish this ideal sense of community.

Members of the early church had some trouble with it, which you will notice if you read further. In Acts 5–6, you discover that some members of this fledgling community of the risen Lord did not live in the power of the Resurrection. Yet amid the several tales of disbelief, we read remarkable stories of power and healing.

The power of the Resurrection and the witness of those first believers is alive today in the lives of those who have experienced the risen Lord. You see it in people who once had no hope but now find joy and purpose in life—those whose lives were shattered by addiction or physical abuse, by distrust and misspeaking. Now they have discovered that they are not alone in their struggle. They have the power of the risen Lord and the fellowship of the Christian community.

Suggestion for meditation: **Reflect upon the community of believers of which you are a part. Write an action you will take to reflect the Resurrection in your life, hence helping someone to believe as powerfully as you do.**

Wednesday, April 2   Read Psalm 133.

Feel the texture of Psalm 133 as you read. I invite you to linger and wrestle with God's word in new ways. The imagery of the psalm causes me to wrestle. When I read these verses, I have to tarry awhile before I move beyond my initial feelings.

The psalm begins with inviting images of a pleasant gathering in community. "It is like the precious oil on the head, running down upon the beard . . . of Aaron." My mind jumps suddenly to memories of my first summer job at an auto parts store. One morning I inadvertently drenched myself with motor oil from head to toe. It was warm and messy; it ruined my clothes and nearly cost me my summer job.

After dealing with that flashback, I can get on with hearing God speak that word of blessing and joy I long to hear. When I read the psalm, I have to focus on the intended imagery: The psalmist is speaking of a high and holy time, similar to the time of ordination or consecration.

The imagery is vivid and touches me at the feeling level. I tarry and wrestle, and the result is worth it. I begin to discover not only the holy anointing but also the extravagant grace and mercy of God. Listen to the psalmist. Do you feel abundantly drenched in God's unending, unrestrained mercy and grace, which is "good and pleasant, . . . running down"?

Suggestion for meditation: **Call to mind your cherished circle of friends, gathered for a high moment of worship. Read Psalm 133 as if you are among those gathered. Pray that each one may feel God's blessed drenching.**

Thursday, April 3   Read John 20:19-31.

"I don't even remember the first half of the trip," Jennifer said, as she described her drive home. Returning home after the deepest heartbreak of her young life, she drove down the interstate highway, unsure of her future's direction. In the midst of grief, it is difficult to conceive of new possibilities.

Surely the disciples' deep grief, as well as their fear of the Jews, hampered their hopes for the future. Perhaps their sorrow so distracted them that no one noticed as Jesus came and stood among them.

Maybe someone looked up. Surely Jesus' presence must have startled them. Maybe it was at Jesus' speaking that someone finally noticed him. He gave the word of assurance: "Peace be with you." What genuine peace must have rested upon them as they saw their Master face to face.

Then Jesus gave the word of recreation, resurrection, and new beginning: "He breathed on them and said to them, 'Receive the Holy Spirit.'" As God breathed into humankind, so Jesus launched the new community of the church with his holy breath.

As dawn creeps onto the horizon, wiping away darkness, so the new day came to the disciples. Though Jesus was no longer with them physically, he would always be with them through the Holy Spirit, the beginning of a new life for the believers.

Suggestion for meditation: **Reread John 20:19-23 while asking God, "What word of recreation are you speaking to me?" Receive the peace Jesus offers in your labors today, or as you release your day to him in blessed sleep.**

Friday, April 4   Read John 20:19-31.

Thomas was absent when Jesus first appeared to the disciples, and he expressed his doubts strongly: "Unless I see the mark of the nails in his hands, . . . I will not believe."

A week later the disciples are together again; Thomas is present as Jesus stands among them. Simply to be in the presence of Jesus convinces Thomas that the Lord has risen from the dead. Thomas's faith statement "My Lord and my God!" is a model for us all.

Noticeably absent is Thomas's probing curiosity. Instead, this encounter with the risen Lord kindles his faith, marking a significant growth point in his life.

Horton, a friend from my youth, was my father's age. He probably never finished public school. Horton worked the night shift at a pipeline pump station. On my way home from a football game one night, I saw his battered pickup truck at the pump station. I stopped and went in. When not checking the gauges and knobs of the pumps, Horton was reading his Bible and working on his Sunday school lesson plans.

We talked. Mostly I listened as Horton shared his deep love for Jesus and Jesus' power in his life. I was sophisticated, a teenager on my way to higher education. That night I was humbled by the strong, simple faith of my friend. "My Lord and my God!" was Horton's affirmation. That night marked a growth point for me toward belief.

Suggestion for meditation: **Thomas thought he needed to touch Jesus' wounds in order to believe. As you meditate on the scripture passage ask, "What do I think I need to bring me to belief?" Then articulate your faith statement. Write it down for future reflection.**

Saturday, April 5   Read 1 John 1:1-10.

When an air traffic controller reports "Traffic at nine o'clock," it means "An airplane is coming at you from your left!" "No joy!" the airplane pilot may reply, meaning "Help! I don't see that aircraft!" Verbal shorthand is essential in an environment where concise, precise communication determines life or death. This point was demonstrated graphically just before I wrote this piece. A pilot flying in South America did not communicate concisely and clearly with air traffic controllers. All on board died in the resulting crash.

There is "No joy" at the prospect that one's life may tragically end. In contrast, the author of First John writes to the followers of Jesus that their "joy may be complete." Reading today's scripture passage may remind one of the prologue to John's Gospel.

The writer of First John convinces me that once I accept the wonderful gift given in Christ Jesus, my "joy [will] be complete." I too will have the profound confidence that I shall live with him forever.

Another apparent connection between the Gospel of John and First John: "These are written so that you may come to believe" (John 20:31), and "we are writing these things so that our joy may be complete." Both relay an invitational message: Those who believe in Christ find their joy complete.

Suggestion for meditation: **List the things that invite you to believe in Christ. Circle those that evoke the greatest joy. Prayerfully thank God for helping you toward making your joy complete.**

Sunday, April 6   Read 1 John 1:1–2:2.

"Been there. Done that. Got the Tee Shirt," she said, as she turned down the opportunity to be youth counselor. Hers was the whimsical if not cynical response of the day.

People often casually dismiss opportunities for fellowship in the church that could begin life-transforming events. Responsibility for this casual attitude must rest, in part, upon church leaders—both clergy and laity. These leaders tend to give committee assignments to anyone who is halfway willing, whether they have a passion or the gifts for the opportunity or not.

By contrast, here the writer describes persons who have an intimate, firsthand relationship with the risen Lord and with one another. There is an invitational passion in his words: "that you also may have fellowship with us."

My friend Tom, a retired state patrol officer, called. "Willis, I want to invite you to participate in an experience that is just fantastic!" There was passion in his voice. Tom (as Lay Director) and I (as Spiritual Director) had led a Walk to Emmaus, so I trusted him completely. This time he was planning a Kairos event (equivalent to Walk to Emmaus but in a prison).

I did not dismiss his invitation casually. I have experienced the intimate, life-transforming power these events can have upon persons. Through the centuries, we have witnessed many different avenues into fellowship with Christ. The most convincing invitation to believe in Christ comes through the transformed lives of his followers living in fellowship with one another.

Suggestion for meditation: **Read John 21:19-31 again invitationally, circling each firsthand experience mentioned. Listen for Christ's invitation into a relationship with him and into fellowship with other believers.**

GOD IN US

April 7–13, 1997   **Pedro A. Sandín-Fremaint✤**
Monday, April 7   Read Psalm 4.

Many writers share an incorrigible fear of the empty page. No matter how many times you have fulfilled a writing assignment successfully, each new task causes you to wrestle with the near certainty that this time you will fail. Writers' anxiety over the empty page may serve as a metaphor for our own spiritual anxiety.

Psalm 4 expresses a tension between the memory and knowledge of what God has done for us and our anguish over present and future uncertainties. The psalmist opens his prayerful song with an anguished cry, immediately followed by his confession of God's grace in previous situations of distress. As we review our own lives, we must acknowledge that God's love and grace have been with us. Yet again and again, we allow anxiety to get the better of us, while God meets our distress with the same reassurance of love and the same exhortation to be still and trust.

One common thread throughout the Bible—despite the many centuries it spans and the diverse perspectives it offers—is its witness to God's unrelenting desire to love us and to make God's self real in our lives. And yet, our disbelief is never greater than before our acknowledgment of this graceful truth.

Prayer: **Dear Lord, may I come to accept the gracious chasm between your love and my lack of merit! Amen.**

✤Professor of French and Associate Dean for Academic Affairs, University of Puerto Rico in Rio Piedras.

Tuesday, April 8   Read Psalm 4:7-8.

There is perhaps no greater obstacle to faith than our reluctance to believe that God could really love us. This is the eternal scandal of the Incarnation, both in the manger and in the cross. How can it be? How can this possibly be the Son of God? How can God become flesh like us in order to win us over to God's love and to the values of the kingdom?

I must confess that in my own journey of faith I have tended toward obsession with my many shortcomings. Guilt has become a most familiar companion! In my difficulty with loving myself, I—almost unconsciously—convince myself that God will *only* love me if I change this or that, if I accomplish another goal, if I become the kind of person that God really loves.

Driving home from work a few years ago, I was consumed, as usual, by introspection. Overwhelmed by the sorry state of our world and feeling guilty over everything that I was not doing in order to improve it, I suddenly heard—deep in my heart—the following words: *¡Descansa en mí!* ("Rest in me!"). What a precious gift these words were, inviting me to accept the gospel of God's free love! It put such joy in my heart, greater than could possibly come from all the riches of the world!

Today's reading is a lullaby for heavy hearts. It invites us to cherish the certainty that we may rest safely in God's arms.

Prayer: **O God, forgive me when I resist the glorious gospel of your obstinate love! Amen.**

Wednesday, April 9   Read Luke 24:36-43.

Many years ago, while watching Franco Zefirelli's magnificent film *Jesus of Nazareth,* the following thought assaulted me: Would I have recognized God in Jesus? With the benefit of nearly two thousand years of Christian tradition, it is rather easy for us to see the Messiah in the man named Jesus. But to his contemporaries, to those who knew him as the son of Mary and Joseph, wasn't it overwhelmingly difficult to recognize the Christ? Have we not been too harsh on the Pharisees?

It is interesting to observe the reaction of the disciples before the risen Lord. They had already heard the news and were even willing to confess to the resurrection: "The Lord has risen indeed!" (v. 34). Yet, before the risen Lord himself, they were startled and surprised and could only suppose that they were seeing a ghost. Mind you, these are the disciples, those who had already believed in Jesus! Once again the Lord must offer proof. Since seeing him is insufficient, he asks them to touch him; and he eats a piece of fish before them so they may realize that God has become flesh . . . again.

This reading reminds us again of God's unrelenting desire to come to us. Dead flesh will rise; there will be no obstacle to God's desire to make God's self real in our lives!

Prayer: **O risen Lord, grant me the grace to recognize you whenever and wherever you cross my path. May the reality of your flesh never become an obstacle to my faith; in your Incarnation, true love comes to me. Amen.**

Thursday, April 10   Read Luke 24:44-48.

Luke is without doubt the "equal opportunity Gospel." It reaches farther and more clearly than the other Gospels in terms of including all persons. From the outset, the beautiful hymns of the first two chapters make it clear that God has become flesh not only for the people of Israel but for all people, and God's love reaches the poor especially. By tracing Jesus' genealogy all the way back to Adam, rather than only to Abraham as in Matthew, Luke presents Jesus as the true light for all nations.

Today's reading emphasizes this truth. The risen Lord presents himself as the fulfillment of the Hebrew Scriptures but also as the gospel to all nations. Thus, the extent of God's love becomes evident.

On this occasion Jesus issues the Great Commission. The risen Lord—God incarnate—entrusts his message of repentance and forgiveness of sins to his disciples. In the glorious itinerary of God's incarnation, it is now ordinary flesh—you and I—that must convey the message of God's redeeming love. Not only are we to evangelize all people, but all believers are to become evangelists: bearers of God's gospel of relentless love!

As we prepare for worship with our faith community, let us meditate on the ways in which we may become the bearers of such wonderful news.

Prayer: **Dear God, in your boundless love, your hope is that I may make your message of salvation incarnate in my life. Grant me the wisdom and the courage to live in such a way that I may bear witness to the risen Lord. Amen.**

Friday, April 11   Read Acts 3:12-16.

The Incarnation embodies the Spirit that is God. We could translate the word *incarnate* (from the Latin *incarnare)* literally to mean "to enflesh": in Jesus, the God of Israel and of all peoples has become flesh.

Acts 2, which precedes today's reading, relates the experience of Pentecost. At Pentecost the believers experienced what we might consider to be the inverse of the Incarnation: the *inspiration* of ordinary flesh. Through God's infinite mercy, the disciples received the gift of the Holy Spirit, which enabled them to carry out the Great Commission. In Acts 3:6-10, Peter performs the first miracle recorded in the book of Acts. He puts his "inspiration" to good use by giving health to a man lame from birth.

In response to the miracle that has taken place in his own body, the man clings to Peter and John and attracts the attention of the multitude. Peter rises to the occasion by resisting the ultimate temptation of all disciples—taking credit for the Spirit's power. Peter delivers the fundamental sermon, the *kerygma*—the gospel in a kernel—and confronts the people with their own participation in killing "the Author of life, whom God raised from the dead." Faith through Jesus has restored the lame man to health. Thus we attend, once again, to God's relentless desire to come to us in Jesus and in Jesus' presence through his disciples.

Prayer: **God Emmanuel, grant me the wisdom to accept your love and your desire to dwell in me. Amen.**

God in Us

Saturday, April 12   Read Acts 3:17-19.

Growing up in the Catholic church and in a Hispanic culture, the yearly reenactment of the events of Jesus' passion played an important part in my early spiritual formation. Through processions (*via crucis*), dramatizations, and other traditional celebrations, I became thoroughly familiar with the stories of Holy Week. Among these, none fascinated or terrified me more than the story of Judas Iscariot.

A great deal of speculation always surrounds conversations about Judas. He had known the Lord personally, had been his intimate friend, and still betrayed him for money. There could be no forgiveness for such a sin! Thus Judas's suicide was inevitable. This concept of the inevitable terrified me the most, especially as I reflected on what might become inevitable in my own life.

In today's reading, Peter, after confronting the people with their guilt in killing the Author of life, addresses them in conciliatory terms. Only ignorance can account for such a crime. Peter asks for their repentance, affirming God's willingness to blot out sin!

Perhaps Judas's mistake was to believe that his sin—awful as it was—was bigger than God's desire to love us. Let us remember that the greatest obstacle to faith, the one that can lead us to Judas's tragic destiny, is precisely our reluctance to accept that God's love overcomes all things.

Prayer: **Lord of mercy, may I learn to accept your love! Amen.**

Sunday, April 13   Read 1 John 3:1-7.

It may be instructive to remember that First John was written in the face of one of the earliest heresies in the history of Christianity, the *docetic* heresy. According to Docetism, the Incarnation was only apparent: Christ only *seemed* to have a body and to suffer and die on the cross. What was not readily apparent is that this belief represented the antithesis of the Christian faith. Without the Incarnation, Christianity becomes a school of thought rather than a movement that grows out of the historical events surrounding the man Jesus of Nazareth. The epistle writer attempts to help believers understand the importance of affirming the truth of God's incarnation in Jesus.

Just as God was literally and physically present in the man Jesus, we who have believed are now literally and physically God's children. This is why John must reject another important tenet of Docetism: the belief that Christians, by definition, do not sin. In practice, this belief became a license to sin. On the contrary, our lives must bear witness to our intimate relationship with Christ in our efforts to purify ourselves as Christ is pure (v. 3). The Christian life is not characterized by sinlessness, as Docetists maintained, but by the awareness of sin.

Reading verses 6 and 7 in docetic terms would contradict other key passages in the epistle (see 1:8-10). Paradoxically, it is only in acknowledging our sin that we remain outside the power of sin!

Prayer: **God Incarnate, grant me the faith to acknowledge the literal truth of Emmanuel!**

BY WHAT POWER?

April 14–20, 1997   **James A. Harnish**✣
Monday, April 14   Read Acts 4:1-12.

Does believing in the Resurrection ever get you into trouble? Living in the light of Easter with the "Hallelujah Chorus" from Handel's oratorio *The Messiah* echoing in our souls, we could assume that everything is fine; God's in heaven and all's well with the world. The Book of Acts, however, is a vivid reminder that the Resurrection is an audacious contradiction of the world's definition of power. The power that broke open the tomb undermines the deadly assumptions of authority and control that put Jesus there.

Nothing suggests that Peter and John ever considered the consequences of healing the lame beggar. The event itself was hardly enough to incur the wrath of the Temple authorities. What got Peter and John into trouble was the power by which they claimed the healing occurred.

Peter's bold proclamation of the Resurrection, his indictment of those who crucified Jesus, and his claim of absolute saving power through Jesus' name was what amazed, annoyed, and angered the council. In the resurrection of the crucified Jesus, they felt the ultimate threat to their power.

What about us? In what ways is the power of life in the risen Christ doing anything in and through us that would threaten the powers of darkness around us?

Prayer: **O Risen Lord, allow your resurrection power to flow through our lives in life-giving and troublemaking ways. Amen.**

✣Senior pastor of Hyde Park United Methodist Church, Tampa, Florida.

Tuesday, April 15   Read Acts 4:14-21.

Although not within this week's lectionary parameters, the story seems incomplete with mention of the response to Peter's action. There is, perhaps, an element of satire in Peter's response to the inquisition. He was probably thinking, *Are we really on trial because a sick man was healed? You would think religious people would be grateful rather than arrest us, put us in jail, and haul us into court. Why should one act of goodness bring this kind of reaction?*

But the powers of death are unconditional; the smallest intrusion of new life threatens undisputed control. One sign of resurrection subverts the absolute power of death.

During the struggle for justice in South Africa, members of Central Methodist Mission in downtown Johannesburg lit a white candle that was surrounded by barbed wire. Every Sunday in worship they prayed by name for people who were imprisoned and suffering under the power of apartheid. Stirring sermons about justice and freedom did not annoy or anger the authorities as much as the lighting of that candle and the calling of those names. That simple act of goodness contradicted the assumptions of evil power.

During some of the darkest hours in the struggle for freedom in South Africa, the pastor of the congregation, Bishop Peter Storey, described the flame of the candle as a sign of protest, a symbol of nonconformity that told the powers of darkness, "We beg to differ." By God's power, the simple light of that candle helped shatter the powers of darkness.

Prayer: **O Risen Lord, allow your power to be the light within my life that contradicts the darkness around me. Amen.**

Wednesday, April 16   Read John 10:11-18.

My earliest images of the story of the Good Shepherd came from Sunday school room paintings. I imagined Jesus sitting on a peaceful hillside cradling a newborn lamb in his arms and speaking softly over the gentle breeze as he shared the story. The reaction to the parable as recorded in verse 19 contradicts that quiet, peaceful image: "The Jews were divided because of these words." What about the good shepherd would be so threatening to those in power?

Five times Jesus speaks of laying down his life, ultimately declaring that he has the "power to lay it down"—no Superman with superhuman powers, no James Bond blowing them away with twenty-first century technology, no lion king destroying his opponent with lionhearted fury—nothing but the power to lay down his life.

Ghandi discovered that power. He called it *satyagraha* or *soul force*, and it threatened the power of the British Empire. Martin Luther King, Jr., found that power in creative nonviolence, the redemptive power of undeserved suffering; it threatened the power of racism. Thomas Merton found it in a life of solitude and prayer. The Methodist Order of Peacemakers in South Africa found it as the power of nonviolence in a world of conflict.

Nothing undermines the power of death as forcefully as the power to lay one's life down, the way the good shepherd lays down his life for his sheep. Nothing is more costly, nothing more like Jesus.

Prayer: **Good Shepherd, help me discover the power that comes in laying down my life in self-giving love. Amen.**

Thursday, April 17   Read John 10:11-18.

Jesus defined a fundamental reality about our lives that can open the way for God's resurrection power to unsettle the powers of death when he said, "I have power to lay it down, and I have power to take it up again."

The difference between the good shepherd and the hired hand is simple and absolute. When the wolf comes, the hired hand's primary concern is saving his or her own skin. By contrast, the good shepherd chooses the welfare of the sheep over personal safety. Everything hangs on that moment of choice between self-giving and self-saving, between taking up life or laying it down.

It was April 3, 1968. In what would be his last sermon, Martin Luther King, Jr., called his followers to "a kind of dangerous unselfishness." Reflecting on the parable of the Good Samaritan, he said the pivotal question is not, "If I stop to help this man, what will happen to me?". . . [The question is,] "If I do not stop to help this man, what will happen to him?" In prophetic words, he said, "Like anybody, I would like to live a long life. Longevity has its place. But I'm not concerned about that now. I just want to do God's will."*

The divine power that unhinges the power of evil is the power to choose to lay one's life down for something larger than self-interest. It is nothing less than the power of the cross.

Prayer: **Good Shepherd, who chose to lay down your life for your sheep, help me choose the way of dangerous unselfishness today. Amen.**

---

*James Melvin, ed., *A Testament of Hope: The Essential Writings of Martin Luther King, Jr.* (San Francisco: Harper & Row, Publishers, 1986), 286.

Friday, April 18   Read 1 John 3:16-24.

"Okay, Jim," the voice said. "It's fine to write about Peter and John. It's important to see Jesus as the good shepherd who lays down his life for his sheep. You love to tell the stories of Ghandi, King, and South Africa. But what about you?"

This epistle was written to people who knew the gospel. It is "the message you have heard from the beginning, that we should love one another." They knew God's love revealed in Jesus' laying down his life at the cross. But the writer would not leave it there. Just as the good shepherd lays down his life, the writer of First John tells us that "we ought to lay down our lives for one another." The Spirit is always asking, "What about you?"

Lest we get caught up in grandiose images of self-sacrificing martyrs of the past, John describes this laying down of our lives in earthy, practical terms: "How does God's love abide in anyone who has the world's goods and sees a brother or sister in need and yet refuses help?"

When he preached his last sermon, Martin Luther King, Jr., was calling people to support the sanitation workers of Memphis. Laying down his life meant walking with the folks who were carrying out the garbage.

I heard the voice again and recognized it as the voice of the Good Shepherd. It reminded me of a call I needed to make, a person I needed to visit, a letter I needed to send, a check I needed to write, a gift I needed to give. What about you?

Prayer: **O God, whose love was revealed in Jesus' laying down his life, show me practical ways in which to lay down my life for others. Amen.**

Saturday, April 19   Read Psalm 23:1-4.

Like the parable of the Good Shepherd, I suspect that the power of Psalm 23 has been weakened by too many romantic paintings of still waters, green pastures, and well-groomed shepherds in long, flowing robes. The perennial reading for funerals and memorial services, we hear it as a word of warm assurance and quiet comfort for people in sorrow or pain—and it is that.

But perhaps we might picture this scene and hear the shepherd's psalm in another way, particularly in light of this week's readings. Shepherding in Palestine was tough, demanding, dirty work. It meant long, hot days in the blazing sun; cold, dark nights on jagged hillsides. Shepherds had to be rugged, muscular, and sturdy; stripped bare in the heat or wrapped in smelly sheepskin against the cold. They had to be gentle enough to hold a newborn lamb but strong enough to walk through a dark valley without fear.

The shepherd who provides, leads, and restores is also the Lord. He lays down his life not in weakness but in strength; in the power that freely chooses to give itself for others, knowing that it could just as easily protect itself. The power of self-giving love threatens the power of death because it is nothing less than the power of God that raises the dead, heals the lame, sets captives free, and will ultimately reign over all the powers of darkness.

The Lord, who shepherds us, leads, us, and restores us is powerful enough to be our comfort and our strength.

Prayer: **Lord, my shepherd, I rest my weakness in your strength. Lead me where you would have me go and restore my soul. Amen.**

121

Sunday, April 20   Read Acts 4:23-31; Psalm 23.

"And now for the rest of the story . . . " In the end, all that the authorities could do to Peter and John was to threaten them and let them go. Then the celebration began. The Christian community praised God and prayed for boldness to make known the good news of the risen Christ. Confronted with the power of death, they celebrated the new life of the Resurrection.

It was a brilliant afternoon in the summer of 1986 when 3,000 delegates of the World Methodist Conference took to the streets of Nairobi, Kenya. Leading the procession, the bishops walked in solemn dignity. Further back, it became more of a march. But bringing up the rear, Archbishop Desmond Tutu and the South Africans were dancing. Back home, they faced the evil powers of apartheid; as people who knew the power of God, they rejoiced in the hope of freedom they knew would come. Looking back now, we know it was a prophetic celebration of the liberating power of God.

The psalmist could see the celebration on the other side of the dark valley. He envisioned a table, set with cups overflowing, in the house of the Lord. And he knew that the goodness and mercy of God would see him through.

Every time we gather for worship, every time we lift the cup at the table of the Lord, we celebrate the power of the Resurrection. Here and now, in a world where the powers of death sometimes threaten to overwhelm us, we rejoice in the life-giving power of the risen Christ. Let the party begin!

Prayer: **Risen Lord, may your power bring joy and boldness as we gather to worship you in the hope of the resurrection. Amen.**

GOD'S GREAT LOVE FOR US

April 21–27, 1997   **Richard H. Schmidt**✤
Monday, April 21   Read Psalm 22:25-31.

The opening verse of Psalm 22 is familiar to Christians the world over as Jesus' cry of abandonment from the cross. The following verses allude to experiences similar to those of Jesus on the cross. However, following verse 21 the mood of Psalm 22 shifts. Gone is the sense of abandonment and persecution. Gone are the graphic descriptions of physical pain. The psalm becomes more ordered and serene and concludes with a ringing affirmation of the Lord's saving presence.

In reflecting on the concluding section of Psalm 22, we should remember the cry of dereliction to which they are an answer. They affirm God's power and goodness to someone who is feeling abandoned, deserted, forsaken. The vivid descriptions of pain and loneliness in verses 1-21 strongly contrast with the confident affirmations of the concluding verses.

Notice the breadth of vision in verses 25-31. The psalmist's experience of deliverance is more than a localized, individual phenomenon. The psalmist bids "all the ends of the earth" and "all the families of the nations" to take note of the goodness of the Lord. This universality is not merely a theological doctrine for the psalmist but a conclusion drawn from personal experience— *God saves*. This is true for all people everywhere. Therefore the psalmist bids those who have already died, and "a people yet unborn" to join him in praising the Lord. Neither space nor time limits the saving power of God.

Suggestion for meditation: **Reflect on the text of the hymn "How Firm a Foundation."**

✤Rector, St. Paul's Episcopal Church, Daphne, Alabama; former managing editor of *The Episcopalian*; amateur musician and composer.

Tuesday, April 22   Read Acts 8:26-40.

The Ethiopian had gone to Jerusalem to worship and was on his way home. Perhaps he was an Ethiopian Jew and wished to make a pilgrimage, or perhaps he had heard of the great temple on Mount Zion. Whatever the reason for his journey, he was moved to read the Hebrew Scriptures as he headed home. When Philip approached him, he asked the Ethiopian whether he understood what he read. "How can I, unless someone guides me?" the Ethiopian replied. He had worshiped in Jerusalem—yet he remained confused.

Visitors and newcomers to our churches often depart confused. We who are inside the church speak in a special jargon, using a vocabulary rarely heard elsewhere and understood only by ourselves. We assume everyone knows how to find a seat; when to stand, sit, and kneel; which book to use and what page to turn to—so we don't bother to explain. We nod cursorily at a newcomer standing three feet from us as we chat warmly with someone we already know.

We scurry around. We're busy. We teach classes on parenting, political and social issues, contemporary literature, and gardening. We organize thrift shops, young people's groups, bazaars, and every member canvasses. We publish bulletins and newsletters, own and maintain property, hire and train personnel, keep records, appoint committees. We bicker among ourselves over money and budgets, worship styles, buildings, ordination, and feelings about our pastor and denominational leaders.

What is the reason behind our action? Do we find the One we seek? Does that One find us? What difference does it make? If a stranger overheard our conversation at church, would he or she be confused? If a visitor asked for directions, could you respond?

Suggestion for meditation: **Reflect on the text of the hymn "The Church's One Foundation" (all five stanzas).**

Wednesday, April 23   Read Acts 8:26-40.

I have a friend who often approaches me and says, "The Lord has laid it on my heart to tell you . . . ." Then comes some opinion about what I should think, say, or do. I want to say to my friend (but have so far resisted saying), "The Lord has laid it on *my* heart to tell *you* to zip it up."

It's not that my friend lacks insight or that I could not benefit from his counsel. The problem is his presumptuousness. Not only does he shroud his opinions in sugary piety, but he offers them unsolicited. He seems more eager to give me advice than to ask whether I need or want advice. He starts speaking before he knows what I think or how I feel. He seems to care more about the sound of his own voice than my well-being. If humility is among my friend's virtues, he does not display it.

Philip approached the Ethiopian in a different way. First he took time to notice what the Ethiopian was reading. Then he asked a question that showed interest in the Ethiopian. Philip waited for an invitation to join the Ethiopian. Finally the Ethiopian asked Philip to explain the scriptures to him. The result was the Ethiopian's conversion and baptism.

What if the Ethiopian had not responded to Philip? He might have said, "Thank you for that explanation. Now I'll be on my way back to Ethiopia." In that case, Philip would have had to accept the disappointment that his words had fallen on deaf ears. The measure of success for Christians is not successful action but faithfulness. Faithfulness begins by doing as Christ did—by accepting people just as they are. Then comes sharing the good news. In fact, accepting people just as they are and letting them know that God accepts them just as they are *is* the good news.

Suggestion for meditation: **Reflect on the text of the hymn "Just As I Am, without One Plea."**

Thursday, April 24   Read 1 John 4:7-21.

The word *love* seems to mean whatever anyone wishes it to mean. We use the same word to describe our fondness for a casserole or a hairdo that we use to speak of the nature of God. Understanding this passage requires us to put aside notions of love that derive from the world around us and let the text speak for itself.

"Love is from God." It is God who defines love. What we say, do, think, or feel has little to do with it. "God's love was revealed among us in this way: God sent his only Son." Love is not an attitude or attribute of God but an action of God, something God *does*. God gives us the gift of God's Son.

"Beloved, since God loved us so much, we also ought to love one another." I once read about a congregational fund drive. One member complained to the pastor, "According to your concept, Christianity is one continual give, give, give!" The pastor replied, "That's it exactly. It all started with God who gave us life and the world. God's been giving ever since. We give now because God gave first."

What is the greatest act of love? The Gospel of John gives the answer: "This is my commandment, that you love one another as I have loved you. No one has greater love than this, to lay down one's life for one's friends" (John 15:12-13). We are to love as God loves, to give not merely our dearest thing but *everything*. For Christ, this meant giving his life; for Christian martyrs, it also means giving their lives. But not all are called to die a martyr's death. Some give everything while living in the world. The important thing is, like God, to hold nothing back. We show our love by what we are *willing* to give.

Suggestion for meditation: **Reflect on the text of the hymn "O Love, How Deep, How Broad, How High" or "Love Divine, All Loves Excelling."**

Friday, April 25   Read 1 John 4:18.

What does it mean to say that perfect love casts out fear? We misunderstand the statement when we take it to refer to our love for God. What a burden to lay on ourselves! How can we love God *perfectly*? But this passage is about God's love for us. The only perfect love is God's love, and it casts out fear.

Consider Job. Often mistakenly called patient, Job is in fact agitated and demanding. He shakes his fist at God, challenging God to a showdown and demanding to know what he has done to deserve the catastrophes that have befallen him. Throughout most of the Book of Job, God remains hidden and silent as Job grows ever more fretful. Job fears God. "Why do you hide your face and consider me your enemy? Will you torment a wind-blown leaf? Will you chase after dry chaff?" (Job 13:24-25, NIV).

At the end of the book, the Lord appears in a whirlwind—but not to answer Job. The Lord ignores Job's demanding questions and instead questions Job: "Where were you when I laid the foundation of the earth? Tell me, if you have understanding. Who determined its measurements—surely you know! Or who stretched the line upon it?" (Job 38:4-5).

God's response silences Job. Some have suggested that Job was browbeaten into silence; but I believe that when he gazed into the whirlwind, Job saw something he had never imagined—a loving face. Job was like the small child who, alone and frightened of the thunder, calls out for its mother. When mother finally comes, the child climbs into her arms, still not understanding the thunder but now resting in a place where understanding no longer matters. Job realized that it was a whirlwind of perfect love, the love that casts out fear.

Suggestion for meditation: **Reflect on the text of the hymn "Immortal Love, Forever Full."**

127

Saturday, April 26   Read John 15:1-8.

The vine and the body (1 Corinthians 12) are the New Testament's two most suggestive metaphors to describe the church's relationship to Christ. Both images are organic, living. The vine image also has eucharistic associations, which links it to the "bread of life" image (John 6).

"I am the vine, you are the branches." The church is more than a gathering of like-minded people seeking to imitate Jesus. The church is organically part of Christ. When the church does the work of Christ, it is Christ working through the church. As the vine nourishes its branches, enabling them to bear fruit, so Christ nourishes the church, enabling the church to do his will.

"He removes every branch that bears no fruit in me." Baptism may be thought of as the grafting of a new branch onto the vine with the promise that the new Christian will bear fruit for Christ. God's throwing of unfruitful branches onto the fire is not an act of vengeance but a natural way to return fruitless branches to earth.

"Every branch that bears fruit he prunes, to make it bear more fruit." God prunes the branches that nourishment may flow into the fruit rather than into useless growth. Pruning is being disciplined by the removal of useless things. This discipline is often painful. Taking no pleasure in afflicting us, God does not withhold a painful chastening when the result will be a more faithful, fruitful discipleship.

"Ask for whatever you wish, and it will be done for you." This is a difficult verse until we understand that the branches ask only for what accords with the purposes of the vine. The church relinquishes self-will and submits all to the will of Christ. The church's prayer is always "Thy will be done."

Suggestion for meditation: **Reflect on the text of the hymn "Shepherd of Souls, Refresh and Bless."**

Sunday, April 27   Read John 15:4-7.

"Abide in me as I abide in you." Persons have translated the Greek verb *meno* as "abide," "live," "dwell," "remain," "make a home." The word occurs eight times in John 15:4-7. It suggests not mere happenstance but an intentional, continuing, long-term relationship. One does not "abide" in a hotel room or a guest room. Those are places of brief visits, more like parking places. A home, or "abode," is something else.

Home is the backdrop of lives, an atmosphere that we breathe in and out. Filled with our own memories and mementos, home is a part of our souls that surrounds and defines us. Home is a place we don't have to think about all the time. It affords us the security and freedom to think about other things, like eating dinner, reading the newspaper, or entertaining friends.

Christ invites us to make our home in him; to allow him to surround and define us; to condition all we say or do, hallowing every moment. He will be with us as a familiar place to abide—a backdrop, an atmosphere—enfolding and embracing us. Other things will often occupy our minds. We must clean, cook, eat, wash, pay the bills, run errands, raise our children, brush our teeth, pick up our clothes, make love, make a living, make do. It is neither necessary nor helpful to think or talk about Jesus all the time—so long as we abide in him.

Christ also tells us that he abides in us. Christ humbly stoops to permit *his* words and actions to be shaped by the cares and anxieties of *our* hearts. Christ allows *us* to define *him*. This abiding is an intimate, long-term relationship, a mutual indwelling where Christ and Christian understand each other so fully and live in such harmony that one cannot distinguish between them.

Suggestion for meditation: **Reflect on the text of the hymn "Abide with Me."**

129

April 28–May 4, 1997 **Chan-Hie Kim✤**

Monday, April 28 Read Psalm 98:1-3.

Many of the psalms praise the name of God for God's unyielding victory over Israel's enemies. Israel is a nation surrounded by many hostile neighbors who threaten her very existence. The Israelites were constantly harassed by their neighbors, thus endangering God's promise to Abraham. But the people of Israel trusted that God would never give them up. Surely God keeps promises and does "marvelous things." God gave the Hebrews the promised land, and the descendants of Abraham became like "the stars of heaven" and "the sand . . . that is on the seashore" (Gen. 22:17). The psalmist of our reading sings a great thanksgiving hymn for God's gracious act of victory and vindication.

God's promise to Abraham is a never-ending promise given to Abraham's spiritual heirs. Often we wonder if God cares about us. At times we shout, "Where is God?" in the midst of our distress and despair.

It is not an easy task to live victoriously. Our journey of life has many ups and downs. Some persons may give up their faith in God; others lead ungodly lives. Yet the Lord will never desert us or abandon us in our hopelessness. God will give us power and courage to stand against the enemies of despair and defeatism. Then like the psalmist we will also be able to sing to the Lord a victorious hymn.

Suggestion for meditation: **What would enable you to live your life victoriously?**

✤Professor of New Testament and Christian Ministries, School of Theology at Claremont; United Methodist clergy, California-Pacific Annual Conference.

Tuesday, April 29   Read Psalm 98:4-9.

The psalmist proclaims with a loud voice that we should make a joyful noise to the Lord for God's coming to the world. But the psalmist's proclamation does not focus its attention on the anticipation of the Lord's presence but God's rule over the world. Despite the many wicked rulers in this world, God will judge the world with righteousness. God's reign will have no inequities, and the psalmist affirms that.

In worship we too praise the Lord with our joyful songs and hymns. We give thanks to God for God's work in the universe and the marvelous work God has done for us. But how many times do we think of God as the righteous judge who does not tolerate the inequities and injustices of our world?

Confronted by the many injustices we experience every day, we may feel powerless. We may be tempted to retreat from rampant inequities in the world and even resign ourselves from engaging them. In a world where bigotry, unfairness, discrimination, prejudice, mischief, abuse, and malicious intentions dominate the minds of people, there seems to be no hope for a better future for us.

But as the psalmist proclaims, the Lord is coming "to judge the world with righteousness, and the peoples with his truth." Because of the coming of the Lord, though the world may seem to be hopeless, God promises us that God will have the final victory over the evils of the world.

Suggestion for meditation: **Envision a just world ruled by God.**

Wednesday, April 30   Read 1 John 5:1-5.

"Jesus is the Christ."—From this most important confessional statement, Christian faith was born. When Jesus asked his disciples about his identity, Simon Peter answered without hesitancy, "You are the Messiah, the Son of the living God" (Matt. 16:16). Upon hearing this bold yet accurate statement, Jesus responded, "You are Peter, and on this rock I will build my church" (Matt. 16:18). Jesus is making more than a pun on Peter's name, which means "rock." Jesus is saying that Christianity is born and built upon this famous confession that we still proclaim to the world.

The writer of our scripture reading further declares that those who confess Jesus as the Messiah are born of God and therefore love God. And those who love God obey God's commandments; and by obeying the commandments, they will be able to conquer the world. Thus our victorious life is the consequence of our faith in Jesus Christ.

Does it really make any difference whether we confess Jesus or not? I believe it does. For me, the gap is wide between those confessing the Christ and those not. It is a matter of death and life.

Suggestion for meditation: **What must I do to live victoriously in this life and to receive the crown of life?**

Thursday, May 1   Read 1 John 5:6.

One of the great mysteries in Christianity, and certainly in the world, is that the blood of Jesus Christ cleanses us from our sins. How can the blood of a man executed as a criminal on the cross wash away the sins of humankind?

The writer of First John is talking about two common liquids that sustain the life of all living creatures on the earth—water and blood. He reminds us that Jesus Christ was baptized and shed his blood when he was nailed on the cross. Jesus' baptism by water and the shedding of his blood on the cross (which we still commemorate through our sacraments) remind us not only of our dependence on these two life-sustaining elements but on the sacrificial love of God as well.

Because Jesus was nailed on the cross, we are able to nail our sins on the cross. Because he died on the cross, we are able to die with him to our sins. Because he was buried, we are able to bury our sins with him. Because he was raised from the dead, we live and enter into the eternal life with him. Dying and rising with him is a great mystery; but since he "came by water and blood," we can go away completely cleansed from our sins.

As Paul says, the crucified Jesus is the one who was never crushed by the force of death but who conquered it. We who believe in him will have life eternal.

Suggestion for meditation: **How can I have a taste of eternity in this world now?**

Friday, May 2   Read John 15:9-17.

The Gospel of John is full of metaphorical images. In this chapter, the writer uses the metaphor of the vine in describing our relationship with Jesus.

For many years I have had a grapevine hanging all along the gutter of my home. It used to produce sweet grapes that ripened in the hot Southern California sunshine. When left on the branch to dry, they turn into high-quality raisins. Strangely enough some of the grapes never mature. On closer examination, I discovered that the tiny branches that support and supply the buds with nutrition were cut off from the main branches of the vine.

Jesus must have observed the same thing. If we are cut off from the vine of our Father, we will never be able to abide in God's love. One of the conditions for abiding in God's love is to keep God's commandments. But unless our lifeline is connected to God and constantly nourished by the word, we will be unable to keep the commandments. Interestingly enough, we can feel the love of God when we keep God's commandments. At that moment our joy will ripen and be fulfilled.

Suggestion for meditation: **How can I connect with God today? Into what am I ripening?**

Saturday, May 3   Read John 15:12-17.

If someone asks me about the essence of Christianity, I will immediately reply in one word without hesitation: *love*. In Mark 12:28-31 Jesus clearly tells us that there is no greater commandment than to love God and to love our neighbors. If we love God and our neighbors as ourselves we need no other commandments; the deed of love is all we need to please and glorify God. It accomplishes the will of God toward us; it satisfies God's demands on us.

But the problem is that loving our neighbors is not an easy task. To consider sacrificing our lives for our friends is an unthinkable demand even though such sacrifice is the highest virtue of love according to Jesus. No one with average intellect and the highest moral conviction can conceive of such outlandish behavior.

But wait a moment! Is it really impossible? By no means! We can realize self-sacrifice for others only with determination and courage by the help of God. I have actually seen it. During the Korean War a communist killed a pastor's two sons. Later this pastor adopted the young man and made him his legal heir. This pastor not only saved the life of this communist young man but gave him a new life as his son. It was possible only because the pastor trusted the goodness of God. He epitomized what love really means in Christianity.

Suggestion for meditation: **How can I attain the power of love in order to accomplish my duty as a child of God?**

Sunday, May 4   Read Acts 10:44-48.

Luke, in his own way, tries to describe a brief history of early Christianity. Of the many stories Luke reports in the book of Acts, chapter 10 particularly intrigues me. In this chapter, Luke presents the exciting drama of Peter's conversion—conversion from his narrow understanding of God's unfolding drama of redemption for humankind. Peter, like other Jewish Christians, could not believe that the Gentiles could become Christians without first being circumcised.

Peter could not believe that Jesus would save Gentiles even if they did follow the instructions of the Torah. Peter's famous confession, "I truly understand that God shows no partiality, but in every nation anyone who fears him and does what is right is acceptable to him" (Acts 10:34-35), is a great statement that deserves our careful attention. When the Gentiles who believed in Jesus received the anointing of the Holy Spirit, Peter could no longer hold his exclusive view of God's redemptive act for all human beings regardless of their religious and ethnic backgrounds.

We proclaim Jesus Christ, and we work hard to make people disciples of Christ. But we often forget that God's gracious gift of salvation comes to us without any other condition but to accept him as our Lord. We do not need to be Jews first in order to become Christians; we do not have to look or act a certain way in order to become Christians. God accepts us as we are. We cannot withhold baptism when the Holy Spirit comes to God-fearing people.

Suggestion for meditation: **In what ways have I been, or am I, a stumbling block for people who want to come to the Christ?**

FOLLOWING INSTRUCTIONS

May 5–11, 1997   **Linda Worthington**✤
Monday, May 5   Read 1 John 5:11-13;
                                                    Acts 1:24; John 17:10-11.

Recently I had to learn a new computer program. After several hours of frustrating trial and error, my son suggested, "Try reading the instructions, then follow them." It worked! I was soon up and running. Throughout this week we will focus on "instructions" for proclaiming Christ as primary in our lives, especially in the family as it extends into our church, community, and world.

Today's scriptures give us a overview of the week. The Gospel of John and the letters of John send the unequivocal message: To know what God is like, one must look at Jesus Christ. In the First Letter of John the "elder" writes the local church community, warning against the false teachings that threaten to destroy the Christian fellowship. His instruction to us is to believe in Jesus as the Son of God.

Later in the week Peter provides us—the community of believers—with a model for decision making. That model is based on prayer, and we will look anew at one of the most profound prayers of Jesus as he turns to his Father and shows his continuing concern for the disciples and their ministry, even as he himself faces death.

Prayer: **Guide me, O God, that I may be open to your instructions today and every day and have the courage to follow you. Amen.**

✤Chair of the Baltimore-Washington United Methodist Conference Commission on the Status and Role of Women; member of Chevy Chase United Methodist Church.

Tuesday, May 6   Read Psalm 1.

The psalms give utterance to the heart of the Hebrew experience with God, covering perhaps a thousand years of that history and mirroring the soul of Israel, God's chosen nation. That heartfelt experience also speaks to us today in poetic, metaphorical language.

Psalm 1 boldly instructs in the following way: Look, friends, there are two possible ways for you to go. Choose the path of righteousness or take the consequences, which, for the unrighteous, are dire indeed. "If your heart turns away . . . you shall not live long" (Deut. 30:17-18). What are the psalmist's instructions? Delight in the law (instructions) of the Lord and meditate on that law day and night.

When the banks of the Shenandoah River flooded my land, the deep-rooted sycamore and walnut trees stood straight and firm, even though the rushing torrential river reached halfway to the tops of the trees. Thus it is with those who are righteous, the psalmist assures us; they will stand and receive nurture from the river.

And if we choose the way of the unrighteous? How many times I've seen the rice drying in the sun along the roadsides in Bangladesh or Thailand; when a breeze stirs the chaff, it is blown away in a swirl of dust. That, the psalmist tells us, is what an unrighteous person faces. Poof! Of no consequence. "For the LORD watches over the way of the righteous, but the way of the wicked will perish."

Prayer: **Help me, God, to see the way of righteousness that you have showed in your Son, Jesus Christ, and give me the strength of heart to follow him. Amen.**

Wednesday, May 7   Read 1 John 5:9-13.

Many churches observe National Family Week this week. One of the phrases that countless politicians have bandied about is "family values." No one would deny that the family is basic to our society.

How do we speak of family today? Not only may the family be the traditional two parents and child(ren); it also may be one parent and offspring; grandparent(s) and grandchild(ren); young single people living together; older folks living in community together; and many other configurations. Church family refers to our congregations and small church groups. These and others are family extended beyond the narrow scope of the politicians who purport to support family values.

The writer of First John instructs us with a stronger message to save the family. The writer's concern with his family—the Christian community of Asia (Ephesus)—is so deep that he wants to give them assurance and confidence in the future as they face a barrage of quite believable false teachings about Christ. "I am writing . . . so that you may know that you have eternal life—you that believe in the Son of God" (TEV), he says.

Do we live our lives within our families—in whatever form they take—as someone who believes as did this writer that eternal life comes to those who believe that Jesus is the Son of God?

Suggestion for meditation: **Pray today for someone in your family who needs to open his or her heart to believe in Jesus as the Son of God.**

Thursday, May 8   Read Acts 1:15-17, 21.

The disciples met frequently after Jesus' death to pray, to console one another, and to support Jesus' family in the grief they all shared—not unlike our church family when a member faces death.

When my husband was unexpectedly killed in a boating accident while we were living in Senegal in West Africa, the small international church of which we were a part quickly came to my side, assisting me in every conceivable way. This embracing community provided an outpouring of love, consolation, and assistance as the members tried to deal with my grief and shock as well as the incredible shock of the whole community.

I believe death is always a shock, no matter how prepared we are, no matter how strong our faith in the Easter resurrection message. Certainly Jesus' death was a shock to the community, and his mother who must have found great consolation from those who "gathered frequently to pray . . . with Mary the mother of Jesus and with his brothers" (v. 14, TEV).

But in spite of grieving I had to go on—prepare for memorial services, finish a job, return to the U.S., and make endless decisions—just as the family and friends of Jesus had to get on with the "job" that Jesus had given them (see Acts 10:42). One of the first jobs was the business of replacing Judas. "Someone must join us as a witness to the resurrection of the Lord Jesus," Peter told them (v. 21, TEV).

Suggestion for meditation: **As you prepare to do your job as a Christian today, be mindful of someone in your community who needs to hear God's instructions for living life fully. Pray for that person.**

Friday, May 9   Read Acts 1:21-26.

As they decided on a replacement for Judas, the disciples were not unlike a church administrative board when faced with an important task. The way they conducted their meeting provides some good instructions for us today.

Look to the scriptures for direction. When Peter stood up to address the group, he was already well-informed of what the scriptures said to their situation (Acts 1:16, 17-21).

Develop the criteria. "He must be one of the men who were in our group during the whole time that the Lord Jesus traveled about with us" (TEV), Peter told them.

Pray. The group, as they so often did together, prayed: "Lord, you know everyone's heart. Show us [who] you have chosen." How important this step is! Whatever decisions we must make— whether it is church finances, the country's leadership, which college to attend, or a personal family matter—sincere prayer made in the full belief that God will reveal the answer will make the decision easier.

Take action. Cast a vote, send in a job application, or discuss the family matter. In this case, fully trusting that God would answer their prayers, "they cast lots." Matthias became the twelfth disciple.

Just as the approximately 120 women and men who made up the group of believers (v. 15) sought God's help in conducting the nascent church's business, so must we continually seek that help in our churches, in our businesses, in our families. And as the answer came to the disciples, so will it come to us.

Suggestion for meditation: **Think of the next important decision you must make and apply these four steps to help you reach a conclusion that reflects God's will.**

141

Saturday, May 10   Read John 17:6-10.

Yesterday we saw how prayer guided the activities of Jesus' followers. Today we will look at Jesus' own prayer for his followers. All of John 17 is a prayer, sometimes referred to as Jesus' High Priestly Prayer or Farewell Discourse, spoken just before his arrest and death. In it, Jesus prays for himself, for his disciples, and for all the world "who will believe in me" (v. 20). Jesus addresses God as Father in the intimate language of the family. He makes it clear: Jesus is God's Son. "All mine are yours and yours are mine; . . . that they may be one, as we are one." Could we have any doubt that Jesus is the Son of God as we read this prayer?

In our reading from the middle of this three-part prayer, Jesus prays for the eleven disciples whom he has nurtured, instructed, and loved; whom he embraces as his family. He now reports to his Father, "I have made your name known to those [the disciples] whom you gave me from the world." They have listened and learned. Jesus says they are now ready to continue his mission and ministry.

Jesus opens the door to all of us whether we have a traditional family or not, no matter how destructive our earth and birth family may be, or how alienated we may be from them. All who believe may be part of this new family by virtue of being children of God.

Prayer: **God, Holy One, may I hear your words, believe your truths, and act as a faithful child in your family, through the name of Jesus. Amen.**

Sunday, May 11   Read John 17:11-19.

The disciples were privileged to hear Jesus' heartfelt soliloquy in which he pleads his case for them. Does this prayer not feel like you're looking through a window into the heart of Christ and glimpsing his very soul in his most private moment?

Jesus knew that it was time for the fulfillment of his mission, that the days were soon coming in which he would leave his beloved disciples (his family). "As you have sent me into the world, so I have sent them," Jesus said as he dedicated his followers to the continuation of his ministry. The disciples had faithfully accepted Jesus' teaching and careful preparation to achieve his mission. He now intercedes on their behalf by asking God to protect them: "While I was with them, I protected them in your name. . . . I guarded them, and not one of them was lost."

By his example, Jesus has instructed us in the importance of intercessory prayer. Prayers of intercession, especially for the sick and grieving, arc frequently a part of our worship services. Many times we personally offer prayers of intercession for those, both in our families and beyond those boundaries, who face painful times or personal crises. Jesus demonstrates that intercessory prayer can come before the fact—to prepare for a coming crisis— as he prayed for his disciples during what would soon be the most grievous time in their lives.

Suggestion for meditation: **Offer your own intercessory prayer for someone who must deal with a crisis in his or her life, keeping in mind that Jesus did not leave his disciples unprepared for the future.**

THE HOLY SPIRIT TODAY

May 12–18, 1997   **J. Ellsworth Kalas✤**
Monday, May 12   Read Acts 2:1-21.

Few religious holidays are less celebrated than Pentecost Sunday. A cynic might reason that commercial interests in general—and greeting card publishers in particular—have not found a way to package and sell it. If that is true, we have a big problem because it is hard to imagine a Pentecost-equivalent to Santa Claus or the Easter bunny.

But the commercial world is not alone in this problem; believers are equally frustrated. Nearly a century ago, a Christian spiritual leader referred to the Holy Spirit as the "unknown member of the Trinity." The definition is only more true today.

That's too bad, because the New Testament indicates that the Spirit is the member of the Godhead closest to us. It is the Holy Spirit that "pursues" us prior to our commitment of faith, the Spirit that works in our conversion, and the Spirit that empowers and indwells us as believers.

Indeed, on the basis of both theology and experience, I dare to say that we know the fullness of the Christian life to the degree that we allow the Holy Spirit to enter our lives. If the Spirit is "God with us," we can hardly imagine the degree of joy, purpose, and effectiveness that can be ours as we are *filled* (what a daring word!) with the spirit of God.

Prayer: **Open our hearts, O God, to the fullness you desire us to know. Amen.**

✤Senior Pastor-in-Residence in the Beeson Program in Biblical Preaching and Church Leadership at Asbury Theological Seminary; Wilmore, Kentucky.

Tuesday, May 13   Read Acts 2:1-21.

Those who witnessed the day of Pentecost were unsophis-
ticated observers, but that makes their observations all the more
fascinating. All they knew was what they could see, hear,
and feel—and of course they processed this data through the
categories of their own experience. Their conclusion? The people
were drunk!—an inelegant observation, but it makes a point.
The incoming of the Holy Spirit had brought an exuberance
the disciples simply could not control and the observers could
not understand.

That runs contrary to our usual experience of religion. We tend
toward religion that stays within the boundaries we have defined.
If it does otherwise, we think it's fanatical.

But you see, the Holy Spirit is really more than we can contain,
so to be filled with the Spirit is to overflow. To overflow is to lose
control, not simply of our emotions—any number of questionable
causes might bring that sort of reaction. The physical events
at Pentecost pointed to far more significant inner happenings.
The spirit of God was now controlling these persons in an
extraordinary way. And with the Spirit's control, they were
enjoying an excitement and a reality that was beyond the religious
vocabulary of the onlookers. No wonder the observers resorted to
secular terms!

Could it be that the rather dull, tame quality of much of our
religious lives indicates that we have not allowed the spirit of God
to fill us? Could it be that in our keeping God under control (what
an absurd concept!) we have missed the best of everything?

Prayer: **Possess me, spirit of God, until I overflow with beauty
and goodness. Amen.**

Wednesday, May 14   Read Psalm 104:24-34, 35*b*.

The Holy Spirit was not invented on the day of Pentecost. As the book of Genesis unfolds the creation story, it is "the Spirit of God" that moves upon the mysterious chaos to bring order (Gen. 1:2, NIV). No wonder then that the psalmist, exulting in God as Creator, sums up the account by saying that it is as "you [God] send forth your spirit" that creation takes place.

When poets, painters, playwrights, and sculptors speak of their work, it is fascinating to see how often they slip into language that is almost theological. They may be utterly secular, perhaps even antagonistic to Christianity; yet as they try to describe the creative process, they find it hard not to say "Holy Spirit" or some secular synonym. Joy Davidman Gresham, who went from militant atheist to passionate believer and who eventually married C. S. Lewis, said that as a young poet she could be shaken by spiritual powers a dozen times a day, yet not realize that there was such a thing as spirit; only after her conversion did she recognize the work of the Holy Spirit in the whole experience of human creativity.

The psalmist sees this creative spirit constantly at work in our world. The creatures of the earth look to God, who then "give[s] them their food in due season"; by this spirit God "renew[s] the face of the ground." The physical sciences tell us that ours is an expanding creation. That fact would not surprise the psalmist; he would use the scientist's report as a call to worship and praise.

Prayer: **Make me your partner in creation, I pray. Amen.**

Thursday, May 15   Read Romans 8:22-27.

Praying is the simplest and most basic of human activities. We do it instinctively. A decade ago, a survey in West Germany revealed that more people prayed than confessed to believe in God. Poets testify to the early instinct to prayer when they say that children "lisp" their prayers. Prayer cuts across every imaginable ethnic, racial, intellectual, and religious boundary. One might define human beings as "creatures that pray."

And yet, simple and instinctive as prayer is, some reaches of prayer are always beyond us. Those who pray best and most often are the first to say how little they know about praying; they are constantly stretching to know more. Paul, who knew a few things about prayer, confessed that we do not know what we ought to pray, so we need help in "our weakness" (Romans 8:26). He seems to be referring to our problem of understanding the will of God. How can we put our prayers on the side of God's purposes if we do not understand those purposes?

The apostle has a solution: When we do not know how we ought to pray, the Spirit intercedes for us "with groans that words cannot express," and does this "in accordance with God's will" (Romans 8:26, 27, NIV).

Groan is the operative word. Strive as we will to use language with grace and precision, the most significant issues of life often reduce us to the inarticulate language of sighs, grunts, tears, and groans. But then the Holy Spirit wondrously takes the groans of our ignorance, our inflexibility, our tentativeness, and shapes it into a prayer! Miracle, indeed.

Prayer: **Spirit of God, teach me to pray! Amen.**

Friday, May 16   Read John 15: 26-27.

The presence of the Spirit seems so often to be marked by joy or tears or deep emotion that we are likely to think that the purpose of the Spirit is primarily to offer emotional fulfillment. But these experiences are results, not purposes; while the experiences may be a source of great satisfaction, they are not the issue.

The Gospel of John tells us a key purpose of the Spirit is to "testify" for Jesus (John 15:26). The Spirit's purpose is not to draw attention to the Spirit or to experiences in the Spirit but to Jesus. The point is that we cannot fully grasp the significance of Jesus or of his work except as the Spirit enlightens our minds. As Paul put it, the things of God are "foolishness" to us, and we cannot understand them because they are "spiritually discerned" (1 Cor. 2:14). If I need a guide to unlock the beauty of an artist's works, how much more do I need a Divine Guide to free me from secular presuppositions and open me to the wonders of the Lord Christ! Such is the Spirit's work.

Then, having been so enlightened, we ourselves become true witnesses to Jesus Christ. Much, if not all of the Spirit's work, is through human instruments. We are introduced to the wonders of Christ through the insights, words, and deeds of others who are used by the Spirit (sometimes without their knowing it) and then we are privileged to "testify" to others with the help of the same Spirit. And so we share the eternal mystery.

Prayer: **Reveal Jesus Christ to me, I pray, that I may show him to others. Amen.**

Saturday, May 17   Read John 16:4*b*-11.

Sin, *righteousness*, and *judgment*. Jesus said the Holy Spirit was coming to convince the world of sin, righteousness, and judgment. As it happens, however, the world is not supremely interested in being convinced of these matters. The words are harsh, old-fashioned, and politically incorrect. They are not seeker-sensitive words; they do not appeal to a modern, secular audience. Come to think of it, they do not appeal even to those of us who call ourselves Christians. We do not rush to have someone convince us of such subjects. Yet it is for this purpose that the Holy Spirit came into our world, and I think it is fair to assume that the Spirit is about the same business today.

We sometimes say that *sin* is an unpopular word in our time. But it always has been. *Sin* is an appealing term only when we can attach it to others; it has never been attractive for personal application. The same can be said for *judgment*. The prophet Amos had to remind the people that they were unwise to call for the day of judgment, because it was going to be judgment for them (Amos 5:18); they had assumed judgment was intended only for their enemies. As for *righteousness*, we hardly know how to define the term, and we do not usually have it high on our must-get list.

Since these terms have so little natural appeal, we will be drawn to them only if the Spirit "convinces" us. That is another reason why we need the Holy Spirit—to convince us of matters to which we are not naturally drawn.

Prayer: **Spirit of God, descend upon my heart! Amen.**

Sunday, May 18   Read John 16:12-15.

Francis Bacon noted that after jesting Pilate asked, "What is truth," he would not stay for an answer. Most of us are equally impatient in our search for truth. So when Jesus tells us that the Holy Spirit is the "Spirit of *truth*" and that the Spirit will lead us into all truth—it is a wonderful promise, but it is also a frightening one.

Our impatience in the search for truth comes not from the length of the search but from the unsettling nature of the truth. Truth comes with a price. Opinions can be received with a shrug of the shoulders or a patronizing nod, but truth demands a yes or no. It was this demand that made Pilate leave the scene. With Truth embodied before him, he had to act when he preferred to philosophize.

But if the Holy Spirit is to lead us into all truth, how is it that we Christians so often seem to miss it? I venture it is because we haven't the humility to receive the guidance the Spirit offers. If our guidance came by direct revelation, we might receive it more gladly because direct revelation is both immediate and special. But the Spirit's guidance usually comes in ways that are more mundane and humbling. It comes through the scriptures and through tradition, and often through the counsel of friends. So if *our* spirit is arrogant, we leave little room for the *Holy* Spirit. No wonder then if we miss the truth—especially the truth as it disciplines and challenges our lives.

Prayer: **Lead on, dear Spirit, and give me grace to follow. Amen.**

May 19–25, 1997   **John O. Gooch**♣
Monday, May 19   Read Psalm 29.

It was a miserably hot afternoon. It had not rained in nearly two months, and the earth was cracked and hard. Then clouds began to darken the sky. Thunder rumbled in the distance. A wind came up that tossed the branches of the huge old maples in our yard. Lightning crashed across the sky, and rain came down in torrents. I danced across the yard in sheer delight, not even caring that I was soaking wet.

That must have been how Israel felt about the coming of the early rains after the long dry season. Probably the Israelites sang this psalm in their celebrations that marked the beginning of the rains. Israel experienced God in the thunderstorm. The psalmist calls on the heavenly beings to praise the Lord, who controls the storm. This is a God of power, who is more powerful than Baal, the Canaanite god of storms.

The "voice of the LORD," mentioned seven times in the psalm, is an echo of the thunder. Thunderstorms are rare in Palestine and more impressive as a result. The Lord sits enthroned over all the waters. God's greatness is not something we hear about; it is demonstrated every year in the beginning of the rain.

Prayer: **God of storms, help me be aware of your presence in the power of the world around me. Help me give you praise and glory for your gifts. Amen.**

♣United Methodist pastor, writer, and teacher; Nashville, Tennessee.

Tuesday, May 20   Read Isaiah 6:1-8.

Do we experience God in worship? Isaiah certainly did. The description of his vision of God suggests that he was in the "holy place," the Temple building itself where the smoke from the incense altars filled the air.

Isaiah says he "saw the LORD," but his description is of God's throne, God's attendants, God's robe. The seraphim who attend God are enough to fill the prophet with awe and fear. But how do the seraphim respond? They cover their faces, because they cannot behold the glory of God. How much more difficult is it for a mere human to behold God's glory?

Isaiah knows immediately that he will die, because he is unclean. He cannot see God and live (Exod. 33:20). Uncleanness may refer to ritual purity, but it more likely stands for the vast gulf between the holiness of God and the ethical and existential failures of humanity.

The key understanding for us is that Isaiah experienced God in worship. Something in the power of the liturgy and the setting drew him out of his own sense of grief and loss to behold God through what was happening in the Temple. I sometimes wonder how seriously both clergy and laity take the possibility of actually experiencing God in worship. Do we expect that we will come to a vision of God in and through worship? Do we prepare ourselves—the liturgy and our participation in it—expecting to come face-to-face with God?

Prayer: **Holy God, give me the gift of expectation. Open me to become aware of you in worship, in work, at home, at school, wherever I am. Amen.**

Wednesday, May 21   Read Isaiah 6:1-8.

Isaiah's life exemplifies the continued relationship between the worship in the Temple and the vision of God. One of the seraphs flew to the incense altar and picked up the gold tongs that lay by the altar. With the tongs, the seraph picked up a live coal, flew to Isaiah, and touched his lips, saying that his sin had been taken away. God responded to the part of Isaiah's life that the prophet identified as the source of his uncleanness—his lips. God speaks to us not generally but specifically. When we confess a sin, cry out in pain, ask for direction or strength, God responds appropriately to our request.

In services of Renewal of the Baptismal Covenant, I invite people to use water in personal ways, often suggesting that they put their hand in the water and then touch the part of their body that symbolizes for them a need for cleansing or a need for God. I am continually humbled by the power of that action as people come to the font, dip their hand into the water, and move it to forehead, eyes, or heart. It is clear to me they are experiencing God in that moment of worship. They are moving from the routine of the liturgy to the freshness and power of God. They are discovering new life.

When cleansed, Isaiah has a new capacity to hear God's word. In his vision, he suddenly finds himself in the heavenly council and hears God ask, "Who will go for us?" With a power born of his experience of God, he cries, "Send me!" His experience of new life leads him to fuller obedience to the call of God.

Prayer: **God of new life, lead me to fuller obedience because you have given me life. Amen.**

153

Thursday, May 22   Read Romans 8:12-13.

Paul is not always easy to read, because he put in so many "by the ways"—and his "by the ways" are sometimes more important than his main thought. These verses seem to be an important "by the way."

We have an obligation, Paul says, but it is not to the flesh, to the world and all the world's temptations. Then comes the "by the way." Look at the parallels he sets up: If you *live* according to the flesh, you will *die*. If you *put to death* the deeds of the body, you will *live*. This sounds like Jesus' saying: "For those who want to save their life will lose it, and those who lose their life for my sake, and for the sake of the gospel, will save it" (Mark 8:35).

The key for us is "If by the Spirit you put to death the deeds of the body, you will live." One would expect Paul to use the word *desires* here, rather than *deeds*. That would fit the grammatical structure. But it would not fit reality as well. We cannot always overcome our desires. They are hidden and come unbidden; we cannot do much about them. But we can refrain from putting them into action. Perhaps the person who struggles with desires (of all kinds) and nearly gives in to them, then rises to struggle again without ever living out those desires, is a stronger and more moral person than the one who never felt the desires in the first place. After all, how hard can it be to do the right thing if one never feels the desire to do the wrong?

Prayer: **Gracious God, give me grace and strength not to act on all my desires but to struggle with them for your sake and mine. Amen.**

Friday, May 23   Read Romans 8:14-17.

It was Saturday night. I, being an adolescent male, was interested in seeking out the company of an adolescent female. My mother came into the room as I was checking out my hair and said, "Remember who you are." At the time I thought, *What a drag! I'm not going to do anything wrong.* Now I know what a powerful statement that was. Who a person is makes all the difference!

Paul says that we are children of God. That probably refers to Roman practices of adopting slaves and making them full members of the family. That is what happens to us in our baptism—God adopts us into the family.

The Spirit is our witness. Whenever we say "Abba," the Spirit is present with us, bearing witness that we are children of God. We experience Father and Spirit in the very use of the word. Those who call God "Father" know that they are heirs of God, that they will inherit the family blessing.

Our adoption makes us joint heirs with Christ, provided "we suffer with him." This phrase has always bothered me. If we must suffer with Christ, do only those Christians who actually face persecution become heirs? That doesn't sound like good news! But that could mean we share in the suffering of his death and resurrection through our baptism (which is a gift of grace in itself). This understanding suggests that baptism is the sacrament of adoption, of being made members of the family and heirs of the kingdom. In baptism we experience Father, Son, and Holy Spirit.

Prayer: **Thanks be to you, O Christ, who with the Father and the Spirit reign eternally. Amen.**

155

Saturday, May 24   Read John 3:1-5.

Nicodemus's conversation with Jesus reflects much of the confusion we feel about baptism, salvation, and God's working in our lives. How can anyone be born again, he asks? (I'm forty-five years old, 5 feet 10 inches tall, and weigh 165 pounds. Can I reenter my mother's womb and be born again?)

Jesus tells Nicodemus that he cannot enter the kingdom without being born of water and the Spirit. Most scholars agree that this is a statement about baptism. Does that mean baptism is necessary for salvation? We don't really want to say that, but neither do we want to say that baptism is only a symbol. Something objective "happens" in baptism. Here, the author of John describes that "something" as "being born from above." The "something" is a gift from God.

The reference to the wind is important. First, the Hebrew word *ruach* can mean "wind," "breath," or "spirit." So the use of the word evokes memories of the "wind from God" sweeping over the waters of creation (Gen. 1:2) and of God's blowing "the breath of life" into the lump of clay that would become man (Gen. 2:7). Life, creation, new life, being born from above, baptism—all are gifts from God, who gives us the Spirit. We experience God in baptism.

Second, Jesus says that the wind blows where it will, beyond human control. We can see only its results. The Spirit works in this way, evidencing the spontaneity of God's nature. God makes us new in a kind of divine playfulness and joy that reminds us of dancing lights and trumpet concertos.

Prayer: **Playful Spirit, blow new life into me that I may be born from above. Amen.**

Sunday, May 25   Read John 3:16-17.

"John 3:16" posters hang in stadiums and sports arenas where they will show up in background shots for the big game. The verse is about God's love—and giving. God's gift was the incarnation of the Son, the Second Person of the Trinity. Out of a dynamic that we can never understand, God gave God's self to the world, and Jesus was born. God became incarnate so that those who believe in the Son will have eternal life. Tertullian and Irenaeus in the second century said it like this, "God became who we are so that we could become who he is."* That's the whole meaning of salvation.

But there's more. Verse 17 is not just another way of saying the same thing. It reminds us that the Incarnation is more than past history. It is a call to make a choice in our own lives. John's Gospel clearly states that judgment came into the world with Christ, and those who do not choose him are condemned. However, condemnation was not the reason Christ came. Christ came inviting all to choose him and find eternal life. So faith is not intellectual but moral. The opposite of faith is not doubt but disobedience.

So we close the week with a question about our own lives and the life of the church. If God's whole purpose in the Incarnation was salvation rather than condemnation, how can we condemn others? If we are called to be like God, how does that likeness encourage our concern for others in our loving, inviting, and caring?

Prayer: **O God, who sends and gives, help me choose Christ and love rather than condemnation. Amen.**

---

*My translation. See Irenaeus, *Against All Heresies*, V; and Tertullian, *Against Marcion*, II, 27.7.

RESPONDING TO GOD

May 26–June 1, 1997   **Trudy Flenniken**✤
Monday, May 26   Read 1 Samuel 3:1-10.

Sensing God's presence

Towering icebergs like sculptured cathedrals glistened in the sunlight; porpoises played hide and seek in the sparkling waters; and seagulls followed in the wake of our ship. In the breathtaking magnificence of Antarctica, I felt the presence of God. Like Jacob at Peniel that long ago morning, I thought, *Surely the Lord is in this place.*

God reveals God's self to us in many ways. Moses first encountered God at Mount Horeb in the burning bush and again in a cloud at Mount Sinai.

Sometimes angels herald God's presence as in the annunciation to Mary, "The Lord is with you" (Luke 1:28). God came to Joseph in a dream and descended from the heavens in the form of a dove at Jesus' baptism.

In today's scripture we find God calling in the night to the boy Samuel, the child dedicated to the Lord by his mother Hannah. Each of the three times God calls, Samuel, thinking it is Eli, responds to the nearly blind priest whom he served in the Temple. In the third call to Samuel, Eli realizes that the voice is that of God.

How often does God call us before we recognize God's voice and sense God's presence?

Prayer: **Ever-present God, open my eyes to see you in your handiwork, my ears to hear your voice in your daily living, and my heart to respond to your call. Amen.**

✤Layperson in the Pacific Beach Presbyterian Church, Presbyterian Church (USA); San Diego, California.

Tuesday, May 27   Read Psalm 139:1-6.

Responding with praise and thanksgiving

The letter tucked away these many years in my worn and tattered high school Bible contained words of totally unexpected praise and thanks that I have treasured. Dated 1934 the letter read, "I wish I had more like you. Thanks for your friendliness and loyalty. You have helped to make many pleasant memories for me." It was from the director of our high school orchestra, a feisty young woman known for her quick temper, one who struck fear in all of us. The signature was simple and informal, "Love from Lucille C." I thought of the letter as I read this psalm in which David, "the shepherd king," praises God not only for God's all-seeing providence and unlimited knowledge but also for God's continuing mercy.

In Hebrew the word *psalm* means "praise." Psalms are sometimes songs of thanksgiving or affirmations of personal faith as in Psalm 23. Often they express a longing for an intimate relationship with God. This particular song of praise is believed to have been one of those sung by worshipers as they journeyed to the Temple on designated feast days.

We find the word *praise* many times in the Bible—more than fifty times in Psalms alone. Used in ancient Israel as a guide for public and private worship, the psalms praise God for the marvelous works God has done and exalt God's majesty and faithfulness.

We all appreciate words of praise for what we have done, but God alone is worthy of our praise.

Prayer: Holy God, today let my heart sing joyful songs of praise and thanksgiving to you. Amen.

159

Wednesday, May 28   Read Psalm 139:13-18.

Responding with awe and wonder

I stood in amazement before the Great Pyramid of Cheops, burial place of that early Egyptian ruler. Believed to have been built some 2500 years before the time of Christ, the Egyptian pyramids were considered by the ancient people to be one of the Seven Wonders of the World. *How incredible*, I thought, *that in those long ago days without modern tools or machinery such a tremendous and long-lasting monument could have been made by human hands!* However, the psalmist marvels at the creative power of God rather than the accomplishments of humanity.

Through modern medicine, we are learning just how intricate our bodies are, how complex our minds. God's creation fascinates the psalmist. Even more unbelievable to him is the knowledge that even before his birth God knew him and had formed days for his life.

The writer expresses astonishment that God's thoughts of him are more numerous than grains of sand and are always with him. He glories that each morning when he wakes, he is still in God's presence.

So it is with us. The God of the psalmist also knows us intimately and is ever-present with us. How wonderful it would be if we, like the psalmist, would begin each day surrounded by thoughts of God!

Prayer: **Creator God, who loved me even before I was born, help me realize how insignificant and temporal are the works of humankind. May my awe and wonder never cease when I consider** *your* **magnificent works. Amen.**

Thursday, May 29   Read 2 Corinthians 4:5-7.

Responding with humility

It was the custom of the church in which I grew up to go forward to the altar for Communion. Kneeling to be served the elements, I never ceased to be filled with a sense of humility and unworthiness.

In this verse Paul declares that his preaching is not about himself but about Christ. He describes himself as a humble servant to the people of Corinth because of what Jesus has done for him, considering himself only a perishable container or a clay jar. Paul declares that the power within him is from God; he simply reflects God's light. Later in Second Corinthians (12:7), Paul also tells them that although he pleaded three times for the "thorn" to be removed from his flesh, it remained so that in his weakness he might serve the Lord with greater humility.

While the Greeks considered humility weak and despicable, the Bible exalts it as a virtue. The Beatitudes assure us the meek (the humble) will inherit the earth. Jesus declares, "Whoever becomes humble like this child is the greatest in the kingdom of heaven" (Matt. 18:4).

As we think of the humble life of Jesus, his lowly birth in a stable, his life of servitude, and his degrading death on the cross, let us remember the words of the ancient prophet Micah, "What does the Lord require of you? To act justly and to love mercy and to walk humbly with your God" (Micah 6:8, NIV).

Prayer: **Gracious God, forgive me for my pride. Remind me that I only reflect your light. Teach me the way of true humility. Amen.**

Friday, May 30   Read 2 Corinthians 4:8-12.

Responding with endurance

Elie Wiesel in his book *Night* tells of the years he spent in Nazi concentration camps in Germany; millions of people perished. The thought filled me with horror. I wondered how anyone could survive the sickness and hunger, the brutality and torture, the sudden disappearance of loved ones, and the threat of death always hanging over them. Yet somehow Elie Wiesel and others endured.

I thought of Paul, "the Apostle to the Gentiles," a survivor who often faced death. In this second letter to the Corinthians, we read of his steadfast endurance as he speaks of the troubles and persecution that beset the members of the Christian community.

Paul had reason to reflect on his own personal afflictions and persecutions: It might have been the frailty of his body or a physical affliction from which he suffered. Perhaps he is recalling his first missionary journey when John Mark deserted him or when he was stoned and left for dead in Lystra. He may have been referring to his flight from Damascus early in his ministry to escape the fury of the Jews, the threatened stoning at Iconium, the shipwreck on Malta, or the times he was in prison.

However, Paul gladly endured the suffering and the constant threat of death to preach the gospel of Christ, and he calls us to become part of this giving ourselves up to death for Jesus' sake. Only in this giving up do we gain life.

Prayer: **Almighty God, grant me the ability to endure in whatever circumstances I may find myself as I serve you. Amen.**

Saturday, May 31   Read 1 Samuel 3:11-20.

Responding with submission

As a child in Sunday school, one of my favorite songs was Fanny Crosby's "Blessed Assurance." The words "perfect submission" in the song's second stanza came back to me as I read the story of Eli and Samuel. Here God prophesies through Samuel that Eli's sin of allowing his sons, Phinehas and Hophni, to blaspheme against God will never be forgiven. Eli replies, "He is the LORD; let him do what is good in his eyes" (NIV).

The Bible contains many stories of those who have submitted to God's will. Abraham, following God's command, prepared to sacrifice Isaac, the beloved son of his old age, as a burnt offering. Moses, after much protest, yielded to God's commission to lead the Israelites out of Egypt. Job patiently suffered through the mocking of his friends and the personal afflictions and disasters that God allowed to be brought upon him, yet continued to praise the name of the Lord. Mary, the mother of Jesus—troubled and fearful—accepted God's purpose for her life.

Surely the greatest words of perfect submission are those of Jesus in Gethsemane as he faced death on the cross: "My Father, if it is possible, may this cup be taken from me. Yet not as I will, but as you will" (Matt. 26:39, NIV).

If we would have our lives be pleasing to God, must we not also surrender our wills to God?

Prayer: Merciful God, forgive my selfish attempts to control my own life. May I have the desire and courage to submit my will to you. Amen.

Sunday, June 1   Read Mark 2:23–3:6.

Responding with compassion

I watched as the young woman knelt beside the man in the wheelchair. His leathery face bore the grime of many days on the street, his eyes dulled by alcohol. Believing his need for food superseded the practice of not serving the homeless who had been drinking to excess, she gently took the bottle from his hands, coaxing him to eat the nourishing supper we had prepared.

In today's scripture Mark tells of the occasion on which Jesus and his disciples, walking through the fields on the Sabbath, picked and ate the grains of wheat. The Pharisees, who consider their actions to be work and thus a violation of the Sabbath, rebuked them. Jesus then reminds the Pharisees of the time when David, fleeing from Saul, unlawfully ate the bread of the presence, sharing it with his companions.

To Jesus and to our volunteer, satisfying the needs of people was more important than obeying human rules. The story of Jesus is an epic of love. God so loved the world that God sent God's only Son. With that same love, Jesus ministered to the needy. With sympathy Jesus healed the sick, with concern he sought the lost, with compassion he fed the five thousand, with tenderness he blessed the little children. Jesus' ultimate gift of love to us was his own life.

Of all the ways in which we respond to God, surely we delight and honor God most when we follow the commandment of Jesus, "Love one another as I have loved you" (John 15:12).

Prayer: God of compassion, make me an instrument of your love so that I may show my brothers and sisters the love you have showed me. Amen.

THE BIBLE'S WISDOM ON LEADERSHIP

June 2–8, 1997   **Grant Hagiya**✤
Monday, June 2   Read 1 Samuel 8:4-9.

Leadership was a constant concern for the people of Israel. Throughout the early history of Israel, great and powerful leaders emerged. In many cases, Israel's leaders were great because of their willingness to follow the ways of the Lord instead of their own self-centered impulses.

In today's reading, the elders gather to demand a new leader. God realizes our human weaknesses all too well and tells Samuel to warn the elders about what a human leader might do to them. But God counsels Samuel to listen to the elders first—an example of God's ultimate openness, of God's willingness to let people make up their own minds. Here God's actions model true leadership—a leadership that is never coercive or dictatorial but always gentle and loving.

All institutions, including the church, expose us to leadership. At times we will lead; at other times we will be led. However, we must remember first and foremost that it is God's leadership that we follow. God's leadership differs completely from any secular form of leadership; God's leadership truly attempts to empower others holistically. By modeling this type of leadership for the church and the world, we *can* make a difference.

Prayer: **Lord, I pray for your leadership in my church and world. Amen.**

✤Senior minister, Centenary United Methodist Church, Los Angeles, California.

Tuesday, June 3   Read 1 Samuel 8:10-20.

This complex passage from First Samuel deals with the issue of power. The people are asking for a king to be appointed over them. It is a practical, civic matter; the priest counsel is old and his sons are immoral and unjust (1 Sam. 2:12-17). God's counsel to Samuel is that the people do not trust enough to allow God to be king over them; rather, they need an earthly power to lead them.

Are we any different in our modern times? Do not the majority of us look to that political leader, business CEO, or senior pastor to provide the necessary leadership to get us out of the many problems we face as a community? We are often too willing to give up our own power to a "leader" who, we think, will get us out of the latest jam we are in.

Perhaps our situations require more trust in the lordship of God in Christ—putting our faith in the Lord rather than in a human leader who might show flashes of brilliance but in the end not have all the answers. We often relinquish our small bit of power, failing to realize that while I alone do not have enough power and you alone do not have enough power, together our power can make a difference in the world. When communities led by the ideals of God's love and justice choose to use their power then we will better reflect the biblical notions of power.

Prayer: **O Lord, enable me to understand that you alone are my guide and leader. My trust resides in you. Amen.**

Wednesday, June 4   Read Psalm 138:1-6.

Psalm 138 is a thanksgiving hymn delivered by an individual who is praising God. The first three verses thank God for answering the psalmist's plea for increased spiritual strength.

The next three verses turn our attention to the theme with which we began the week—trusting in God rather than political leaders. The psalmist states that all the political leaders of the world will praise the Lord, for they will hear and know the ways of God. Why? Because of the Lord's great justice: "For though the LORD is high, he regards the lowly."

Does not the true worth of any leader lie in her or nis compassion for those being led? Is not this compassion borne out in the humility of leaders who realize that they are in a position of leadership to serve? True leadership always comes from the bottom up rather than the top down.

In this sense, all of us can become great leaders in our own families, churches, and communities. All it takes is the willingness to serve and be for others. Most of all, we must put out trust in God and allow the Lord's ideals of love and justice for all to lead us. Let us model God's leadership as we strive to serve those whom we lead.

Prayer: **O God, move me to see where I can be a servant leader in the coming weeks and months. Let me trust in your ways and your leadership forever. Amen.**

Thursday, June 5   Read Psalm 138:7-8.

Persons often decline leadership positions because they do not want to be the object of criticism, and criticism comes to those in leadership. People in any organization, community, or church often rationalize that it is much safer to be a quiet, unassuming member rather than the one who leads.

But whether we lead or not, how many of us can escape conflict and criticism? The psalmist seems to imply in verse 7 that receiving criticism is a natural part of life. Those who take on the mantle of leadership undoubtedly will face criticism and second-guessing at one time or another.

But the psalmist contends that God will preserve and defend us. No matter how strong the criticism, God's "right hand delivers" us. Then comes the challenging call in verse 8: "The LORD will fulfill his purpose for me. . . . Do not forsake the work of your hands!"

At certain times in our lives, God calls us to leadership. It is one of the many ways we fulfill God's purpose for our own lives. Let us not fear criticism as we weigh decisions to assume leadership roles; God will protect and preserve us. May those in leadership know that no criticism can harm them, if they are truly fulfilling the God's purposes.

Prayer: **Let me not fear assuming leadership, O Lord. Enable me and protect me. Amen.**

Friday, June 6   Read Mark 3:20-35.

At the heart of this story is the scribes' accusation that Jesus is in alliance with Satan. We must remember that the scribes were the learned religious leaders of their society; they spent a lifetime in study of and devotion to the faith. Most likely, Jesus challenged their traditional way of thinking and acting. So they condemned him, even though they witnessed the marvelous things he could do. Their minds were so full of their own understanding of what is right and good that they could not see the new possibilities that Jesus offered.

As members and leaders of local churches and community organizations, we must heed the important message here. Often we get locked into a certain way of doing things; when someone or something comes along that offers a new way, we close the door on the possibility of changing—even if it is for the better.

Those who have been in the church for years have a great legacy and history behind them, but they must guard against falling into the same trap as the scribes in this story. Longtime members should not allow their knowledge and church standing to be a stumbling block to positive change and growth. True openness to God's leading in Christ affirms positive change. In fact, strong leadership demands that the church keep growing and becoming spiritually stronger. Christ is the model for creative newness and transformation. Being faithful to Christ means being open to such newness and change.

As we pray and work for our church, let us embrace the Lord who makes all things new.

Prayer: **Lord, may the closed minds of the scribes teach me a lesson. May I recognize and welcome the open creativity of your Spirit. Amen.**

Saturday, June 7   Read 2 Corinthians 4:13-15.

In management theory, one of the key elements is identifying your basic foundation, missional purpose, or deepest value. In other words, it is knowing what is the most important thing to your organization or company. Once this is clear, all of one's energy, activity, and programs can be focused on this one main value or goal. Obviously, this central focus makes everything flow much more smoothly.

Often we in the church forget this basic principle. We are so busy carrying on the traditional functions of the church that we fail to remember why we are here in the first place. This leads to a kind of self-absorption as we carry on the functions of institutional maintenance without the burning passion to fulfill the church's mission. Ultimately lack of focus may lead to disillusionment, burnout, and leaving the church.

We should thank God today for Paul's reminder of our basic foundation and missional purpose. Our foundation is Jesus Christ! We believe this, so we speak of this truth. We invest our energy in activity and programming for the Lord's sake, "so that grace, as it extends to more and more people, may increase thanksgiving, to the glory of God."

If we can focus our entire energy on this basic purpose and task, our churches will be filled with those who are ready and eager to extend Christ's love to the world in which they live.

Let us remind one another of our purpose as the church. Then let us go out and fulfill the ministry to which God has called us.

Prayer: **Lord, give me clarity of purpose and the burning desire to fulfill our mission and ministry for your kingdom. Amen.**

Sunday, June 8   Read 2 Corinthians 4:16-5:1.

As a leader, it is easy to lose heart—especially in the church, where our successes are small and the workload is large. What makes the church unique is the fact that the tasks never end. As one church season ends, another follows. This is the nature of our Christian ministry and mission: We are to love God and neighbor with our whole selves, and our neighbors have so many needs that our job seems endless.

Paul puts our ministry and mission in its proper perspective. He tells us not to "lose heart," for our burdens are only slight and temporal. In fact, they are preparing us for a greater glory that God has in store for us. We as Christians live not only for the moment where things can be seen and touched, but we also live for a greater vision that is eternal and cannot be seen with the human eye.

What is this greater vision that cannot be seen? We glimpse it in words such as *love, peace, justice, liberation, righteousness, joy*—abstract words that hold the meaning of our Christian mission. This is what is at stake when we engage in the work of the church.

In our leading and working in the church, we may become weary and disappointed. At these times may we remember not to get bogged down in the temporary and the visible. We have a greater vision—an eternal vision that guides and sustains us.

Prayer: **Lord, enable me to know a greater vision that cannot be seen or touched. Give me a hunger for this vision that will not cease with any human disappointment. Amen.**

GOD ALWAYS HAS A PLAN

June 9–15, 1996   A. Safiyah Fosua♣
Monday, June 9   Read Psalm 20.

Today's psalm is one of intercession. The petitioner is confident that the Lord will always answer those who are troubled. The psalmist has no doubt that we will receive support. We are assured of God's constancy. God rewards the faithful; victory and favor are certain. The psalmist encourages us to pray with the assurance that God always has a plan that benefits humankind.

Listen to the strong closing affirmation of verse 7: "Some take pride in chariots, and some in horses, but our pride is in the name of the LORD our God." Human interventions, like the chariot, often fail to win the battle. Horses eventually need rest. What certainties can we rely upon? None of our solutions is sufficient. Take pride in the Lord our God, who always prevails.

This week's readings reinforce a common truth: God always has a plan. There is no need to be perplexed by the disposition of our bodies or the disposition of the kingdom of God. What we see today is not the final disposition of either. It does not matter if we are discouraged by human depravity or by the failure of human leadership; we are reminded that God is never caught unawares; we have no reason for alarm. God always has a plan for growth and restoration.

Prayer: **Help me, Lord, to trust in you when I am tempted to put too much confidence in my own solutions. Amen.**

♣Writer; United Methodist clergy and missionary, Ghana, West Africa.

Tuesday, June 10   Read 1 Samuel 15:34–16:3.

From the start, Samuel could foresee the risk involved in having an earthly king. Neighboring kings had abused the people, keeping them from undivided worship. However, the Israelites had insisted, and God had granted their request. Their first king looked the part; he was tall, handsome, and well-regarded. He was also strong-willed and disobedient. Saul quickly proved that he was not the right person for the job. Israel needed a king who would follow God and present God's will to the people.

Even though Israel's having a king was never God's ideal, God had an alternate plan. Samuel was to anoint David as the new king, while Saul was still alive. Imagine Samuel's fear. What if Saul heard of it? In another historical context—the Middle Ages or even modern times—what Samuel was called to do could have been considered an act of treason.

The ministry of modern-day prophets also toes the delicate line between political loyalties. Prophets in our day often are called upon to proclaim God's will for people, communities, nations, and the world. Samuel was not called to overthrow a corrupt government; he was called to proclaim God's alternate plan for leadership—David.

As we look around us, we see that human governments are still flawed. Human nature continues to prefer styles of leadership and decision making that do not always involve God. Israel's example proves that God continues God's active involvement in human history—even when human systems are flawed or become corrupt.

Suggestion for mediation: **What plans might God have for intervention in modern governments? What is my role as a faithful disciple in helping work out God's will through my government?**

Wednesday, June 11   Read 1 Samuel 16:4-13.

Israel's future lay in the hands of one who was not even invited to the sacrifice. Even David's father considered him small and insignificant. The sons with great physical stature and reputations were invited to meet the prophet. David was left to tend the flock. Yet the great prophet could not speak God's word until David was present.

Later we learn that God had been preparing David, even as a youth, for the leadership Israel demanded. To protect the sheep, the young shepherd took on lions and bears. He became skillful in the use of a sling. He learned to play his harp. To a casual observer, none of these activities would appear to offer training in leadership of a people, but God obviously saw something different in David's heart.

Human nature has changed very little. When we are looking for God's solutions to human problems, we often look in tried and "true" places: We question the experts; we consult analysts. We conduct large, expensive meetings with consultants. Perhaps God is attempting to tell us that the answers often lie in those persons we consider small, insignificant, or even bothersome. Who do we fail to invite to our great meetings? What might they have to offer?

The strong leadership of today's children will shape our future. They, like David, are often left off the invitation list when adults plan great meetings; yet they bear responsibility for leadership in the future.

Suggestion for meditation: **God is preparing today's children and youth for the awesome leadership tasks of the future. How am I helping them? How am I hindering them? In what ways are we, as faithful disciples, ignoring our responsibility for children and youth?**

Thursday, June 12   Read 2 Corinthians 5:6-10.

We hide from our aging bodies. For proof, look on the shelves of your local pharmacy or cosmetic supplier. We dye hair, tighten skin, and replace missing teeth—often to *appear* younger. Aging is the natural result of normal wear and tear on the human body. Why do we deny its beauty?

The predictable coming crisis for baby boomers is that of aging. The first of those boomers born in the post-Korean War years have reached the age of fifty. Those of us who unexpectedly overcrowded elementary schools, threw colleges into a frenzy, and immortalized rock and roll are slowly moving toward the sunset. As we go, our preoccupations include both the span of our lives and apprehension about what lies on the other side of the grave. What hope does God offer for our crisis of mortality?

Seen in this context, Paul's words remind us that—whether in our bodies or away from them—we belong to God. The bodies that preoccupy our thoughts are not our ultimate destination. They serve as vehicles for our sojourn on this earth. Verse 1 of today's chapter reminds us that the body is merely a house for the soul, "the earthly tent we live in"; our ultimate destination is the presence of God.

Paul reminds us that our aim is to please God. Knowing that we will eventually appear before Christ's judgment seat, encourages us to live faithful lives. We do this with the assurance that God has made provision for our souls when the time comes to shed our rapidly aging bodies.

Prayer: **Lord, as my body ages and eventually wears out, comfort me with the fact that your plans include provisions both for my body and my soul. Amen.**

Read 2 Corinthians 5:14-17.

"I'm not sure that I would have done it! It's just too risky."

"What do you mean, Gabriel?"

"I'm talking about this 'free will' business, Michael. Do you really think that they can make it all the way through life without making a mistake?"

"I seriously doubt it. What do you think God will do when they fail?"

"I don't know Michael, but I'm sure that God has a plan."

As noted by the two angelic observers in today's simulated conversation, the design of the human will is risky. Humankind possesses the power to reject evil and choose good or to choose evil and reject good. Sometimes we "miss the mark"; at other times we cast caution to the wind. We cannot help but make poor choices at some time in our lives. Eventually, most of us become aware of our tendency to err and need a way to experience restoration. Fear not, friend, because God indeed has made provisions to restore each of us.

God's plan for human redemption involves re-creation. We were created initially in both the image and likeness of God. As a result of humanity's poor choices, both individually and corporately, that image became distorted. But those in Christ are created anew. "So if anyone is in Christ, there is a new creation: everything old has passed away; see, everything has become new." The language of this verse suggests that such a person is altogether new. Before we were born, before we ever became aware of sin, God had plans for our restoration.

Suggestion for meditation: **God in Christ offers me an opportunity for renewal. What portions of my life have already become new? What still needs renewal?**

Saturday, June 14   Read Mark 4:26-29.

I once tried to start an avocado plant from an enormous seed that I carefully extracted from the fruit. Day after day, I passed by the contraption that I had concocted for rooting the large seed, looking for signs of a sprout. After days of disappointment, like the farmer in the parable, I too slept and rose night and day, going about my life's activities. Eventually, the anticipated sprout did appear—without my help.

Only Mark's Gospel records this parable about the mysterious growth of seeds. Here Jesus describes the kingdom of God in similar terms. Once we have done our part, the kingdom eventually comes without our help. God allows us to scatter the seeds and do our part to enhance growing conditions; but in the end, we can do nothing to *make* the seeds (or the kingdom) grow.

How does this principle translate into daily life? God's kingdom is neither a thing of the past nor a mere future hope. Something about God's kingdom intermittently peeps into our present. Sometimes signs of the kingdom show forth in an unexpected renewal of interest in God and the church. Attempts to duplicate such a unique manifestation of God's will in human history usually fail. When the dust of our human activity finally settles, we find ourselves—like farmers scattering seed—staring at the ground again, looking for sprouts.

Like the seeds' growth, the kingdom's growth is often secret, imperceptible, and somewhat unpredictable. Perhaps Jesus is encouraging us to scatter seed and watch expectantly for signs of the kingdom that are sure to follow.

Suggestion for meditation: **What unseen activity of the kingdom do I discern in my home? in my workplace? in my community?**

Sunday, June 15   Read Mark 4:30-34.

Today's parable addresses the impatient soul. Three of the four Gospels include this parable, which compares the kingdom of God to a mustard seed. In each of the three Gospels the emphasis is the same: The kingdom of God often has small beginnings. Eventually the kingdom grows to large proportions, becoming a place of shelter for many.

The writer of the Epistle to the Romans defines the kingdom of God using the terms *righteousness*, *peace*, and *joy* in the Holy Spirit. In what other ways might we discern the kingdom's small beginnings in our modern context? Several historical movements were clearly visible manifestations of the kingdom of God.

Modern historians would agree that the Civil Rights Movement had small beginnings. Rosa Parks just sat down and refused to get up. She refused to ride in the back of the city bus because of the color of her skin. The movement did not begin with appeals to the public or with lobbying or with debate. These came later. One woman's simple act of resistance was the mustard seed. The chain reaction of events that followed challenged the moral conscience of the United States.

As this movement grew, other marginalized groups of people took refuge in its shelter. Other racial and ethnic groups rallied for their rights. Women, children, and the elderly rose to the forefront. In those movements, we catch glimpses of the kingdom of God in our midst.

The symbol of the mustard seed challenges us to watch God's kingdom as it shows itself in many small ways around us.

Suggestion for meditation: **Which parables have contributed to your understanding of God and God's kingdom? Read one or more of these parables again and meditate on the message.**

COURAGE IN THE FACE OF OPPOSITION

June 16–22, 1997   **Robert V. Dodd**✤
Monday, June 16   Read 1 Samuel 17:1*a*, 4-11.

Once again the Philistine army aligned itself against Israel and prepared for battle. The battlelines were drawn on both sides; defensive and offensive strategies were planned. But the Philistines, instead of attacking, engaged in a strategy of psychological warfare. Goliath, one of their best soldiers, stood over nine feet tall, wore heavy bronze armor, and brandished both spear and sword. Goliath challenged the Israelites to send out their best soldier to fight him one-on-one. The winner of this two-person combat would win the battle for his respective army.

But this enormous man frightened Saul and the other Israelites. The sight of the giant who stood before them struck fear in their hearts. Who among them could stand up to such a powerful opponent? Their situation seemed hopeless. Surely they must have considered retreating.

Whenever we face a life-threatening situation, our basic survival instincts take over; our bodies automatically prepare us either to fight or to run away. Sometimes neither option seems available to us. This presents us with the challenge of how to express courage in the face of opposition. We must never let our fears prevent us from courageously pursuing God's will under difficult circumstances. This is the challenge of living as Christians in a world that is often hostile and un-Christian.

Prayer: **Lord Jesus Christ, help me to know that you are with me and strengthen me when I must face the challenges of life. Amen.**

✤Senior pastor of Trinity United Methodist Church in Kannapolis, North Carolina; writer of "The Sunday School Lesson," a regular column in the *North Carolina Christian Advocate*.

Sometimes in life the stage is set for a hero to enter the scene. Such was the case with the Israelites as they faced the army of Philistines and Goliath's taunting and teasing, "Give me a man, that we may fight together." Then David, the shepherd boy—a most unlikely hero—approached the field of battle. He expressed courage and youthful idealism. He declared that Goliath was seeking to defy the armies of the living God and therefore was an insult to God.

When David volunteered to accept Goliath's challenge, he explained to Saul, "The LORD, who saved me from the paw of the lion and from the paw of the bear, will save me from the hand of this Philistine." David's confidence apparently convinced Saul of David's courage, skill, and faith. Saul sent him into battle with his blessings in the desperate hope that the shepherd boy would somehow manage to defeat the giant. He even gave David his own armor to wear, but it proved to be heavy for the boy. Instead, David took the weapons with which he was most familiar: his shepherd's staff, five smooth stones, and his sling. Following a verbal confrontation with Goliath, David killed the giant by striking him on the forehead with a stone wielded by his sling. When Goliath fell to the ground, David used the giant's own sword to cut off his head.

In times of trial and opposition, we must remember that we fight with the Lord at our side to strengthen us. The Lord has been with us in the past and will continue to be with us. We must also seek to use weapons and strategies that are suitable to our personality and skills. As we do this, the Lord will see us through to victory.

Prayer: **Lord, help me to see that the battle is not mine but yours. Give me your strength and strategy for the battles of life. Amen.**

Wednesday, June 18   Read Psalm 9:9-20.

The Hebrew Scriptures attribute many of the psalms to David. This particular psalm speaks of the Lord as being utterly trustworthy and able to provide protection for those who seek refuge in him. The Lord is said to fulfill the roles of defender, judge of one's enemies, and vindicator. God responds to the cries of the afflicted and delivers them from their sufferings. The nations that oppose God's people will be caught in their own trap or net, snared by the work of their own hands. The Lord God in glory, majesty, and power will make them painfully aware of the limitations of their humanity.

While this psalm—like many others—alludes to God's vanquishing the enemies of God's people, the overall theme is that of God's ability to protect and defend God's people. This psalm's hope and reassurance enables the reader to see beyond the immediate opposition to the future victory. Because David knew that the battle and the victory belonged to the Lord, he could already see Goliath's defeat.

Sometimes we become so overwhelmed by the stress and strife of our present situation that we fail to appreciate the hope of salvation that is ours in the Lord our God. We are unable to look beyond the sin and see the Savior. Overwhelmed by the stormy sea, we cannot see Jesus walking on the water, coming to rescue us. George Bernard Shaw, famous British dramatist, once wrote, "You see things; and you say 'Why?' But I dream things that never were; and I say 'Why not?'" Faith that expresses courage in the face of opposition looks beyond the things that are, to dream the things that can be.

***Prayer:* Lord God, enable me to look beyond the limitations of the present moment and see the victory that is just beyond the horizon. Amen.**

Thursday, June 19   Read 2 Corinthians 6:1-2.

Often we think of salvation as either a past event or a future accomplishment. But salvation also has a present tense. David summoned the courage to face Goliath by recalling times in the past when the Lord had enabled him to triumph over a lion and a bear. Then he reminded himself that the Lord who had been with him in the past was with him now and that the Lord would also deliver him from Goliath's spear and sword. This same Lord who saves and delivers would be with David in all his future endeavors.

Paul, writing to the Christians in Corinth, reminded them that God through Christ had reconciled them to God. Paul and his colleagues were Christ's representatives, announcing to the Corinthians that the time to respond to God's great initiative and to experience God's deliverance is now: "Now is the day of salvation!"

Some people tend to postpone making the most important decisions of their life: choosing a spouse, selecting a college, or deciding upon a vocation. Perhaps they fear making the wrong choice. But Paul sought to reassure the Corinthians that being reconciled to God through Christ was the right choice and that they could not afford to postpone that decision.

In times of trial and tribulation, God's power to save, deliver, empower, and protect seems at best to be either a clouded memory from the distant past or a vague hope in some far-off future. We need to remind ourselves that now is the day of salvation. God stands ready and willing to help us in our present crisis, if we will call on God. Help is ours for the asking.

Prayer: **Merciful God, help me experience the power of your salvation in my present situation. You promised always to be with those who look to you and trust you. I look to you and trust you now. Amen.**

Friday, June 20   Read 2 Corinthians 6:3-10.

Sometimes our experience of pain, suffering, tragedy, and misfortune strengthens our faith and gives credibility to our testimony. We then can speak not as those who affirm the highest ideals of Christianity but as those who have proved in their own life the difference Christ makes.

When Paul confronted the Corinthians with the immediate availability of God's salvation, he spoke as one who had been through the fire of testing. His faith had proved to be strong and true. He and his colleagues had experienced "afflictions, hardships, calamities, beatings, imprisonments, riots, labors, sleepless nights, hunger" for the sake of the gospel.

They had endured it all in a spirit of patience, kindness, holiness, and authentic love for those whom they sought to introduce to the Lord's salvation. In spite of their circumstances, they had been able to express a joyous and triumphant attitude. For them, mere survival was not enough. They would accept nothing less than ultimate and total victory in Jesus. They had learned how to be overcomers in Christ, and they wanted others to join them on their spiritual journey of victorious living.

The finer points of theology and doctrine have been debated for centuries. But it is difficult to discount the power of a faith that is sufficient to give us strength and courage in even the worst of circumstances. The faith that we live speaks louder than the faith we proclaim. The apostles were living examples of the value of courageous and triumphant faith for all of God's people to witness and follow.

Prayer: **Lord Jesus, through all the ups and downs of life, keep me courageously faithful to you. Enable my life to be a positive example for others, a living gospel. Amen.**

Saturday, June 21   Read 2 Corinthians 6:11-13.

For people to make an authentic response to the message of salvation in Christ, they must have open minds and responsive hearts. Our Lord's parable about the sower and the seed reminds us that the condition of the soil is as important as the quality of the seed and the climate in which it is planted (see Matt. 13:3-9). Whenever someone is trying to sell me something, I often ask myself, "Does this person really believe in the product that he (or she) is selling?" The openness, genuineness, and sincerity of the person communicates as much as the content of the message. Somehow people know whether we believe in the product we are selling or the gospel we are telling.

Because Paul cared for them and wanted them to grow in their knowledge and love of the Lord Jesus Christ, he encouraged the Corinthians to enlarge their hearts to embrace the good news. He spoke to them openly, frankly, sincerely, and affectionately; as one who cared a great deal and had sacrificed in order to bring the message to them.

In an interview with Barbara Walters, actor Christopher Reeve, who became a quadriplegic after falling from a horse, explained his reason for not being bitter. For him, the game of life was worthwhile, and therefore he opted to play the hand he was dealt; it wasn't the hand but the game that mattered. In the larger scheme of things, Paul's hardships were not worth comparing to the salvation that was being announced to all. His courage along with his obvious sincerity proved to be a winning combination.

Prayer: **Living Lord, light me up and set me on fire for you. Let my enthusiasm for the gospel be contagious. May the genuineness of my faith be obvious to all who know me, and may it serve to bring others closer to you. Amen.**

Sunday, June 22   Read Mark 4:35-41.

One evening the disciples and Jesus were returning to the other side of the lake when a storm threatened to capsize their boat. But Jesus was sleeping soundly in the back of the boat. Fearful and frustrated, they woke him up and said accusingly, "Teacher, do you not care that we are perishing?" Then Jesus spoke to the wind and the sea and said, "Peace! Be still!" Immediately the wind died down, and the sea grew calm. Jesus said to his disciples, "Why are you afraid? Have you still no faith?" And they wondered among themselves about his true identity and the nature of his power to command even the wind and the waves.

Nothing, with the possible exception of death itself, reminds us of our own powerlessness more than witnessing the forces of nature that are unleashed in hurricanes, tornadoes, floods, volcanic eruptions, and earthquakes. Yet Jesus proved to his disciples that he was more than adequate to deal with these naturally occurring phenomena. The One who expressed such courage in the face of the potentially destructive forces of nature would express even greater courage when the whole world seemed to have turned against him or deserted him, and he faced personal pain, suffering, and death alone.

In the version of this story in the Bible storybook that I read to my children at bedtime, Jesus is reported to have said to his disciples, "Why are you afraid? God is with you in the storm." We too can weather any storm on the sea of life if we know that Jesus is in the boat with us. His presence gives us strength, courage, and reassurance. Because of Jesus, we can also express courage in the face of conflict and opposition.

Prayer: **Lord Jesus, throughout the storms of life stay close to me and help me to stay close to you. Let me hear you saying to me in the midst of life's turmoil, "Peace! Be still!" Amen.**

IN GIVING, WE RECEIVE

June 23–29, 1997   **Robert K. Smyth✛**
Monday, June 23   Read 2 Samuel 1:1, 17-27.

The opening verse calls to mind past history: "After the death of Joshua" (Judg. 1:1), "After the death of Moses" (Josh. 1:1), and "Then Joseph died" (Ex. 1:6). The opening verse of 2 Samuel 1 signals a pivotal point in history. Saul is dead, and history has favored David in the turn of events. In verses 17-27, David laments the loss both of Saul and Jonathan. Despite his differences with Saul, he now clasps him to himself in death. War has taken its toll. The repeated refrain "How the mighty have fallen" sounds a note of both praise and judgment.

As you view your past history, what have been your pivotal points—points that have affected your personal history? For what or whom do you grieve?

Evidence of our being Christian is not in the words we speak but in the way Christ's nature permeates our whole being. The grace, mercy, light, and truth of God incarnate in Jesus must permeate our lives as dye permeates cloth.

We hold in esteem those whose living fosters peace and puts an end to warring factions. We feel the deep pain of warring, its cost of good lives, its waste of earth's resources. We can echo David's lament not just for Saul and Jonathan but for all those who have fallen.

Prayer: **Lord, make me an instrument of thy peace; where there is hatred, let me sow love; where there is injury, pardon.* Amen.**

✛Clergy member of the Southern New Jersey Annual Conference of The United Methodist Church; currently interim pastor, Holy Trinity UCC, Willingboro, New Jersey; councilman, Borough of Riverton.

*Prayers for this week adapted from the Prayer of Saint Francis.

Tuesday, June 24   Read Mark 5:24-34.

Human existence is so complex that we can seldom center on one aspect of living to the total exclusion of everything else. Jesus' ministry bears this out: While he is teaching, persons come with hunger; while he is praying, persons come for healing. Today's reading is about a woman in dire need who comes for help while Jesus journeys to Jairus's home to heal the synagogue official's daughter. The Savior accepts both needs as opportunities to reveal the grace and goodness of God as cures for doubt and despair.

The Gospel tells us this unnamed woman spent twelve years and all her resources in her search for a cure. In her desperation and poverty, she believes what she hears about Jesus. "If I just touch his clothes, I will get well" (TEV). Her faith is the remedy to her doubt; her hope overcomes despair. She elbows her way to be near Jesus. She reaches to touch his cloak.

The power flows from Jesus into her as a chemotherapy of the spirit that cures her ailment. The woman feels the surge of wholeness, the joy of redemption from her twelve-year anguish. She gives Jesus faith; she receives his redemption in return.

Jesus feels the power leave him. He stops. His eyes search for the one face showing an answer to his asking, "Who touched my clothes?" Our sister kneels, looks into his eyes and hears, "My daughter, your faith has made you well. Go in peace, and be healed of your trouble."

Prayer: **Lord, make me an instrument of thy peace; where there is doubt, let me sow faith; where there is despair, let me sow hope. Amen.**

Wednesday, June 25   Read Mark 5:21-24, 35-43.

The diverse gathering by the water's edge is understandable. After all, local interest in Jesus is high. But just as Jesus steps out of the boat, an unexpected person arrives. It is Jairus, one of the top-drawer men in town, a chief officer in the synagogue. He is highly respected for his personal integrity and his loyalty to God. Why does Jairus ask to speak with Jesus? He even kneels before him!

The other elders will be in a rage when they learn of this, but Jairus's desperate personal need far outweighs his concern about what others will think. His precious twelve-year-old daughter is near death. "My little daughter is very sick. Please come and place your hands on her!" (TEV). Jesus feels Jairus's urgency and fatherly concern. He starts off with Jairus only to feel a hand from the crowd touch his cloak and draw healing power from him. For Jesus, it is the teachable moment to show love to one newly healed. For Jairus, those moments are an eternity of wasted time; his anxiety fueled by the arrival of messengers who say it is too late.

But Jesus lives in *kairos* time, God's time. As he and Jairus hurry on, Jesus assuringly says to all, "Don't be afraid, only believe" (TEV). Jesus enters that home as calm for the weeping, as light for the darkness, as joy for the sadness, as healing for the ailing daughter. Jairus had asked Jesus to take her hand, and Jesus did. "Little girl, I tell you to get up" (TEV). As she gets up, Jesus asks that she be given something to eat. Another opportunity, another healing.

Prayer: **Lord, make me an instrument of thy peace; where there is darkness, let me sow light; where there is sadness, let me sow joy. Amen.**

Thursday, June 26   Read 2 Corinthians 8:7.

The nature of Christian gratitude leads us to build our Christian courage and stamina on blessings received rather than on what we think we want. This spiritual wisdom seems to be in Paul's mind when he appeals to the new saints in Corinth for support on behalf of the struggling saints in Jerusalem. "You are so rich in all you have" (TEV). Paul intends that his sincere affirmation awaken awareness within these sisters and brothers, awaken them to the innumerable gifts of God's grace within each one.

When Harry Emerson Fosdick wrote a dedicatory hymn for Riverside Church in New York City, he began at the center of true praise and adoration: "God of grace and God of glory, on thy people pour thy power."* Later in this hymn, Dr. Fosdick gives a valid assessment of many Christians, observing that we while we have many possessions, we are spiritually poverty-stricken. We need Jesus' lordship to guide us in overcoming our poverty of spirit. The standard we always hold before us is the depth of Jesus' faith and trust in and love for God.

Although "poor in soul," we have many blessings already within our spirit and mind; for Jesus offers us richness in faith, speech, knowledge, and love. Our part of the covenant is to employ the inventory of riches we have by giving away all the love with which we are blessed. Then we can experience the inexpressible joy of discovering our cup filled anew—always to overflowing.

Prayer: **O divine Master, grant that I may not so much seek to be consoled as to console. Amen.**

The United Methodist Hymnal (Nashville, TN: The United Methodist Publishing House, 1989), No. 577.

Friday, June 27   Read 2 Corinthians 8:8-9.

My wife, Barbara, and I experienced five summers of joyous Christian service from 1990 through 1994 when we led teams of volunteers in mission to North Pole, Alaska. There teams of fourteen to eighteen persons gave two weeks each summer to help the New Hope Methodist Presbyterian congregation construct a beautiful new sanctuary. This suburb of Fairbanks is experiencing growth; the enlarged facility is providing a loving, inclusive community for individuals and families hungering for God.

One of the fundamental tools in any building project is the plumb line (see Amos 7:7-8). It is an implement used to measure how true all vertical walls are to God's invariable force of gravity. Our building volunteers frequently employed the plumb line for constructing the twenty-two facets of the exterior walls as well as for the interior walls. By building correctly, these walls, the roof they support, and the shelter they provide will endure.

In Paul's appeal to the Christians in Corinth to help others, he placed the crucified and resurrected Jesus as the plumb line in their midst. He implored Christians to always measure every act of love by this standard of the grace of our Lord, Jesus Christ. All the wealth of God's spirit was made to reside in Jesus; yet for our sake and our salvation, he chose the cross. He chose to be God's servant who suffered on our behalf; he became the Lamb of God to atone for all our sin. He gave all of himself for the redemption of each one of us. Jesus is the plumb line, the sole standard by which we understand and measure how real the love we have for God and for neighbor is.

Prayer: **O divine Master, grant that I may not so much seek to be understood as to understand. Amen.**

Saturday, June 28   Read 2 Corinthians 8:10-15.

God's creation bears witness to an alternating rhythm, an orderly cadence in the flow of the universe: day and night, warmth and cold, peace and upheaval. Ecclesiastes 3, which begins with the memorable phrase, "For everything there is a season," acknowledges this cadence. The chapter goes on to name various happenings in the human condition as a biblical reminder that nothing on earth is forever.

Paul knows all too well that this life contains uncertainties. This truth applies to financial resources as much as to anything. At the time of writing his letter to the Corinthian Christians, he encourages them to carry out this desire "If you are eager to give, God will accept your gift on the basis of what you have to give, not on what you don't have (TEV) Sometimes circumstances change, and those now able to share resources may come to a time of being the ones in need. Paul recalls the blessings of God during the Exodus, when God's manna became food in the desert. Paul's spirit recalls his own experience of being sustained by God in all circumstances, and he writes to the Philippians, "My God will supply all your needs" (4:19, TEV).

God's love for us in Jesus motivates sharing within the Christian community. This creates what some describe as the economics of equality. By the grace of God, we share our blessings with sisters and brothers in their moment of need. "We love because God first loved us." "The command that Christ has given us is this: 'whoever loves God must love his [or her] brother [and sister] also'" (1 John 4:21, TEV). We never know when we may be the one in need.

Prayer: **O divine Master, grant that I may not so much seek to be loved as to love. Amen.**

Sunday, June 29   Read Psalm 133.

Every Sunday Christians remember and celebrate the resurrection of Jesus Christ. When Christians are equipped with Christ as "God with us" and as Christ resurrected, we as the body of Christ will fulfill the words of the psalm: "How wonderful it is, how pleasant, for God's people to live together in harmony!" (TEV). God has done all that God can do for us while allowing our human individuality.

Yet as we near the completion of this magnificent century, we see increasing evidence that God's people are not living together in harmony. High councils laud ecumenism; but in reality, the body of Christ is more fractured than it is united. Diverse convictions can weaken denominations. Independent nondenominational congregations are increasing. In the church, trust is declining, morale is at a low ebb, financial support either barely holds its own or dwindles, membership statistics fail to match population growth, and mission enterprises are struggling or disappearing. Psalm 133 expresses vitality; contemporary Christianity is struggling.

Suggestion for meditation: **Where in your life within a faith community have you experienced the "precious oil" of unity running down over the collar, falling on all? In which relationships do you find the blessing of the Lord? In your understanding, how might unity bring about increased vitality?**

Prayer: **O divine Master, grant that I may believe it is in giving that I receive, it is in pardoning that I am pardoned, and it is in dying that I am born to eternal life. Amen.**

June 30–July 6, 1997   **Mamie Ko♣**
Monday, June 30   Read Psalm 48:1-8.

The psalmist wants us to envision the magnificence of the city of God—a city built on a mountain. Jerusalem was a fortress city built of stones. Yet the fortified city is not the source of Israel's strength. God serves as the city's defender. Within its walls is the source of joy for the Jewish people.

God had chosen a special place on earth to call God's abode. The people process through the city, recalling and proclaiming God's wonderful intervention for the faithful. The glory of God shone around Jerusalem in such a powerful manner that enemies panicked and trembled. They were overwhelmed by the majestic power of God. This holy presence scattered the enemies.

Today Jerusalem is divided into four quarters: the Jewish quarter, the Muslim quarter, the Christian quarter, and the Armenian quarter. Each group claims a part of this holy city. One day the Son of God will come again and the joy of God will fill this place. Some day, the earth will meet together in unity and harmony in the city of our God.

Prayer: **God, come and establish your world soon! Amen.**

♣Pastor of the English-speaking ministry in the Chinese United Methodist Church of Los Angeles, California.

Tuesday, July 1   Read Psalm 48:9-14.

In the temple court of Yahweh, we ponder the steadfast love of God for all of us. The psalmist invites us to envision ourselves walking around Jerusalem, considering all the fortresses and ramparts. Although it was a secure place, the stones, chiseled by human hands, could still tumble down. Neither the strength of the city walls nor the cleverness of the city's people are the source of success.

For centuries, Israel was trampled by many countries. This small nation has been invaded many times. The Jewish people were scattered all over the world. It was only in 1948 that the nation of Israel was reestablished and the Hebrew language was reinstated. Even though Israel has achieved independence, this nation lacks peace and security. We may wonder if God really is watching out for God's people.

Whatever the threatening force may be in our lives, we know that God is our only sure defense. There is no secure place in the world, no hiding place. In this unstable world, we know that God is still our guiding force. God loves and cares about what is happening around us. No matter what befalls us today, God still towers over us, ready to give us refuge.

Prayer: **O God, be my refuge and hiding place especially today. Amen.**

Wednesday, July 2   Read 2 Samuel 5:1-5; 9-10.

God intended that the shepherd boy David become the shepherd of Israel. The people of Israel discerned God's plan, and they anointed David as king.

The narrative asserts that God was with David every step of the way. David was the vehicle of the providential will of God.

Proverbs 19:21 says, "The human mind may devise many plans, but it is the purpose of the LORD that will be established." When David became king, he must have had many plans. One of his plans was to take Jerusalem as his own. Despite rejection by the inhabitants of Jerusalem, David acquired that city. It was in God's plan. If God wants something done, it will be accomplished ultimately.

All through history God has asked men and women to fulfill God's plans—men and women who in their daily lives listen and obey the sovereign will of God. Presidents and dignitaries are in a position to accomplish what is needed at the time. But most of us are ordinary people. We are not all called to be kings or presidents of a nation.

Our task is to discern whether or not we are with God. This is a two-way relationship. It speaks of the importance of daily communion with God. To sharpen our senses to God's presence, we need to have daily worship, prayer, and scripture meditation.

Suggestion for meditation: **What plans have I made for myself or my family? Have I checked my plans with God first to see if they are feasible?**

Thursday, July 3   Read 2 Corinthians 12:2-7*a*.

Paul could boast about many things: He was a successful evangelist. He was a church builder. He was handpicked by Christ in a special way on the Damascus road. He probably had a glimpse of heaven and could boast of his visions and revelations. Paul had every right to boast about his success. He deserved to be praised, but he did not want to brag about such things. Instead he wanted to boast about his weaknesses.

If our friends praise us—even if the praise is not quite true—our hearts may accept it with gratitude. This is human nature. Paul did not want anyone to say or to think better of him than what was seen or heard from him. He did not want any credit and merit put on him at all.

Why is Paul so rigid about receiving praise from others? Today's reading encourages us to give credit to others when credit is due. Yet many of us speak and even boast of our own achievements. In meetings we sometimes hear people say, "It was I who influenced the change." "It was I who made it possible."

Paul does not say "It was I." He refrains. In not boasting about his achievements, Paul looks squarely at his own humanity; he faces his limitations. He understands that achievement and success belong to God.

If we, like Paul, want to share our weaknesses, with whom can we share them? Can we "boast" to the bishop, the superintendent, or our congregation? How will they accept the information? How may we rejoice in our humility of weaknesses and stand in support of one another?

Prayer: **Dear God, in moments when I believe I have done well, please remind me of your sovereign hands in everything. Amen.**

Friday, July 4   Read 2 Corinthians 12:7*b*-10.

No one likes hardship in life. No one wants to be in an uncomfortable position. Unpleasant circumstances may hold us back.

Paul had a thorn in the flesh: It could have been anything—illness, pain, an uncomfortable situation. Paul asked God to remove it from him; God did not.

Today our thorns may be losing a job, rebellious children, disrespectful individuals, gangs, drugs, alcohol, gambling, and so forth. Sometimes the thorn becomes extremely painful; sometimes death results.

At these trying moments, God says, "My grace is sufficient . . . my power is made perfect." In time of need, God's unceasing favor pours upon us, and Christ's power perfects our weaknesses. When life is difficult, we can rely on God's power to make us strong.

In this passage Paul is talking specifically about the calamities, persecutions, hardships, insults, and weaknesses he had to endure for the sake of Christ. In this society, we may need to think about this. Do we find ourselves in situations where we have to suffer for our faith?

We hear stories from missionary organizations about Christian leaders facing death or persecution in many different parts of the world because of their faith in Christ. Where will you allow yourself to be vulnerable so that Christ's power can be manifested through you?

In these few decades, we have taught ourselves, as well as our young, to be strong, to speak out vehemently, and to stand up for our rights. How can we learn to accept insults for Christ's sake? How might we relearn this truth?

Prayer: **Dear God, you suffered for my sake to give me new life. Help me to suffer for the sake of new life for others. Amen.**

Saturday, July 5   Read Mark 6:1-6*a*.

Day in and day out we serve in the same local churches. We may question our effectiveness. Things do not seem to happen as fast as we want. People do not seem to appreciate what we do. Jesus did not receive honor in his hometown. Tragically, he could not do any deed of power there. The scripture says that Jesus was amazed at their unbelief. Nothing should amaze Jesus at all. Yet they did not believe in things they saw. Reality check for us today: How many times does the church stop Jesus' power because of its unbelief?

How many times do we say to God, "These things cannot be today. There is no such thing as supernatural healing, no demonized persons, no miracles." Jesus is amazed at our unbelief today. How can we believe if we only have a scientific explanation? Isn't God's realm beyond earthly understanding?

The people recognized Jesus as special: "What is this wisdom . . .? What deeds of power?" The world is made up of many good people; people who do good to others and who serve and love the poor, the sick, the homeless. Every religion has its good points. But none can point to one like Jesus and say, "What wisdom, what power."

As Christians, do people evidence God's power and wisdom in us? in the church?

***Prayer:* Dear God, help my unbelief! Amen.**

Sunday, July 6   Read Mark 6:6*b*-13.

Yesterday's unbelief becomes today's belief. The disciples Jesus sent out relied solely on Jesus' instruction. He asked them not to take money, food, or extra clothes with them. They were to depend totally on the family with whom they were staying. At the time of Jesus, the road was rough and the distances between villages were long; yet, Jesus asked them to take nothing with them. This was living by faith.

When the disciples were not welcome in a village, they were to leave that place. They had fulfilled their responsibility, and those who rejected the mission would have to answer to God. Clearly, Jesus expected some people to reject the gospel.

By faith, the disciples engaged in mission. First, they were to preach the gospel of repentance. Second, they were to minister to people's physical needs. Before being sent out, Jesus gave the disciples authority to cast out unclean spirits. They were equipped to battle anything in the name of Christ.

Words and actions are necessary today to invite others to Christ. The church needs to provide the words of God to people and to minister to their earthly needs. Christ has given us the power he gave to his followers. He expects the casting out of demons and the curing of the sick.

We need to explore these missions again.

Prayer: **Reveal to me the truth about this passage again, O God. Amen.**

July 7–13, 1997   Mary A. Avram✤
Monday, July 7   Read 2 Samuel 6:1-5.

Successful in battle, David had united all Israel under his reign and had established Jerusalem as his new capital. The time had come to fulfill his vow to "find a place for the LORD" (Ps. 132:5). The time had come to move the ark of God from the house of Abinadab to its "place" in the tent of worship David had prepared in Jerusalem.

David gathered a great escort for God's ark and placed it on a new cart—unpolluted by previous use. The procession to Jerusalem began. Thirty thousand chosen men of Israel with musicians, dancers, singers—and David himself in the midst—danced and sang with all their might before the Lord. Joy, ecstasy, rapture—what a glorious procession of rejoicing it must have been!

An old gospel hymn invites Jesus into our heart; it declares that there is room in our heart for him—a "place" for Jesus in our heart just as David had a "place" for God's ark in Jerusalem. Let us also choose to rejoice with all our might in the presence of our Lord.

Prayer: **Gracious God, fill my heart with yourself; there is a place in my heart for you. Amen.**

✤Spiritual director, author, educator, speaker; Spiritual Guide for the Academy for Spiritual Formation; member of the Wider Quaker Fellowship and The United Methodist Church; Signal Mountain, Tennessee.

Tuesday, July 8   Read 2 Samuel 6:12*b*-19.

As often happens in our own lives, an unexpected event interrupted the journey of the ark of God. Following this incident David took the ark to the house of Obed-edom where it rested for three months or so. God blessed the household of Obed-edom as it sheltered the ark. David then returned with all the house of Israel and took the ark from Obed-edom to continue the journey to its place in Jerusalem.

There is an old saying that the longest journey begins with the first step. For David, this journey began with the first six steps. For, after six paces, it was evident that God favored the journey and David made sacrifices to the Lord in gratitude. And David danced before the Lord with all his body, mind, soul, emotions— with all his might.

The procession continued into Jerusalem with all the house of Israel shouting and with trumpets blowing. David, clad in a small linen apron leapt and danced in exaltation, enthusiasm, frenzy, and transport of joy. Michal, David's wife, saw him from her window; from the leanness of her soul, she despised him in her heart. How sad.

Yet we are to remember that the focal point of this narrative is not King David or Michal or Jerusalem's becoming the center of Israel's worship. The heart of this story is the ark of God, a sacred object venerated as a visible sign of God's presence among the people. We look at David, we look at the procession of the house of Israel, we look at Michal—each represents a way of responding to God's presence. We can be self-centered or we can be God-centered—and every day we are called to choose.

Prayer: **Blessed God, this day I choose you. Guide me, enliven and inspire me in all my comings and goings—in all my thoughts and actions—to seek you continually as my center. Thank you. Amen.**

Wednesday, July 9   Read Psalm 24.

Psalm 24 is a liturgy of entrance, a processional liturgy most likely used by the Israelites on festival days when the ark was taken out of the Holy of Holies, processed through the city or countryside, and then returned in joyous procession. Perhaps it was written for the entrance of the ark of God into the tent of worship when David first brought it to Jerusalem.

Verses 1 and 2 are a hymn, proclaiming the Lord as owner and master of all that is—for God founded and established it. Verses 3-6 may have been chanted by two priests or choirs as questions and answers regarding the qualities necessary in those admitted to Temple worship. And verses 7-10 are an antiphonal song sung between those within the Temple and those outside the gates who are bringing the ark of God, the symbol of God's presence, into the place of worship.

As I read this psalm I am taken back to the moment I stood in the silent, lonely sacristy of the chapel at Keble College, Oxford, and gazed upon William Holman Hunt's "Light of the World," which Hunt painted in 1854. The basis for the painting was Revelation 3:20.

I saw the glorified Jesus in priestly garb with kingly crown entwined with thorns. He stands in a weedy garden before a door with no knob. His right hand is raised, knocking on the door. In his left hand he carries a lantern lighting the way. His face and form encounter the one who views the painting and ask the ancient question: Will you open the gates and doors of your heart that the King of glory may come in?

Prayer: **Loving and saving God, may there be nothing in my heart this day that keeps you outside. Come into my heart, Lord Jesus; it is yours. Amen.**

Thursday, July 10   Read Mark 6:14-20.

The scripture readings for today and tomorrow recount the death of John the Baptist in Mark's Gospel. Matthew also relates this narrative, and Luke briefly tells of John's imprisonment and beheading.

As the text opens, John is already dead; rumors about Jesus, a man with great powers, are flying all over the place. Herod's response to Jesus indicates that he is a man of superstitious nature with a guilty conscience, for he says, "John, whom I beheaded, has been raised."

Herod was a man with choices, even as we have choices every day of our lives. Somewhere in his soul he knew John was a righteous and holy man, and although he was greatly perplexed or disquieted when he heard him speak, he liked to listen to him. But because John condemned Herod's incestuous relationship with his brother's wife, Herod had him bound and thrown into prison.

Herod had a choice: follow his soul wisdom, the inner nudgings in his spirit that led him to a reverential fear of John, or follow the egotistical way of the world around him. Herod, in his moral weakness, chose expediency and silenced John by throwing him into prison—yet he protected him. Those inner nudgings would not abate and maybe, just maybe, Herod could have it both ways: John silenced but unharmed.

Prayer: **Loving and gracious God, open the ears and eyes of my heart today that I may recognize the nudgings of your Spirit. Lord Jesus, come in your Holy Spirit and strengthen and encourage me not to ride the fence but always to choose your way. Amen.**

Friday, July 11   Read Mark 6:21-29.

A birthday party. A rash vow. A bloody banquet platter. Rage, revenge, misplaced obedience, grief, pride—choices. Herod solemnly swore, made a promise equal to a vow, and backed himself into a corner where his moral weakness prevailed. Even though he was "deeply grieved" he chose to save face before his guests and do the unthinkable—a drama played out to the final verse of this text, which evokes a sense of love and tenderness, "When his disciples heard about it, they came and took his body, and laid it in a tomb."

The flamboyance of Herod and his court; the grandiosity and hubris; the feasting, dancing girls, and vengeance all seem to overshadow the simplicity of John the Baptizer who is the central figure of this text. Yet with prayerful listening we hear the prophet speaking truth to power. We hear again that the Gospels do not promise a rose garden to followers of Jesus, who is Truth. Rather, we remember that the promise given is, "I am with you always, to the end of the age" (Matt. 28:20).

In this narrative of John the Baptist's death—the only death other than that of Jesus recorded in the Gospel of Mark—we can see again the profound importance of the choices we make in our lives. Throughout, the Hebrew and Christian Scriptures call upon us to *choose*. May God grant us the strength and courage to choose with Joshua, "As for me and my household, we will serve the LORD" (Josh. 24:15).

***Suggestion for meditation:* Add the above words of Joshua to your daily prayer time and seek God's grace to live them out day by day.**

Saturday, July 12   Read Ephesians 1:3-10.

The Letter to the Ephesians was probably a "circular" letter, a letter that "made the rounds," traveling from one church to another. Our text today is a portion of one long, complicated sentence in Greek—the original language—that stretches from verses 3 through 14. Gratefully, the English translators formed multiple sentences to make it easier to read.

This prayer of praise and blessing reminds me of a question raised in a Bible study I attended: "How can we bless God? I thought that God was the one doing the blessing." As the man spoke, my heart filled and overflowed and I responded, "How can we *not* bless God who freely and lavishly pours out blessings and grace upon us without measure?"

This prayer tells us who we are, where we are, how we got here, and why. The language is sublime and lifts the willing heart into the heavens.

God chose us, says the author, before anything that is existed. We are a part of the very heart of creation, chosen "to be holy and blameless before him in love." Glorious grace is lavishly bestowed on us through Jesus the Beloved; bestowed like precious oil. It calls to mind the oil poured on the head of Aaron—running down, dripping off his beard onto the collar of his robes, soaking him through and through (Ps. 133:2). In this prayer of blessing we know ourselves filled with, immersed in, overflowing with, surrounded by our blessing God.

Prayer: **I am blessed by my glorious God. Thank you, thank you for choosing me in Christ and for the blessings in him you lavishly pour out upon me endlessly and without price. Amen.**

Sunday, July 13   Read Ephesians 1:11-14.

"Bless the LORD, O my soul, and all that is within me, bless [God's] holy name," cries the psalmist (Ps. 103:1). On this Lord's day, these four verses in the Ephesian prayer of blessing join with yesterday's reading, and the waiting heart soars in Christ.

In Christ, the opening words of our text today, runs through this epistle like a golden ribbon weaving it all together. This phrase, along with its alternatives, "in him" and "in whom," appear more than thirty times within the six short chapters of Ephesians.

We who have set our hope on Christ—we who have heard the word of truth, the gospel of our salvation, and believed in him— are marked with the seal of the promised Holy Spirit, says the author. The age-old questions of Who am I?, Why am I here?, and What is life all about? are subsumed into our destiny in him of living "for the praise of his glory."

All day long, every day, for all the days and nights of our lives, we are faced with choices. Some are quick, made in the flash of a moment. Others become sources of anguish and struggle, and we may seek and yearn for holy guidance. These opening verses of Ephesians offer us a direction to use always and everywhere in our lives: I am called to live to the praise of his glory. Am I?

Prayer: **Gracious, redeeming God, I know you hold me close in your heart in Christ. Thank you. Please live your life in me in such a way that my life may be lived to the praise of your glory. Thank you. Bless your holy name. Amen.**

July 14–20, 1997   **David Lowes Watson**♣
Monday, July 14   Read 2 Samuel 7:1-14*a*.

Today's passage offers two important insights into how God
intends to accomplish the redemption of the world. The first
insight comes from David's choice of Jerusalem as a royal
headquarters for the tribes of Israel. This move was a stroke of
political genius. Jerusalem previously had been a Jebusite
fortress, aligned with neither northern nor southern territories.
Thus it was an ideal place to hold court for all the tribal leaders.

Yet to foster genuine unity among the people of Israel, David
knew that Jerusalem had to be more than a political base. It had to
be a place where God was honored; thus he made the procession
of the ark of God into the city a profoundly symbolic celebration
(see 2 Samuel 6). We would do well to take note of David's
priorities. We must ground our efforts to bring God's redemption
to our neighbors and even to this planet in the honoring of God,
not in the meeting of political minds.

The second insight follows from the first. David was concerned
that the ark, the most powerful symbol of the presence of God,
have a permanent dwelling place in this new center of religious
and political union. God's response through the prophet Nathan
was disconcertingly direct: "Thanks all the same, but I will
determine my own dwelling place" (AP). Once again we should
take note. God is God; David is only king.

Suggestion for meditation: **How blessed we are to know that God
intends to redeem the world! How blessed we are when we
remember that redemption is God's initiative!**

♣Professor of Theology and Congregational Life and Mission, Wesley
Theological Seminary, Washington, D.C.

Tuesday, July 15 Read 2 Samuel 7:1-14*a*.

The same passage gives us several additional insights into God's redemptive plan. To begin with, the method is quite astounding. Instead of some grandiose scheme that will impose a new order on planet earth, the salvation offered to all the world has very small beginnings in a nation that has only begun to sense its identity. The Israelites, no less and no more, are chosen to be the foundation of God's new household. It is a strategy fraught with risk, but this is how God intends to set about reclaiming the wayward world.

The scope of the plan is no less astounding than the method. David makes clear that the city of Jerusalem will be a place where *all* the people of Israel are welcome, not just their tribal leaders. In the same way, God intends planet earth to become a household in which *all* of humanity is made to feel at home. The message could not be more straightforward. We must set about making everyone—*every* one—our neighbor. We must do this just as soon as we can—if, that is, we want to feel at home in God's eternal household.

There is yet another insight. When God refuses to accept the offer of a permanent dwelling place (vv. 8-17), David is rebuked but not snubbed. He may have smarted a little over God's rejection of his proposal, but he is promptly overwhelmed by a gesture beyond all his expectations: a covenant that establishes his line forever and binds him to God as son to father and as father to son. We should remember this whenever we feel snubbed by God. It will not be long before major generosities make our minor resentments embarrassingly unbecoming.

Prayer: **O God of Israel and of David, teach me the ways of your new household and help me remember that your reproof often precedes your blessing. Amen.**

Wednesday, July 16   Read Psalm 89:20-29.

These verses affirm the covenant made with David and tell us even more about the nature of our Redeemer. This is a God who wants to lavish love on those who are willing to accept it. Just consider what God promises to do for David: exalt him, anoint him, strengthen him, protect him, and make him the highest of the kings of the earth. David has honored God, and this is all the pretext God needs to shower him with more blessings than anyone could ever imagine. Why does God do this? Because God is parental. God rejoices to hear David cry, "You are my Father, my God, and the Rock of my salvation!" The God who lavishes love also thrives on love.

Elsewhere in the Hebrew Scriptures we find that God's parental love is destined for a much larger family than the Israelites—indeed, for all nations (see Isaiah 42:5-7). The house of David is the paradigm for God to lavish countless blessings on the whole of planet earth. The relationship between God and the peoples of the world will be that of a household in which the head of the house will distribute infinite wealth to everyone's advantage. This affords the people of God the clearest possible identity. They know who they are because they belong to a family in which there is a plentitude of parental love.

The day will come when everyone will know this, from the least to the greatest (see Jeremiah 31:34). In the meantime, those of us blessed with a foretaste of God's eternal household must declare God's limitless generosity that awaits their homecoming to the whole of humanity.

Suggestion for meditation: **If the love and affection of a child can cause a human parent to pour out love in return, how much more will God respond to my love and affection?**

Thursday, July 17   Read Psalm 89:30-37.

In the midst of such generosities, it seems incongruous, if not mean-spirited, for God to remind David that this new household has rules. The covenant relationship is not without conditions. When the people of Israel step out of line, they can expect to be called to task, their intimacy with God notwithstanding. The punishments for their misdeeds are fearsome and certainly unacceptable today. Can this be the same loving, parental God?

The idea is jarring. Most of us would question such methods, not least because of the abuse that takes place in so many homes, not least because of the random violence of society at large. Yet in a household governed by a loving parent, punishment has a positive purpose: to keep the family centered on the love that holds it together. Those of us who forget this and become selfish with our household privileges sometimes need a sharp reminder of the household rules. The quickness and firmness with which this happens will be in direct proportion to God's parental care and concern, and it will always be remedial.

There is a pitfall to be avoided as we wrestle with this passage. We must be careful not to confuse the routine ups and downs of life with divine favor or disfavor. This is a slur on God's love and minimizes God's rightful displeasure over weighty lapses in "family manners." As we grow in grace, we learn to tell the difference. The trusting child of God knows instinctively that when God disciplines, it is never over trivialities.

Prayer: **Most Holy God, help me to become more sensitive and responsive to your loving, parental promptings.**

Friday, July 18   Read Ephesians 2:11-22.

This passage discloses an exciting development in God's redemptive plan. Having entered into covenant with the people of Israel, God now makes clear that the Gentiles are to be included as well. They key to this new phase of the plan is Jesus of Nazareth. He is the cornerstone of a household that will incorporate all the peoples of the earth. God also makes clear that the new covenant in Christ is in direct succession to the covenant made with David. The genesis of God's plan is linked quite explicitly with its glorious fulfillment.

All too often Christians find it difficult to accept their Jewish pedigree. We take exception to the idea that they were once "strangers to the covenants of promise" and have now been "brought near." It is much more reassuring to think of Jesus as a personal savior or a social redeemer without all the cultural baggage that comes with the Hebrew tradition. If truth be told, we still have to deal with the residue of anti-Semitic prejudice in our Christian history. Yet the point is incontrovertible: Jesus was a Jew, making us heirs to the household of David no less than to the household of God.

Two observations are in order. First, the Jewish particularity of God's redemptive plan is also its genius. Far better that the course of our salvation be plotted by the worldly wisdom of God than by the celestial utopianism of humanity. No less significant is the quantum leap God takes with this new covenant. Our redemption is no longer a matter of mere reconciliation. Christ inaugurates a whole new humanity for God's new household.

***Prayer:* O God of David and Nathan, of Mary and Elizabeth, give me the grace to acknowledge and honor the Jewishness of Jesus. Amen.**

Saturday, July 19   Read Ephesians 2:11-22.

A phrase in this same passage raises a serious question. When we read that Jesus has "abolished the law with its commandments and ordinances," does it not contradict his admonition, "Do not think that I have come to abolish the law or the prophets; I have come not to abolish but to fulfill" (Matt. 5:17)?

It helps to understand that the law, or the Torah, was more than a set of rules and regulations for the Hebrews. The Torah was the very means of their salvation. It was a divine revelation to guide their daily living and the bedrock of their covenant relationship with God. In the rabbinical tradition, one understands the law only by seeking the spirit of God that shaped it. Without this Spirit, the Torah is forensic and restrictive. As the expression of God's covenant love, however, it is salvific and liberating.

In Christian tradition, the Torah becomes even more relational in and through the person of Jesus. God does not merely show us the way home but comes in person to *bring* us home. God's salvation now is set firmly in the context of a family reunion. The letter of the law was never the point of the Torah, but in a household it becomes altogether pointless. In this sense the commandments of the law have been superseded.

In another sense, however, the law remains in place. As we noted earlier in the week, God's household has rules; and God expects us to follow them. Good behavior is all the more to be expected, now that we are Jesus' siblings.

Prayer: **Thank you, most gracious God, that in Jesus I have a role model for living in your household. Help me to remember what he taught by word and deed as I seek to follow his example. Amen.**

Sunday, July 20　　　　　　　Read Mark 6:30-34, 53-56.

These events reveal even more of God's redemptive plan, and the revelation is dramatic. Not only does God promise to establish a new household for humanity in which there will be limitless blessings and boundless love, but God also attests to the dependability of this promise in the miracles of Jesus. The hungry are actually fed (vv. 35-44); the sick are actually healed (vv. 55-56). Indeed, so all-encompassing is God's salvation that the whole of nature responds to the divine power in Jesus of Nazareth (vv. 47-51).

We also see the consistency of God's redemptive method. A few are called into a particular covenant, and through them the wider human family is invited into God's inclusive covenant of salvation. As the house of David was called, so the disciples of Jesus are called to be apostles of the new Israel, the church. The privilege of entering into this new covenant is to walk with the risen Christ in the world; ministering to the hungry, the thirsty, the stranger, the naked, the sick, and the imprisoned (see Matt. 25:35-36). The obligation is to embody the Holy Spirit's welcome home to all the peoples of the world (Acts 13:47).

This should leave us in no doubt at all about our identity as Christians. We have a place in God's new household, but we also have the divine calling and commission to invite the rest of the world to join us. With Christ we can anticipate the heavenly feast, but we will not begin to eat until all of God's promises are fulfilled (see Isa. 65:17-25). In the meantime, Christ greatly needs our help.

Prayer: **Dear Jesus, thank you for calling the church to help with your unfinished work. May we be trustworthy servants, true friends, and loving sisters and brothers to all who abide in your kingdom. Amen.**

EMPTY OR FULL?

July 21–27, 1997   **Trudy M. Archambeau**✣
Monday, July 21   Read 2 Samuel 11:1-5.

David's rooftop stroll at the royal palace in Jerusalem was probably accompanied by cool evening breezes. Amid scented shadows and fading light of a springtime day, one of biblical history's most familiar stories unfolds. With winter rains over, the ground was dry, the grain harvested, and the time ripe again for another military campaign. About twenty miles away, the Israelites were attacking the Ammonite capital of Rabbah. After the siege, the Ammonites would be subject to Israel.

A different battle was being waged in the heart and mind of David, the king chosen by God to reign over God's people. According to Samuel, David was a man after God's own heart (1 Sam. 13:14). David's life exemplified fullness with God and God's ways. Yet in this incident with Bathsheba, his undivided intention to live as God's person breaks down in the face of his openness to sin. It becomes apparent that David has emptied himself of God and has become full of himself instead. Seeing Bathsheba bathing, David yields to the alluring fascination of his fantasies. No matter how closely we walk with God, no one is exempt from temptation.

Prayer: **When tempted, O God, help me to stand firm in your strength. Empty me of myself and fill me with yourself. Amen.**

✣Active layperon at Christ United Methodist Church, Lansing, Michigan; writer; certified lay speaker; Worship Liturgy Coordinator, West Michigan Conference of The United Methodist Church.

Tuesday, July 22   Read 2 Samuel 11:6-15.

David, a man after God's own heart, is pictured here as self-centered, drawn into the web of sin. Attempting a cover-up, he becomes trapped in the quagmire of deceit and finally murder. David's life is falling apart as his sinful choices suck him into an ever-quickening downward spiral. His life rapidly disintegrates.

In contrast to David's fragmented spirit, Uriah (whose Hebrew name means "is a light") maintains his integrity. He remains dedicated and faithful to the point of unwittingly carrying his own death sentence to the army commander. This incident clearly illustrates abuse of power. Bathsheba is seen less as a consenting adult and more as the victim—powerless in the face of the king's desires, unable to say no to his demands. Joab, a loyal pawn, seems incapable of questioning David's orders.

But the good news for David and for us today is that God's grace always exceeds human sin. David was not exempt from the painful consequences his actions brought upon himself and his family. God still confronts us with the stinging indictment, "*You* are the [one]!" (2 Sam. 12:7, emphasis added). But in that same moment, we can know the miracle of God's cleansing pardon. In the power of God's spirit, we too can discover the humility and courage to say with trust-filled assurance, "Create in me a clean heart" (Ps. 51:10).

God's recycling grace can bring good out of our worst failures. God beautifully wove David's sin into the genealogical tapestry of the ultimate good, Jesus Christ (see Matt. 1:6).

Prayer: **According to your constant and unfailing love, O God, have mercy on me, I pray. Amen.**

Wednesday, July 23   Read Psalm 14.

During the "God Is Dead" movement of the sixties, I remember beginning a speech in a college course with the words, "The Bible says, 'There is no God.'" I then completed the context from Psalm 14 and its parallel Psalm 53 and identified the words as coming from the fool's heart. In Hebrew thought, a fool is one who is morally bankrupt. In sharp contrast, the psalmist defines those who are wise as seekers after God.

Presenting a sad commentary on the human condition, the writer mourns, "They have all gone astray.... There is no one who does good, no, not one." The evidence of human experience teaches that, to some extent, we are all fools. Using different imagery, the prophet Isaiah recognized the same truth: "All we like sheep have gone astray; we have all turned to our own way" (Isa. 53:6).

Human motives and actions combine to confirm the psalmist's lament that fools take no account of God in their hearts. Today foolish ones still attempt to live as if God does not exist. Whenever you and I rely more on ourselves than on God, we are practicing a form of atheism.

The psalmist continues by condemning the deplorable abuse and victimization caused by those whose foolish lives are evil and devoid of God. Today injustice and oppression, indifference and neglect still dehumanize persons, stripping away dignity and worth. But the psalmist's hope is not shaken, for it is God who provides a shelter. In genuine humility, wise ones continually search for ways to extend that refuge to all persons.

Prayer: O God, forgive my foolish ways. Make me an instrument of justice and wisdom this day. In Christ I pray. Amen.

Thursday, July 24   Read Ephesians 3:14-19.

With fervent feeling, the writer picks up the unfinished train of thought begun in verse 1 by praying for the church, the spiritual dwelling place of God. The Greek words used here make it clear that the family of God derives its being and identity from God. Relationship within this household issues from relationship with God.

The writer petitions God for the Ephesians' inner strength. Set in the context of fellowship, the community of believers is individually and collectively empowered by the spirit of Christ. Strength is produced by the indwelling spirit of Christ—Christ in *me* and Christ in *us*.

The prayer continues that Christ may dwell in believers' hearts, be at home there and take up permanent residence. We appropriate this wonderful experience by faith as our roots grow and as we are more firmly grounded and established in love. By definition, such faith is a dynamic, growing thing.

The writer then prays that a drenching, soaking rain of understanding might fall on believers. Recognizing the inadequacy of words, these verses try to expand the terms *high*, *deep*, *wide*, and *long* to cover the immeasurable love of God. But no human expression can fully contain a love whose limitless dimensions cannot be defined or explained by words.

Breathless and exhausted, perhaps the writer now laid down his writing tool for a moment before admitting that the love of Christ passes all knowledge. Then he feverishly continues, praying that believers may be "filled with all the fullness of God." In the final analysis, we need not attempt to understand further. We cannot grasp the love of God with our minds, but we can know it with our hearts.

Prayer: **Come, spirit of Christ, make your home in us and fill us with yourself. Amen.**

Friday, July 25   Read Ephesians 3:20-21.

Shifting from rather abstract ideas concerning the love of God to the experiential arena of God's constant activity, the writer finally turns to doxology. In the preceding spirit-expanding verses, he has struggled to theologize in prosaic words and phrases. Finding that task impossible, he turns to a tumbling avalanche of poetic expressions in his attempts to stretch his readers' imaginations.

"To [God] be glory"—not because of who God *is* but because of what God *does*. God is able to *do* more than we could ever expect or anticipate. He uses terms variously translated into English as "immeasurably more than" (NIV) or "abundantly far more than" all we ask or imagine. God's power at work within us is able to do greater things than all our highest hopes, desires, or prayers.

People in our pews and in our world today need to know that God is one who continually intersects human lives. The eternal God is ever breaking into time. God is actively present in every song and every silence, every hurt and every hope, every dream and every darkness. People need encouragement to look beyond and behind the circumstances to see the activity of God's spirit. All of us need to be challenged to ask the question, "What is God doing here and now?"

All through these words written to the Ephesians is the compelling assurance that God is not passive. God is always active. People today are hungry to be filled with the knowledge of God's activity on their behalf. The Spirit enables the church to meet that hunger.

Prayer: **O God, what do you have for me here? What is your word to me today? Amen.**

Saturday, July 26   Read John 6:1-15.

All four Gospel writers record the miracle of the feeding of the five thousand. John's account of the story opens with Jesus' sitting down alone with his disciples, away from the crowds. However, intent on pursuing the worker of signs and wonders, the crowds will not be left behind. Seeing the approaching multitude, Jesus asks his disciples to solve the food shortage problem. From this dialogue comes Andrew's seemingly ridiculous suggestion of the small boy with his five barley loaves and two fish.

Instructing the disciples to invite the people to be seated in groups, Jesus blesses, breaks, and multiplies the cheap bread and meager fish. Then he distributes it; all eat until filled and satisfied. Recognizing the need, Jesus himself initiates the miracle of grace. The scene is sacramentally flavored, offering a foretaste of the church's celebration of Holy Communion. Jesus, in meeting the physical need for food, opens a window through which to glimpse his self-identification as the bread of life, giver of spiritual nourishment (6:35). Recalling Israel's history as a people wandering in the wilderness, fed by God through Moses and manna, Jesus points toward the fulfillment of messianic expectations.

Twelve baskets of scraps are gathered. Now, as then, nothing is ever wasted in God's economy. God's definition of "adequate" is always "abundant," far exceeding human need and expectation. Jesus is present in the fragments and broken pieces of our lives, spreading a banquet of blessing before us daily. God never serves us leftover grace or scraps of love or crumbs of compassion; God serves us life—in all its fullness.

Prayer: **Bread of life, help me always remember that your fresh supply of grace is new every morning, feeding and nourishing my hungry spirit. Thanks be to God. Amen.**

Sunday, July 27   Read John 6:16-21.

The Sea of Galilee is often subject to unpredictable shifts of wind and sudden storms. But the disciples were unprepared. Into the darkness of nightfall came the darkness of their fear as the sea became rough, tossing their small boat about in the turbulent waves and fierce winds. Their fright increased when they saw Jesus coming to them. Contrary to all rules of nature, Jesus was walking on the water, and they became terrified.

Scholars like to argue about whether the Greek words translate into English as "on the sea" or "by the sea"; but whatever the case, the fact of the disciples' distress is undeniable. They were filled to overflowing with fear. Jesus answered their fear with what amounted to the divine name of God. "It is I," Jesus assured them. "Do not be afraid." The crashing waves and shrieking wind become the setting of a theophany, an appearance of the God of peace and shalom in the midst of the storm. Then, in a dramatic fashion, the boat arrived at the sheltered shore.

In the feeding miracle, the crowds witnessed the divine display of grace. Here only the disciples were witness to the revelation of Jesus' glory, a miracle addressing the fears that plague human experience. We in the church still need to encounter the glory of God—to hear the words, "I am with you," whether we fear the storm of painful circumstances or the inner turmoil of doubts and insecurities." Jesus still comes to us, identifying himself with the strength-giving words, "It is I."

Prayer: **Let me see you walking on the stormy seas of my life, O Christ. Empty my heart of fear and fill me with faith that I might know it is you. In the power and majesty of your name I pray. Amen.**

RAGS TO RICHES

July 28–August 3, 1997   **Alec Gilmore**♣
Monday, July 28   Read 2 Samuel 11:26–12:6.

This week we explore the familiar theme of how faith may lift us from the depths of sin to the heights of life in Christ. We begin by reflecting on Nathan's parable to David. Certainly Nathan did not like what he saw in David's actions, but he knew that his job as prophet was not to condemn but to help David see. Nathan could then leave the rest to God and David's conscience.

Telling someone the truth in this sort of situation is never easy. Notice the skill with which Nathan handles his task. In a world where intimacy has played a cruel and selfish role, Nathan speaks of the intimacy of a truly loving relationship. In a world where the wrong kind of intimacy has destroyed a family, Nathan points out the emotions of love and loyalty within the family of the poor man. And Nathan portrays a world in which the rich man has used his power and position to help himself, while the poor man is obliged to surrender even the little that he has.

Suggestion for meditation: **To whom do you need to speak the truth in love? Reflect on the way Nathan handled this situation.**

Prayer: **Father, when I am more ready to spot injustice in others than in myself, please send me a Nathan. Amen.**

♣Baptist minister; writer, and lecturer; West Sussex, England.

Tuesday, July 29   Read 2 Samuel 12:7-13*a*.

Does Nathan have to spell it out for David? It seems so, for even at the end of verse 6 David has not recognized himself in the story. Perhaps afraid that David will fail to appreciate the enormity of what he has done, Nathan details the offense. Ponder the depths of David's wrongdoing.

First, David's action was much more than a physical offense against a woman or a cruel crime against a man, though either would have been bad enough! It was a crime against humanity because David had treated people in a way that permanently changed their character and relationships. Second, David had forgotten that everything he had he owed to God. Had God not rescued him from the hand of Saul and endowed him with all the blessings and benefits of kingship? Third, though blessed in every way with this world's goods, David had wanted more; in his greed, he had abused his position of trust and responsibility. In short, David's action was an offense against God: "Why have you despised the word of the LORD?"

The repercussions do not stop there. What David has done, others will now do. Where David has set off, others will follow. For David there is no escape—not because God will punish him but because the consequences of his misdeeds will follow him to his own front door. David's confession at least begins the process of healing.

Suggestion for meditation: **Focus on something you have done wrong and try to understand how it is an offense against God.**

Prayer: **Father, keep me constantly aware that when I sin against my fellow human beings, I sin against myself and against you. Amen.**

Wednesday, July 30   Read Psalm 51:1-12.

It does not matter much whether this psalm arose directly out of David's sin, was just one he happened to use, or was one that later editors thought David might have used. Clearly it is intended that we read it against a certain background, but that must not blind us to other contexts. What is more important is our understanding that true repentance requires a straightforward acknowledgment of our wrongdoing. Is it not better that we show penitence for *our* sins than eavesdrop in the confessional while David pours his heart out? Read today's scripture twice: first in relation to David; second, in relation to your own wrongdoing, which you identified yesterday.

The confession in verses 1-5 follows our readings in 2 Samuel 11–12; these verses characterize the sin as a sin against God. The psalmist then acknowledges (vv. 6-7) that only God can help; it is God who desires truth and God who can make him clean. The cleansing and purging then leads to a spiritual "filling": "Create in me a clean heart, O God, and put a new and right spirit within me." This "clean heart" and "new and right spirit" comes as a result of God's initiative.

Suggestion for meditation: **As you reflect on the wrongdoing identified yesterday, of what do you need to be purged? How might you experience God's cleansing? Imagine what "a new and right spirit" within you might actually look like.**

Prayer: **Father, may the damage that I have done be turned into something good. Amen.**

Thursday, July 31   Read Ephesians 4:1-6.

After confession and (even more) after penitence, the next temptation is satisfaction—the feeling of being right, self-righteousness. And when too many Christians begin to feel self-righteous and associate together, it can spell danger. So think of the church at Ephesus not so much as a divided church (the result of quarrel and discord among friends) but as a disunited church (the result of too many people's all being right). The question is this: In the interests of unity how much diversity can you tolerate? Today we will consider unity; tomorrow we will consider diversity.

They were not getting along too well with one another and that was bad enough. All human relationships have their problems, and the relationships among the Christians in Ephesus were no exception. Undesirable as they may be, the problems could be tolerated and the Christians had ways of handling the friction. What was more worrisome was that they were trying to drag God into their divisions.

Three qualities were missing in the church at Ephesus. *Humility:* The different factions all claimed God was on their side, and they were making ultimate claims for their own group or for their own interpretation. *Gentleness:* At best they were treading on one another's toes, and at worst they were riding roughshod over other people's feelings. *Patience:* It was not so much that they were rushing on ahead but more that they were showing signs of irritation with those who took a different view.

Suggestion for meditation: **Avoid dwelling on what is wrong in your relationships with other people, whether in the church or elsewhere. Instead try to identify ways to nurture and develop unity among various groups.**

Prayer: **Lord, where there is discord let me bring unity. Amen.**

Friday, August 1   Read Ephesians 4:7-16.

We need to avoid two problems in dealing with today's passage. The first is that verses 8-10 are difficult to understand and seem to interrupt the flow of thought. The quotation from Psalm 68:18 is changed, and the issues are complex. The second is avoiding involvement in the specific gifts of verse 14 and concentrating on their diversity.

The first step towards true unity is coming to terms with diversity, which requires more than simply recognizing that we are all different. We all have different gifts, and we all have to learn to live together. That is a *grudging* acceptance of diversity. It implies that things would be better if we were all the same, but since we are not we have to find a way to deal with it.

We need to see diversity as something positive rather than something that pulls us apart. Diversity brings us closer to one another as we learn to appreciate the gifts, skills, and qualities of others. We need a complex body (not a single cell) because of the many and varied duties the body has to perform. Diversity not only produces a balanced and mature community but also is the means by which each one of us develops his or her own unique maturity. In this way we grow to "full stature," and the reference to children suggests that unless we mature in our diversity, "children" is what we are and are likely to remain.

Suggestion for meditation: **Pray for a friend with whom you find it difficult to relate; consider how your friend's gifts can help you become more like Christ.**

Prayer: **Lord, bring me through diversity to the full stature of Christ. Amen.**

If you can handle a crowd of excited people in the desert, armed only with a dozen dedicated followers, five loaves, and a few fish, you can hardly be surprised if the next day the world is beating a pathway to your front door. The miracle and the wonder, the way-out and the zany, rumor and gossip have an unfailing appeal and create an insatiable curiosity.

But do not become so obsessed with the extraordinary, says Jesus, that you miss the true message. The feeding of such a large number of people from such a little bit of food was miraculous but temporal; giving people food for their souls is eternal. Look beyond the obvious sign.

An artist encouraged his students to allow their eye to fall on any one thing before them, then to close their eyes for five minutes. After that time, they were to open their eyes and focus once more on the object, looking at it until they had a sense of the object's returning their gaze, acknowledging that the object contained the riddle of life and death. Only then might they move from looking to seeing.

Once we learn the skill of moving beyond looking to seeing, we can meet God any day, anywhere. Miracles, wonders, and signs surround us; look beyond them to the true message. Develop a new way of seeing.

Prayer: **Lord, teach me to "see," to look beyond the obvious so there is no time when I am not aware of your presence. Amen.**

Sunday, August 3   Read John 6:30-3_.

We began the week in rags—"all our righteous deeds like a filthy cloth" (Isa. 64:6)—but we have learned how God can use us, change us, and help us grow through diversity to unity so that we are constantly aware of God's presence. "Riches" in the form of a life lived in tune with God's will cannot be far away. But there are two more hurdles.

First, when you believe in a God who is always doing a new thing (see Isa. 43:19), it is a mistake to be looking for the old signs. Old rules, old categories no longer apply in the new situation when the Messiah is there before you. If you spend too much time looking for old signs, you may miss the riches he has to offer.

Second, how is Jesus to tell them that when you have the real thing in front of you and it is working, you need neither the glossy brochure nor the guarantee certificate? The thing authenticates itself. Verse 35 (today) completes verse 29 (yesterday). Why look for Moses? The manna came not from Moses but from the Father. Can they not see that the same Father who gave them manna in the wilderness is now giving them the Messiah in the desert?

All they need is faith in what is clearly there before them. Of course, mistakes will happen. Of course, others will take a different view. But then the riches of maturity in Christ is the ability to live like a full human being and to know that when we fail, God is still one who forgives but never deserts.

Prayer: **Sir, give us this bread always. Amen.**

OFFERING UP MY RELATIONSHIPS

August 4–10, 1997
Monday, August 4

Gerrit Dawson✤
Read John 6:35, 41-51.

And with him is plenteous redemption

If you are in the northern hemisphere as you read this, the air outside is warm. The trees are full of leaves. Crops are in the fields. You would not think of putting on a coat and gloves to go outside. It is hard to imagine that the land is ever leafless and brown. But the thought of autumn during these dog days is tantalizing.

As I write, however, winter is deepening around us. I can see to the tops of hills once dense with impenetrable green. I get chilly just thinking about being outside in a T-shirt. It is hard to imagine that I will be hot again and that the land will be full of bright colors. Still, I hunger for the turn of the seasons.

Such is life in this world that we are ever thirsty for the next thing. We constantly need to replenish body and soul. Many of us are restless for what is just around the corner. Our relationships are in flux; we hunger for more intimacy, more harmony.

In John 6, Jesus offers his disciples the bread of life: "Whoever comes to me will never be hungry." This week we will explore how Christ himself is the constancy for which we long. In all our relationships, his love is the basis for forgiveness, intimacy, and joy.

Prayer: **Lord Jesus, make me aware that my hunger is for you. Amen.**

✤Minister of First Presbyterian Church of Lenoir, North Carolina; author of *Writing on the Heart: Inviting Scripture to Shape Daily Life.*

Tuesday, August 5   Read 2 Samuel 18:5-9, 15, 31-33.

King David's cry for his son Absalom echoes still in the pain of all relationships between parents and children. None of us escapes that grief. O my son Absalom!

In the best relationships between parents and children there is still the ache that the cuddly, closely held child must become a separate, independent adult. Even when parents and grown children become friends again, there is the inarticulate memory of a primal closeness that can never be.

A parent who has lost a child will cry out like David, "If only I had died instead of you—O Absalom my son!" Loving parents feel the impulse to offer themselves to spare their children pain. But most times, they cannot make such a substitution. They watch and wait in anxiety and hope. O Absalom!

David and Absalom, however, were not candidates for Family of the Year. David's adultery with Bathsheba tore through the integrity of all his relationships. From that moment deception, neglect, incest, murder, and rebellion rippled through the years and the family.

So many of us know full well how the "sins of the fathers" pass through the generations. We have not been the kind of children or parents we want to be. Through the veil of anger, across the valley of separation, we still cry out for one another, "My son, my son Absalom!"

Suggestion for meditation: **Consider your relationship with your parents through the years and with your children, if you have them. Which places of memory still cause you to cry out? Which losses still sting? Offer these to God with prayers for healing. Keep these relationships in mind through the week.**

Wednesday, August 6 Read Psalm 130.

Meditating upon our relationships with parents and children can cause upheaval. Even good memories can keep us awake with pain in our hearts for what is passed. Recognition of unresolved issues can awaken anger, seize us with guilt, or knock us into the depths of a low, sad mood.

Our natural tendency then is to avoid the subject and keep the pain at bay. But scripture seems to point us in a different direction for healing.

"Out of the depths I cry to you, O LORD." We may tend to avoid God when we feel out of kilter. We fear that God does not want us in the shape that we are in, particularly since so much of it is our own fault. But the psalmist was bold—and faithful. He knew that the deepest cries of the soul are for God. And he did not hold back. From the depth of his pain, he called for God.

So we may follow the ache of the heart to such prayer. Precisely in the moments when we feel most separated from others and God, we may cry out for attention and mercy from our Lord.

The psalmist had to overcome the same fear we have in order to pray, "If you, O LORD, kept a record of sins, O Lord, who could stand?"(NIV). We know that if receiving God's grace was a matter of worthiness, then none of us would. We meditate on our primary relationships and find an ocean of regrets, shame, and longing.

Thankfully though, we may also pray with the psalmist, "But there is forgiveness with you." There is grace with God.

Prayer: **O Lord, you know the depths in which I am sinking. Give me strength to cry out and faith to grasp the lifeline of your grace. Amen.**

Thursday, August 7   Read John 6:35, 41-51.

Today, we return to Jesus' offer of the bread of life. We know that we are restless and hungry. And much of this soul-thirst arises from the pain in our relationships.

Jesus invited his disciples to be taken up into the wonderful relationship of harmony and love that he had with his Father. There exists an eternal, intimate communion between the Father and the Son. The incarnation of the Son in Jesus Christ is God's invitation to include all humanity in this love.

The bread of life is Jesus himself. But Jesus lived in relationship to his Father in heaven. By coming to Jesus we enter the love between the Father and the Son. In that love, there is no betrayal, no deception, no neglect, no ignoring, no abuse, no dismissal. Rather there is harmony and exchange, the seeing and hearing of one another in love.

Christ said that it is the Father who draws us to Jesus. We come to him and eat the bread he offers as we invite his life to come into ours. He offers us himself for the life of the world, for Jesus is fully human in right relationship with God and fully God in loving gift to the world.

Suggestion for meditation: **So now hold up your intimate relationships to this Christ, thinking especially this week of parents and children. Invite him to come in and transform them. Ask him to enter and flow through every part. Here is mysterious, but real, hope for healing.**

Friday, August 8   Read Psalm 130.

This psalm provides the prayerful backdrop to the theology of yesterday's lesson. We know that our relationships are not what they could be. We also know that Jesus Christ revealed the perfect, intimate love that exists between the Father and the Son. Christ takes us up into that relationship. But before we fully experience such communion, there is a long period of active waiting. During these years of our spiritual journeys, we continually invite— through the cries of prayers and the watching of expectant eyes— God's redemption in all our relationships.

Such transformation in our relationships is rarely instantaneous. Grief is salved by peace only after years. Brokenness is set right only after time, hard work, and the slow movements of grace.

The psalmist understood this process. After crying out to God from the depths of his pain and claiming God's mercy, he acknowledged the necessity of waiting.

Five times in two verses (vv. 5-6, NIV), he uses the word *wait*. We can almost see the psalmist pacing the perimeters like a nightwatcher. He is waiting, waiting, waiting for the Lord to act and change his situation.

This waiting is not without a basis for hope. The psalmist encourages all God's people to put their hope in the Lord as he has. The reason for hope is that "with the LORD there is steadfast love, and with him is plenteous redemption"(RSV). God is the source of the faithfulness we could never sustain alone in our relationships. God is the one who can redeem even the most twisted, lost relationships.

Prayer: **O Lord, give me patience as I wait for your work to be completed in my life and confidence to know it will be so. Amen.**

Saturday, August 9   Read Ephesians 4:25–5:

The psalmist gave us hope that with the Lord there is forgiveness, unfailing love, and redemption. In today's passage, Paul gives us the basis for applying this love to our intimate relationships. He writes, "Live a life of love, just as Christ loved us and gave himself up for us" (NIV).

In the shame of our own part in broken relationships, we hear this word of grace. Christ loved us and gave himself up for us. He forgave our sins. He offers to replace our guilt with his love, our anger with his peace, our blame with his acquittal.

When we receive that good news in faith, we are ready to begin to make amends. We find strength to act in love toward those who have done their part in breaking our relationships. We can "be kind and compassionate to one another, forgiving each other, just as in Christ God forgave you" (NIV).

We could, of course, live in bitterness and rage the rest of our days. Enough has been done to us to warrant such hostility. We could live in guilt all our years, as well, for we know the damage we have done. But Christ calls us to leave blame and shame behind. He has paid for it all; he gave himself for us; he forgave us. That love is the bread of life that fills the hunger in the depths of our souls. On that basis, we move toward others, even as we know healing takes time; and we live as those not finished but still waiting for God.

Prayer: **O God, you have forgiven me in Christ. Now soothe the wounds of my hurt and help me act towards my loved ones as you acted toward me. Amen.**

Sunday, August 10   Read Ephesians 4:25–5:2.

God alone can bring the healing in our intimate relationships for which we long. It occurs on the basis of God's forgiveness in Jesus Christ who loved us and gave his life for us. Of course, God's work of transformation takes time. We have to wait for it. But in the interim, we can perform some practical, daily tasks.

"Putting away falsehood, let all of us speak truthfully. . . . Be angry but do not sin; do not let the sun go down on your anger. . . . Put away from you all bitterness and wrath and anger and wrangling and slander, together with all malice."

If only David and Absalom had heeded such advice! Their relationship unraveled when justice was not served. They did not express their anger in open conversation, so violence erupted. In malice the son's life was lost. And it was too late for love.

But it is not too late for us! We are called to put away wrath and bitterness. We are done with them, not because we put on a happy face, but because we deal with them through the costly gift of Christ's life.

Casting our anger on the cross, binding Jesus' love to ourselves, we begin to "be kind to one another, tenderhearted, forgiving one another." Now is the time to take positive steps to cease hostility in our relationships. Now, though we are not perfect and never will be, we can offer to mend fences and rebuild bridges. The Bread of Life is our food in this difficult work. Healing and love are our goals.

This Lord's Day is a good time to start. Pray. Make the call. Write the letter. Begin anew.

***Prayer:* Our Lord, make me bold to take a step toward love today. Amen.**

August 11–17, 1997   **Catherine Gunsalus González✤**
Monday, August 11   Read Psalm 111:6-10.

God is the source of all wisdom. Those who seek to be wise must turn to God. Our temptation is to trust in our own wisdom. That often means seeking what is good for us, even at the expense of the rest of the community.

The psalm rehearses God's works. It especially praises God for the laws—the ordinances—that God has given. God's laws are the "manufacturer's instructions" for human life. God is our creator and therefore knows how human life works best. We often rush ahead (without reading the instructions) and try to operate or put together human creations. When things don't work—then and only then—do we go back and read the instructions. We try to live our lives without reading the "instructions," without studying what our Creator says about how human lives are to work.

"The fear of the LORD is the beginning of wisdom." Such fear is not cringing terror but rather the awesome recognition of God's majesty and greatness. It involves recognizing that we are creatures. When we turn to God and are open to God's precepts, we are on the path to true wisdom—not a surface fulfillment of commandments in a legalistic fashion but a deep awareness of God's purposes for all humanity.

Prayer: **O God, teach me to love your will for me and to seek it eagerly all my life. Amen.**

✤Professor of Church History, Columbia Theological Seminary; Ordained minister, Presbyterian Church (USA).

Tuesday, August 12   Read 1 Kings 2:10-12; 3:3-9.

David, flawed as he was, had been a great king in God's eyes. Now his son Solomon has become king. Solomon wanted to be faithful to God, even as his father had been. In a dream God invited him to ask for what he wished. He could have asked for many things; his response is instructive. First, he acknowledged God's faithfulness in the past. Then he made clear his own smallness in the face of God's greatness—the proper "fear of the Lord."

Finally Solomon makes his major request: that God would give him "an understanding mind" so that he may govern the people wisely. He asks for the ability to distinguish between good and evil. Remember, it was eating the fruit of the tree of the knowledge of good and evil that led to the fall (Gen. 2:16-17; 3:1-6). That eating implied humanity's attempt to make its own decisions about good and evil without turning to God. Solomon asks for such discernment from God, not from himself.

Solomon's invitation came in a dream, but God invites all of us in prayer to ask for what we want. What is it we really desire? Does our prayer seek God's will for our lives? Our constant study of God's word will shape our prayers and our requests.

Prayer: **O God, my vision of the good is so often clouded by my own selfishness. My view of evil often overlooks what is to my advantage. Instill in me a desire to seek your view, so that my prayers and my life may be wise. Amen.**

Wednesday, August 13   Read 1 Kings 3:10-14.

Solomon prayed for understanding and wisdom. Solomon's concern to be a good king—based on God's idea of goodness—pleased God. God therefore assured Solomon that he would receive the understanding to discern what was right. In addition, God would give him the things he had not included in his prayer: riches and honor.

Most faithful Christians discern a significant lesson in Solomon's request: If we center our life on what we believe will lead to our own happiness, we will never find what we really seek. Happiness, security, fulfillment are by-products of a life centered on God and therefore also on others. "Those who want to save their life will lose it, and those who lose their life for my sake will find it" (Matt. 16:25); "Strive first for the kingdom of God and his righteousness, and all these things will be given to you as well" (Matt. 6:33).

God gave Solomon "a wise and discerning mind." Kings are not the only ones that need such a gift. Everyone needs that. Solomon understood that those who have responsibility for the lives and well-being of others are in particular need. Public officials of all kinds, pastors, parents, teachers— all could benefit from a vision of what is good and evil from God's perspective.

Prayer: **O God, may your Spirit guide me to seek the welfare of others before my own. This I ask in Christ's name, who came to fulfill your will and not his own. Amen.**

Thursday, August 14   Read Ephesians 5:15-20.

One can live wisely or unwisely. The Christian is called to live wisely. What does such living include? First, it means using the time wisely. That implies not going along with prevailing opinions and custom but guiding our lives by God's values and goals. Second, it requires seeking the will of God who will give us these goals. Third, it means avoiding all things that would lead to debauchery, to forgetfulness of God and God's will.

It might appear at first glance that such a life avoids all the fun, all of the good times that this life affords. But that is not the case. The letter goes on to say that our lives should be lived with songs and hymns to God. Those who make "melody to the Lord" in their hearts can hardly be thought of as missing out on good times.

Praising God is not another requirement; it is the center of living wisely. We live in a world that is God's good creation, but it has fallen from its original goals. We live in a world where living unwisely is the prevalent mode. How do we become attuned to wisdom? We become attuned by seeking God, by studying God's word, and by associating with God's people.

When God's people gather, all we need to live wisely is present. There is a seeking of God's will, repentance and forgiveness for not having done so, joyful praise, and songs of thanksgiving. Above all, living wisely means joining with the rest of God's people, trying to be a model of God's desire for all human life.

Prayer: **Join me tightly to your people, O Lord, so that I may be wise. Amen.**

Friday, August 15   Read Psalm 111:1-5.

What does it mean that God "provides food for those who fear him," because God is faithful to the covenant? In one sense, this promise is truthful. Those who are part of faithful congregations have the support of a loving and sharing community when times are hard. Where members of Christian communities share what they have with one another, more people have food. Those who live a wise and sober life are more likely to have food than those who live their lives in a careless and dissolute fashion.

But it is also true that in a sinful world, those who truly follow God may well not have food—as other parts of scripture make very clear. In spite of this, the faithful pray for daily bread and believe that God is faithful, gracious, and merciful. However, the food may not always be what we wish. It may sometimes be a hidden manna that feeds the soul even as the body remains hungry. A gospel that centers on the cross is not always a comfortable one.

Jesus said, "My food is to do the will of him who sent me" (John 4:34). If that is our ultimate source of sustenance, indeed we will find God faithful to the covenant. The truth of God's promises rest on our seeking to be part of the faithful congregation.

Prayer: **O Lord our God, I often expect that you will fulfill your promises to me in the way I wish. May my greatest desire be to fulfill your will. This I ask in the name of the faithful one, Jesus Christ. Amen.**

Saturday, August 16   Read John 6:51-56.

Jesus announces that he himself is the living bread. Unlike ordinary bread, unlike even the miraculous manna in the wilderness, this bread leads to eternal life. That is a promise that no ordinary bread can give.

How do we obtain this bread? It is a gift, even as the manna was a gift. We cannot create it for ourselves. Jesus says that he is the source of this miraculous bread. Yet it is not a simple gift.

How do we receive gifts? Some come by mail; we have no direct, physical contact with the giver. The gift may involve bonds of love as well as great distance between the gift and the giver. Even when we receive a treasured gift from a close family member in person, a distance remains between us. We are not always with them. The gift remains, but the giver goes away—at least part of the time.

It is not so with the gift of bread that Jesus gives: He gives himself as our food. Those who receive this gift become part of him, and he becomes part of them. For this reason this gift leads to eternal life. Though these words were spoken during his earthly ministry, his Resurrection is the guarantee of ours. The promise is astonishing; the gift is a miracle. But it means a life of discipleship, for the gift cannot be received without receiving the Giver also.

Prayer: **Lord Jesus Christ, make me worthy of the gift of yourself. Let others see you in me, and let me see myself in you. This I ask in your name. Amen.**

Sunday, August 17   Read John 6:57-58.

There is a continuity of life on the human, creaturely level. Parents produce offspring, generation after generation. There is no interruption in the chain, no generation arises without biological connection with the previous one. In a strange way, a similar process exists in the Christian life. It is not only that one person tells another of salvation in Christ, though that link is important and essential.

Jesus says that his saving work is the result of God's own life, so those who follow him will live because of his life. We receive this life by receiving Jesus himself in our whole being, not simply a message about him that we accept in our minds.

The image of receiving the flesh and blood of Jesus as the bread from heaven obviously has overtones of the sacrament of the Lord's table. What matters in the sacrament is not only receiving the bread and cup but, above all, receiving Jesus himself. The manna the people of God ate in the wilderness was a gift from God, but it did not bring eternal life. It was an important gift *of* God, but in it the people did not receive God's own life.

Jesus promises that those who eat the bread he gives them will indeed receive him. In faithfully eating this bread, we are made part of that living chain, the generation of the children of God, begotten by God through Christ.

Prayer: **Give me an open heart, O Christ, to receive the gift of yourself. Let me be born anew, so that my life shows forth that I am one of your people, and others may be brought to you through my words and my deeds. This I ask in your name. Amen.**

A REFUGE FOR THE REDEEMED

August 18–24, 1997   Kenneth L. Waters, Sr.✤
Monday, August 18   Read 1 Kings 8:1-11.

Solomon had assembled the people for the dedication of
the Temple in conjunction with the celebration of the new year.
After seven years of building, the Temple had been completed
the previous year in the autumn of mid-tenth century B.C.
Transferring the ark of the covenant from a historically obscure
site in Jerusalem to the Holy of Holies was the centerpiece of the
festivities. God had spoken to David concerning Solomon saying,
"He shall build a house for my name" (2 Sam. 7:13). God's word
was fulfilled.

Completion and dedication of Solomon's Temple were
significant milestones in the history of God's people. The Temple
provided a model for all future houses of God, and eventually a
metaphor for the human body as the temple of God was
bequeathed to Christian language (1 Cor. 3:16-17).

Mysteriously, however, God dwells in us only when we
dwell in God. We become God's temples when we seek God as
our refuge.

Beneath the dry descriptions of the Temple and the rituals
surrounding its dedication lies the reminder that God does not live
in temples fashioned by hands (see Acts 7:48). More than a
reminder, it is an invitation to find our abode in the One who
abides in us.

Prayer: **Lord, I live in you when I allow you to live in me. Teach
me to be open to your indwelling Presence. Amen.**

✤Pastor of the Vermont Square United Methodist Church of Los
Angeles and Spiritual Director of the Los Angeles Inner City Walk to
Emmaus Community.

Tuesday, August 19   Read 1 Kings 8:22-26.

Solomon's prayer at the Temple dedication was a tribute to God's unique character as the One who keeps covenant with Israel. God's promise to David concerning an offspring who would build a house for God's name was fulfilled. For Israel, this was confirmation that God would also keep the divine promise to forever sustain a successor from the house of David on the throne.

However, obedience to God was the condition for the fulfillment of God's covenant; Solomon acknowledged that this condition had not changed. God's steadfast love would continue to be upon those who walked before God with the hearts of servants.

God's promise—as much as God's presence—was a refuge for the people, provided they obeyed the mandates of the covenant that God had made with them. Solomon's prayer was both an expression of faith in God's promise and assent to God's call to obedience.

Obedience is no less required of us who still look to the Lord for sustenance. God's promise to be with us is nowhere more fully realized than in the lives of those who submit to the Lord. Adverse situations may break in upon us, but we can find shelter in God's promise to the obedient.

Wonderfully, a divine promise fulfilled is also confirmation of promises not yet fulfilled; God is faithful in the keeping of promises. When we see God's hand in the unfolding of our lives, we can celebrate that presence as well as the promise of good things to come.

Prayer: Faithful God, I rejoice in your promises already kept and in promises yet to be honored. Your promise is a refuge for me in anxious times. Let your word be confirmed in my life once more as I obediently submit myself to you. Amen.

Wednesday, August 20   Read 1 Kings 8:27-30.

Solomon's acknowledgment of a glaring irony became the theological core of his prayer on the day of the Temple's dedication. He had constructed a magnificent edifice of stone and wood as the house of God, yet no house of any size can contain God. Even "heaven and the highest heaven" cannot hold God.

Therefore, Solomon's prayer included the reminder that the Temple was built as a house for the *name* of the Lord. In this way, Solomon evades the theological difficulty of assigning the infinite God to a dwelling on earth. Modern believers would say that God could be present in the Temple without being limited to the Temple, but Solomon's concept of God's exalted, unbounded nature did not allow him this perspective.

God's name therefore becomes crucial as the people's route of access to the transcendent God. Prayer must take place facing in the direction of the Temple, if not actually in the Temple, because *there* is where God's name dwells.

Our understanding of prayer and God's presence may be less rigid, but we still need Solomon's example of reverence for God's name. From Solomon's view, God's being is so exalted and removed that it is God's name that becomes a refuge for us when we need help, healing, and forgiveness.

When we invoke God's name, we also invoke God's presence and power in our lives. In this way, we, who are living temples of God, become the place where God's name dwells. As we become living houses for God's name, God's name becomes a refuge for us.

Prayer: **Dear God, may I find refuge in your presence, promises, and name. May I remember all the ways you make yourself available to me in both comfortable and critical times. Amen.**

Thursday, August 21   Read 1 Kings 8:41-43.

Facing the Temple as one prayed from afar was a signature of Jewish piety from the time of the Temple's construction until its destruction in the sixth century B.C. Prayer toward the Temple was expected in times of war, drought, famine, plague, and disease (1 Kings 8:31-40).

Solomon prayed that when the people entered the Temple or looked toward it from afar that God in heaven would hear their prayer (1 Kings 8:30). Astoundingly, Solomon included the "foreigner" among those to be heard when that person prayed toward the Temple. *All* the peoples of the earth would then know and fear the name of God.

Inclusiveness is the hallmark of a universal faith. Since God is God of all people, the house of God must be a beacon of faith for all people. There were areas of this Temple that only Jews could physically enter, but all could *spiritually* enter the Temple through prayer and faith in the God of Israel.

Beneath the cultural overlay of ritual practice in Israel's religion lies a significant message: regardless of who or where one was, that person could find refuge in Israel's prayer and faith tradition.

Hardship can come upon us anywhere at any time, but we can also turn to God in prayer anywhere at any time. It matters not which direction we face as long as our hearts are turned heavenward with faith. In this way, prayer and faith become as much a refuge for us as any fortified building.

Prayer: **Lord, I thank you. In crisis I have a refuge in prayer and faith because you hear my prayer and affirm my faith. Receive me into your protective embrace. Amen.**

Friday, August 22   Read Psalm 84.

The pilgrims' song ascribes beauty to the house of the Lord as they approach Zion, the site of the Temple. Deeply felt yearning is expressed by those whose souls long to tarry in the courts of the Lord.

Sparrows and swallows share the blessedness of the servants who reside and sing praises in the house of the Lord. Blessed or "happy" also are the pilgrims whose strength is in the Lord and who move from one stage of spiritual strength to another as they pass through the Valley of Baca and draw nearer to Zion.

For the psalmist, one day in God's house is acknowledgedly better than a thousand elsewhere. Lowly service in the Lord's house is preferable to an opulent life among the ungodly.

The end of Psalm 84 affirms the reason for the pilgrims' joy: God is our light and protection, the One who bestows good upon those who walk uprightly.

As suspected, to abide in God's house was, in the thoughts of the pilgrims, also to abide in God's presence. Solomon's question over how the infinite God could dwell in an earthly house did not seem to trouble the masses.

Like Solomon, we know that God cannot be contained in any house of worship; but like both Solomon and the pilgrims, we also know that God is there in some sense. For many of us, church is a refuge to which we flee after a harrowing week because God is there. For this reason, our journey to church can be just as joyful and exciting as the pilgrimages of old.

Prayer: **God, I long to be in your presence when I come to your house. May our gathering be especially healing for me and for those with whom I worship. Amen.**

Saturday, August 23   Read Ephesians 6:10-20.

The writer of Ephesians exhorts us to be "strong in the Lord and in the strength of [God's] power" by putting on "the whole armor of God." Some of the "armor" language comes from Isaiah 11:5 and 59:17. However, in Isaiah, God wears the armor.

Earlier the Temple was both a house for God and a haven for God's people; now it is armor that is both the panoply of God and protection for us. A significant implication follows this shift in metaphor. We cannot always flee to the refuge of God's house; we must also wear protection.

Wearing armor also implies greater mobility in a hostile environment and readiness for combat in wartime. The concept of spiritual warfare makes this metaphor most appropriate.

It is often observed that the sword of the Spirit or word of God is our only offensive weapon against evil. Actually, this passage identifies a second offensive weapon: "Pray in the Spirit." The writer abandons the metaphor when it comes to the weapon of prayer.

Rather than speak of "the battle ax of prayer" or some other metaphor, the writer becomes urgently literal—indicating the importance of prayer to the writer.

Prayer, we see, has a fluid character as both a refuge for the redeemed and a weapon against evil. Prayer serves us well as a shield from evil that allows us to destroy it.

Prayer: **O God, clothe me in your armor and heighten my passion both for your Word and for prayer, that I may be fully equipped for battle against evil. Amen.**

Sunday, August 24   Read John 6:56-69.

The eucharistic language of eating the Lord's body and drinking his blood is so familiar to us that we may not realize how repugnant such language was to Jesus' first hearers. Jesus, of course, spoke of eating his body and drinking his blood as symbolic expressions for receiving him with wholehearted faith and trust. His first hearers, however, could not get past the literal shock of Jesus' words. Even the disciples had difficulty seeing below the literal surface of the Savior's language.

Jesus suggested that the disciples may not see the spiritual meaning of his words until he ascended to heaven; that is, until they had faith. Spiritual insight is the key both to understanding Jesus' words and to receiving his gift of eternal life. Faith, in turn, is the key to spiritual insight.

Despite their difficulty with Jesus' teaching, the disciples had faith and the beginnings of spiritual insight. They knew that Jesus had the words of life and that he was "the Holy One of God."

Spiritual insight and growth is a pilgrimage that begins with faith. As pilgrims of old grew "from strength to strength" (Ps. 84:7) as they journeyed to the Temple, we grow deeper in the Lord as we journey with Jesus.

Jesus is our ultimate refuge. But it is not a physical journey to an earthly place that brings us to him; it is a spiritual journey from unbelief to faith that enables us to live in him and he in us.

Prayer: **Lord Jesus, abide in me even as I abide in you. Make me an instrument of salvation and healing for those who are hurting. Amen.**

THE INTERNALS OF FAITH

August 25–31, 1997   **Will H. Willimon**✤
Monday, August 25   Read James 1:17.

We are at summer's end—gracious time of relaxation and rejuvenation. What makes summer is the sun. In the year's longest days, we bathe ourselves in the glow of this life-giving gift of God, sunshine.

James uses an August analogy. All gifts come "from above," from "the Father of lights" in whom there is no "shadow." James speaks of God, the giver of all good gifts, as one might speak of the sun. Just as we could not live without the sun and its gifts, so we cannot live without the gifts of God.

Furthermore, all of our gifts and acts of generosity have their source in God, says James. Yesterday when you put your money in the offering at church, one reason for your giving is that you have received. Because God is so gracious to us, we know how to be gracious to others.

This morning I was awakened by a blues singer on the radio belting out an old favorite, "This Little Light of Mine." She exuberantly sang of letting her little light shine, shine, shine. That's who we are. Our little lights shine in a sometimes darkened world only because God's light has shone upon us. Gifts beget giving. We shine as grateful reflection of that light, which comes down from "the Father of lights."

Let your light shine.

Prayer: **Father of light, give me the grace to let my light shine. Amen.**

✤Dean of the Chapel and Professor of Christian Ministry, Duke University; Durham, North Carolina.

249

Tuesday, August 26   Read James 1:22; Mark 7:6.

I read the story in *The New York Times*, of all places. The African-American family had moved into an all-white neighborhood in the Northeast. While no one welcomed them, they were relieved that at least none of their neighbors seemed openly hostile. Then they awoke one morning to find that someone had painted a blatant racial epithet on the front wall of their new home.

The police investigated, but no one in the neighborhood could offer any clues as to who had done this terrible act of hate. No one knew anything. Then a ten-year-old boy stepped forward. Starting on nis paper route early one morning, he had seen a man painting the words. He gave a complete description of the perpetrator, and the police arrested and imprisoned the man.

What struck me was the reason the boy gave for his courageous deed. "I am a Christian. I am supposed to tell the truth." As Jesus once said to his critics, it is one thing to honor God with the lips but another to give our whole heart.

The Letter of James has been criticized for being simplistic, undeveloped lists of truisms and proverbs. Yet simple truth is still truth. Let us ponder the direct truth offered by this beloved verse from James. Jesus does not want us just to *know* his truth, to *understand* his truth. He wants us to *do* his truth.

The truth of Jesus' word is in the doing.

Prayer: **Jesus, lead me from hearing your word to courageously doing your word. Amen.**

Wednesday, August 27   Read Song of Songs 2:8-13.

I work on a university campus with young adults. Love—romantic love—is a major preoccupation of this age group. After all, they are nineteen and the sun is shining and the woods are green. The library will still be there tomorrow!

So forgive me if the Song of Songs has become one of my favorite books of the Bible. It is a strange book when compared with most other biblical literature. It is an ancient Hebrew love poem in which two young lovers take turns waxing poetic about all the lovable details of one another's personalities—comparing one another to gazelles, young stags, trees in bloom. If you have never been nineteen and in love, the Song of Songs can seem boring and repetitious. If you have, then you will love this book.

Although it is one of the few books in the Bible that never mentions God, do not judge Song of Songs too harshly for that. It is an exuberant, joyous, unrestrained song of love—romantic, physical, passionate, mushy young love as a gift of God.

We began this week's meditations with a word from the much more sober Letter of James. James says "every perfect gift, is from above, coming down from the Father" (1:17). Surely that includes the gift of love.

So relax. You will learn nothing new from today's scripture; it will not make you a better person or help you make it through the week. Yet it may remind you of the glorious gift of romantic love; and if it does, give thanks to God for the gift.

Prayer: **Loving God, give me the grace to love and to be loved in my relationships as you have loved us. Amen.**

Thursday, August 28   Read Mark 7:1-8, 14-15, 21-23.

Pity the poor Pharisees. They were only doing what the Bible told them was right. Isn't it important to follow your faith, to put it into action in your daily life? That is what the Pharisees believed; so do we. Going to church, tithing, Bible reading, daily use of the Upper Room *Disciplines*—these are all worthy, essential religious acts that nurture the Christian life.

Yet in this episode from Luke's Gospel, Jesus criticizes the Pharisees for having perverted the faith of Israel. He tells them that Isaiah was talking about them when he charged, "This people honors me with their lips, but their hearts are far from me." They have the externals of faith but not the internals. They are so concerned to avoid the impurities without that they have overlooked the more troublesome impurities within.

Probably that is why we often begin our service on Sunday with a prayer of confession. We admit up front that we are capable of doing the right thing for the wrong reason, of allowing our religion to become a way of avoiding God rather than getting close to God. "Look at me, Lord; see how well I'm doing?"

Lord, have mercy.

So consider this passage as an invitation to look at our lives, to ponder the ways in which we pervert the faith even while we are busy doing the faith. I expect that you have your list; I certainly have mine.

Prayer: **Lord, help me to love you as I ought to do. Amen.**

Friday, August 29   Read James 1:26; Mark 7:1-8.

James, after talking about getting our hearts right with God, now focuses upon another much more troublesome organ of the body—the tongue. Bridle your tongue!

Evil tongues do more damage in congregations than clenched fists. Sometimes it is the deceitful, "I don't mean to be spreading rumors but . . ." Or it's the old, "Have you heard . . .?" knife-in-the-back.

Our thoughtless, insensitive speech about others can hurt as deeply as a blow across the face. There are those who have spent their lives discredited, lonely, and rejected—not because of their bad deeds but because of the thoughtless, malicious speech of others.

I, who do lots of talking, ought to take note. Am I careful in what I say about others? When am I guilty of "bearing false witness," accusing someone of something for which I have no real proof? Am I too quick to report a rumor rather than waiting to verify what I have heard?

James does not say that our tongues are evil, just that, like an unruly, undisciplined horse, tongues need an appropriate "bridle." What is the tongue's best bridle? James doesn't say, but I think James would agree that the bridle is the love of Christ. To love as Jesus loved, this is our task—to want the best for others, to be fair and restrained in our judgments upon them. Loving.

Prayer: **Lord, I love to talk. In love, bridle my tongue so that I may speak about others in the same loving, forbearing way you have spoken to me. Amen.**

Saturday, August 30 Read James 1:27.

Loving God rightly can be so complicated. Here at the seminary it takes us at least three years of rigorous study after college to prepare someone to lead a congregation as pastor—church history, doctrine, theology, pastoral care. There is so much to know and to understand.

Yet I wonder if sometimes we are guilty of overcomplicating the Christian faith. "It's just all so confusing," we say. "I hardly know what to do or believe." Let's keep having detached discussions about the Nicene Creed, keep pondering the finer points of Deuteronomy, delay judgment on Jesus until we get clear on the facts.

James, who has a genius for pithy, direct statements, cuts to the heart of the matter: "Religion . . . is this: to care for orphans and widows . . . , to keep oneself unstained by the world."

There you have it. Faith in Jesus involves care for the most vulnerable among us and the practice of holiness in the world. It's so succinct you could put it on a bumper sticker or write it on your wrist.

Might our congregations be made more faithful if we took a moment and evaluated our life together on the basis of this little verse? What do we do that is essential? Might each of our lives be made more faithful if, rather than having these eternal discussions, we simply tried—in all we do or say—to be faithful to this one little verse?

Sometimes following Jesus is not as confusing and complicated as we would like!

Prayer: **Lord, help me simply, directly, straightforwardly to follow you. Amen.**

Sunday, August 31   Read James 1:25.

The angry young man had been speaking for nearly an hour, castigating the church for its cowardice, its lethargy, its avoidance of the AIDS crisis. When he finally concluded, he asked if anyone had anything to say.

A woman stood up and said, "I'm a member of our church's Wednesday Women's Bible Study. We meet, have punch and cookies, and study the Bible. One day, one of the women said, 'It's so hard to understand Jesus sometimes. So confusing. You just don't know what he wants of us.'

"Another spoke up and said, 'That's not true. We already understand more of the Bible than we don't understand Sometimes I think we sit here and talk about the Bible to avoid really living the Bible. The difficulty is not in the understanding; it's in the *doing.*'

"Her words struck us. When we prayed at the end of our study, we prayed that God would show us what we ought to do. The very next week after our punch and cookies, one of the women told us how she had befriended a young man in her apartment building who is dying of AIDS. His family has deserted him. He has no friends. She visits him, shares a couple of meals each week with him, runs errands.

"We knew what we had to do. Each of us has now become an adopted grandmother for someone in our community with AIDS. We do cooking, errands, light cleaning. Sometimes we just talk. We can't do much, but we can do that. It has really changed our Bible study!"

Thus in our hearing, James 1:25 was fulfilled.

Prayer: **Lord, help me to be a doer of your word and not only a hearer, debater, procrastinator, and avoider of your word. Amen.**

FAITH ENACTED

September 1–7, 1997   **John Indermark***
Monday, September 1   Read James 2:14-17;
           Proverbs 22:8-9.

In labors

Labor in the year 1997 differs significantly from labor in 1894, when Congress declared Labor Day a holiday in the District of Columbia. Paving information highways and surfing the 'Net did not occupy many (if any) laborers then.

But labor remains a key component of faith. Words and pop-down menus alone do not embody faith for those in need of its witness, much less its compassion. Twice in the text from James, "What good is it?" and "What is the good of that" become the objection to faith's possessing no "energy." (James's favorite word for work is *ergon*, so we may accurately render faith's enacting as *en-ergeia*.) Congregational benedictions and denominational social pronouncements bring no good word, no matter how finely wordsmithed or well-intentioned, without actions that embody them. Why? Unlabored faith is dead (James 2:17).

While the nature of labor may change from generation to generation, works of injustice still reap the whirlwind, and acts of generosity still bring blessing. So Proverbs reminds us that our labors have consequences for ourselves and others.

What do you make of your life's labors on this day? Or, even more risky, what might a neutral observer make of the links between your faith words and your faith works?

Prayer: **Sovereign God, whose grace fashioned all creation, whose love labored in incarnation: empower our faithful works and so enable our working faith. In Jesus' name. Amen.**

---

*Ordained U.C.C. minister, free-lance writer, and supply pastor in Presbyterian churches in northwest Oregon.

Tuesday, September 2   Read Mark 7:24-30;
                                                             Psalm 125:4.

In persistence

   She apparently did not know her place: Jesus wanted seclusion, and the woman barged into the house unbeckoned. She apparently did not know her standing: the Nazarene Jesus came for the sake of Israel, and this Gentile Syrophoenician came for the sake of her daughter. She apparently did not know her role: the male rabbi Jesus intoned solemn words of exclusion, and she challenged him for a still-unspoken crumb of grace. At story's end, Jesus not only exorcised the demon from her daughter, but in Matthew's parallel text declared to the woman: "Great is your faith!" (15:28).

   The story raises questions, to be sure. Why would Jesus not heal a child at the outset? Why would God's Messiah offer the harsh-sounding imagery of children and dogs as a euphemism for the relationship between Jews and Gentiles? Parable-like, the story does not answer every question it suggests. And parable-like, it pushes us inward.

   The need of persistence in faith owes not to awakening God's sense of the right, which doubtless far exceeds our awareness of it, much less our ability to manipulate it. More likely, persistence is evoked for our own sake. What do you value so much that you would be willing to badger God about it? What so consumes your sense of justice and compassion that you would give God no rest until the plea of the psalmist, "do good, O LORD" (Ps. 125:4), finds fulfillment? A woman came to Jesus for her daughter . . . for whom do you come? And how long will you persist?

Suggestion for meditation: **Think of those you know who are in need of God's help and healing, those otherwise forgotten persons who need your voice.**

Wednesday, September 3   Read James 2:1-4;
                                              Psalm 125:1-3.

In community

   The communion of saints. In the Apostles' Creed the phrase
sounds sufficiently noble. The intrigue comes in discerning traces
of that heavenly communion in its earthly counterpart. James
noted disturbing trends of favoritism (the Greek word literally
means "to receive the face") based on wealth, or the lack thereof,
in his community. He takes to task those who make such
superficial distinctions, even questioning their faith.

   Fortunately, we have moved beyond such distinctions in our
modern ecclesiastical environs. We no longer court the rich,
taking special notice and fawning over those whose funds endow
this pulpit or that chair of theology. We no longer shuffle those
ill-suited to our congregation's profile to the side, moving them
out of the more-visible ranks of teachers or ushers or council
members, lest they give new prospects the wrong impression of
us. Right?

   Communities of faith have an uncanny ability to be as human
as those who comprise them. The psalm, in its own way, makes a
similar point. It explains the wicked will not exercise their rule
"so that the righteous might not stretch out their hands to do
wrong." Even the righteous can veer to the wrong, given the
(im)proper climate; even the righteous community can veer that
way, if favoritism rather than faith defines it.

   Faith gives communities more than just a name to call
ourselves. Faith seeks embodiment with integrity in community,
respecting *all* the people of God.

**Prayer: Holy God of Zion, may our trust in you fashion not only
persons but communities of faith, so we may together stretch out
our hands to do right. In Jesus Christ. Amen.**

Thursday, September 4   Read James 2:5-7;
                                             Proverbs 22:1-2.

In surprise

It is the sort of philosophy one might expect to encounter in some now-discredited manual of Marxist principles: oppression by the rich, favored status of the poor. Yet those very ideas catch us by surprise in James 2:5-6. What do we make of such a text in scripture?

Actually, the discipline of interpretation forces us to ask the related but harder question: What does such a text in scripture make of us? The communal sharing alluded to in the Book of Acts had apparently passed from the scene as quickly as it arose. Consequently, the church in the time of James struggled with how to deal with disparities of wealth and poverty among members.

James used those disparities to illustrate the upside-down nature of the gospel, a frequent theme in Jesus' teachings and parables. The riches of faith stand out in far greater contrast when set against the backdrop of poverty. The inheritance of God's sovereign realm seems all the more bountiful when possessed by those who have no other estates or endowments to claim. The letter's warnings against abuses by the rich were due not to classist rhetoric but the sad state of affairs that undermined the church in that day . . . and in too many days since.

So again: What does this scripture seek to make of us? It might make of us persons whose eyes and hearts are set on that which lasts; communities whose regard is cast not on what glitters and seduces with power and prestige but on the One who fashioned rich and poor alike: with grace, for love.

Prayer: O God, grace those whom the world writes off, love those whom the world ignores—and renew our surprising call to be the agents of that very grace and love. In Jesus Christ. Amen.

Friday, September 5   Read Mark 7:31-35.

In healing

A deaf man with a speech problem interrupts Jesus' journey. How well do you deal with interruptions? How easily do you drop the schedule in favor of an unplanned interlude of unknown duration? I once saw ministry (clergy or lay) judged by the capacity to be interrupted—by life, by need, by grace. The journey pauses for the sake of this man. For whom, for what, do you pause?

Oddly the text portrays the plea for help coming not from this individual but from an anonymous "they." Perhaps the speech impediment made the fellow self-conscious about asking for help. Perhaps he had already been dismissed as a nuisance too many times before. The text does not say.

But it does say this. Jesus took him aside: in private, away from the crowd. This would not be a public display of power, certainly not a gimmick to attract crowds. Healing resided between this individual and Jesus. The crowd brought him for healing. It did not need to be its audience.

When healing came, it did so in steps recognizable to the deaf man. The pressure of fingers, the moistness of spittle, the sight of a face lifted upward. Jesus made the healing the man's experience, not the crowd's spectacle.

The church may still heal. We may still touch human lives in ways that bring "openings." Think of your own life. How, and through whom, has God touched you in healing ways? How does your congregation, and how do you, bring that touch to others—even, and especially, to those who might be discounted as mere interruptions?

Suggestion for meditation: Where does your life still need God's "opening"? Pray for that healing. And seek to be its instrument for others.

Saturday, September 6 Read Proverbs 22:22-23;
James 2:8-13.

In justice

The Wisdom literature of the Hebrew Scriptures, of which Proverbs is but one work, aims to instill the living of righteous lives before God. Whereas other traditions connect wisdom to intellectual attainment or special knowledge, Judaism sees wisdom revealed in faithful conduct.

These verses from Proverbs address how one lives in relationship to those who are vulnerable. The robbing of the poor is a story as old as Ahab and Naboth's vineyard (1 Kings 21), a story that never seems to lack for contemporary recurrences. The crushing of the afflicted at the gate raises the specter of judicial injustice. In ancient Israel, judges held court at the city gates. The crushing of which Proverbs speaks refers to the rendering of their decisions in blatant disregard of impartiality and righteousness.

The objection of Proverbs (and prophets like Amos) to such treatment of the poor is not based on social etiquette for the "less fortunate." The objection is that such conduct represents bad faith. Even more ominous, the objection is that such conduct places one squarely in opposition to Israel's God (Proverbs 22:23). James raises the same issue when declaring that partiality, previously identified in this chapter with dishonoring the poor, jeopardizes one as a transgressor of the law. The wisdom of God insists on justice for those who cannot ensure it for themselves.

By what wisdom do we conduct our lives—especially our societal commitments? Do we conduct our lives by the wisdom that people get what they deserve; the wisdom that says you can't fight city hall; the wisdom that cannot separate justice for the poor from living in covenant with the God who pleads their cause?

***Prayer:* Give me a heart and voice for justice, Sovereign God, to feel and speak and work as you would have me do. In Jesus Christ. Amen.**

Sunday, September 7   Read Mark 7:36-37.

In witness

Has the news ever been so good you just couldn't keep it to yourself, you *had* to go out and tell someone? A new grandchild, a promotion, a magnificent sunset . . . or what happened in church last week? I suspect most of us are more comfortable on the former than the latter—to our detriment. Faith means to be infectious, even though many latter-day disciples seem skilled at quarantine.

Take the scene summarized in Mark. As in other instances, Jesus attempts to stifle the news about a healing. But the folks will not have it. The more he insisted on keeping things quiet, the louder they got. And to their credit, the praise has a point. They recognize that he does good things. They announce that he gives hearing to the deaf and speech to the mute: perhaps not a simple recitation of the miracle just past, but a realization that they have witnessed something like the promised words of Isaiah 35:5.

Scholars say Jesus' wish for silence on occasions like these, as with the messianic identity, stems from his desire not to set loose ideas prone to popular misunderstanding. But have we become too adept at heeding Jesus' call for quiet? When was the last time you heard about a pastor having to admonish church members to keep quiet about their faith and the presence of God at work in their lives—or vice versa?

Has faith, has grace, ever been so good you just couldn't keep it to yourself, you *had* to go out and tell someone? If not . . . why not?

Suggestion for meditation: **Consider ways in which you and your congregation can give voice and witness to faith's joys so that others may share in it with you.**

1998

Now is the time to order your copy of
The Upper Room Disciplines 1998

Published for over 35 years, Disciplines is one of the most popular daily devotional books available. Year after year, Disciplines continues to appeal to more and more Christians who, like yourself, desire a more disciplined spiritual life. Be sure to order your copy today, while the 1998 edition is still available.

THE UPPER ROOM DISCIPLINES 1998
$7.95 each — 10 or more copies $6.76 each
Ask for product number UR811

To Order Your Copies, Call: 1-800-972-0433
Tell the customer service representative your source code is 98D.

Or Write:
Customer Services
The Upper Room
P.O. Box 856
Nashville, TN 37202-0856

Shipping Charges:
On **prepaid** orders, we pay postage.
On **"bill me later"** orders, the shipping charges will be added to your invoice.

Please prepay if your order is under $10.00.
All payments in U.S. funds, please.

THE UPPER ROOM DISCIPLINES 1998
is also available at most bookstores.

GOD'S WISDOM

September 8–14, 1997
Monday, September 8

Wightman Weese✤
Read Proverbs 1:20-28.

Listening to the right voice

The word *wisdom* in these verses means more than just accumulated philosophic or scientific learning. It is knowledge put to practice; insights that result in learned behavior, insights derived from a proper reverential fear of God. To be wise is to learn how to live in obedience to and respect for God and God's revealed truth. Proverbs describes how a godly person in the writer's day would live out the principles of the Torah, applied to every area of life.

Here the writer speaks of wisdom as a person, persistently attempting to woo the simple—those not yet trained in the skills of godly living to listen, to follow, and to find God's favor. These verses personify wisdom as female. In later chapters the proverbs use the imagery of a wicked, enticing woman to personify the entrapments of sin.

These verses clearly set out the roads to life and death. We listen to the heartfelt entreaties of wisdom, or we ignore the warnings and face disaster, the storms of life that come as the consequence of disobedience.

Prayer: **Dear God, above the clamor of many enticing voices, may my ears be open to hear the clear voice of your wisdom to guide my steps today. Amen.**

✤Ordained Baptist minister; book editor at Tyndale House Publishers for fifteen years; currently recruiting, training, and leading work teams to Third World countries.

Tuesday, September 9   Read Proverbs 1:29-33.

Love wisdom and live

The warnings of God's impending wrath against those complacent ones who hated knowledge and scoffed at God's advice are placed side by side with God's promises to enrich those who listened to the voice of wisdom to "live in safety and be at ease, without fear of harm" (NIV). The offenses mentioned here are not merely the result of ignorance of the truth. The warning is to those who "hated knowledge," "did not choose to fear the LORD," "spurned my rebuke." The age-old alibi, "I didn't know," is not an acceptable excuse.

Notice that God is not arbitrary, showering benefits on certain of the creation and serving up blight on others. The reward and punishment of obedience and disobedience are inherent in God's nature, which God reveals in God's word. It would be contrary to God's nature to overlook the behavior of those who spurn rebuke. A disrespect for God's wisdom carries its own consequences. The writer warns, "They will eat the fruit of their ways and be filled with the fruit of their schemes."

We can compare certain principles of spiritual growth with the time-tested rules of planting and reaping. Well-tended seed and plants produce good fruit. Neglected, untended orchards and vineyards produce worthless fruit. That is the nature of agriculture. For the same reason, we cannot rail against the Creator when spiritual harm comes to us because of our own disobedience. That is the nature of God's wisdom.

Prayer: **Dear Father, I thank you for the wisdom revealed in your word that shows me the way of life and eternal blessing. Amen.**

Wednesday, September 10   Read Psalm 19.

God speaks to me everywhere

This psalm explains why the Paul could speak with such certainty about God's revelation. He concluded that we have no excuse for not knowing and worshiping God. Paul wrote, "For since the creation of the world God's invisible qualities—his eternal power and divine nature—have been clearly seen, being understood from what has been made, so that [all] are without excuse" (Romans 1:20, NIV). The beautiful description of nature, the intricacies of creation, the heavens and skies that "pour forth speech . . . [and] display knowledge" lead to a logical conclusion to be drawn from the wonders of creation: "The law of the LORD is perfect, reviving the soul. The statutes of the LORD are trustworthy, making wise the simple."

Important theological arguments are grounded in these and similar passages of scripture about the nature of God's revelation. While we cannot dispute that many have never heard the clear message of the atonement made by God in the death and resurrection of Jesus, this psalm and Paul's teaching in Romans show that no one can claim ignorance of a wise divinity who created the world, a divinity to whom we owe allegiance and obedience.

We must leave it to God to respond to those, wherever they are and how much or little they know about the gospel, who seek to respond to the wisdom they may learn from God's fingerprints in creation.

Prayer: **Dear Father, thank you for speaking so clearly—through your word and your works—to bring me to yourself. Amen.**

Thursday, September 11   Read James 3:1-6.

A warning about human wisdom

James's warning to teachers about the human tongue was given in the context of their responsibilities as guardians of the truth. By their teachings they could steer others to the truth or lead them astray. James wrote that the teacher's place of authority adds great responsibility, especially in spiritual matters. The teacher instructs others in the truth both by what is said and by what is practiced.

Sharing the truth about God is a tremendous privilege but also a terrible responsibility. The difference between a teacher of truth and one who leads others astray is determined by who is in control of the tongue. An uncontrolled teacher's tongue, as James warns, can set "the whole course of his life on fire, and is itself set on fire by hell."

God's gift of wisdom is available to all who seek it, but by nature we allow human wisdom to control us. Human pride makes us think we have something to say. But humility and dependence upon God gives us the benefit and blessing of wisdom from above. Unless God is in control of our lives, we deprive ourselves of God's wisdom with the result that we become purveyors of the world's wisdom. God's wisdom brings life; worldly wisdom brings death and destruction. How it behooves us to ground ourselves in God's wisdom! It would be better for us to remain forever silent than to become the instrument of destruction for others through our worldly wisdom.

Prayer: Father, may my tongue always be filled with your wisdom that I may be an instrument of life to others. Amen.

Friday, September 12   Read James 3:7-12.

The answer to the uncontrollable tongue

The writer of James understood human nature and its proneness to inconsistencies well. The uncontrollable—or the uncontrolled—tongue is a great source of trouble because it is so difficult to control. The tongue can build up or destroy; humanly speaking, it is uncontrollable. The tongue's inconsistent message is evidence of someone's trying to please God with worldly wisdom—one minute acting pious and blessing God; the next moment cursing humanity. James said, "This should not be" (NIV) and suggested a better way.

Early in the Book of James, the writer offers an invitation: "If any of you lacks wisdom, he [or she] should ask God, who gives generously to all without finding fault, and it will be given to him [or her]" (1:5, NIV). A wise and understanding person who desires to please God will "show it by his [or her] good life, by deeds done in the humility that comes from wisdom" (3:13, NIV).

Perhaps no theme of scripture, from beginning to end, is more consistent than the teaching about the wisdom that comes from above—heavenly, God-given wisdom. It appears as a seamless garment, unchanging in all it says about its availability and about God's desire that we partake of it and walk in its truth. There seems to be only one requirement: We must seek it in humility, with our whole heart. God's wisdom fills our tongues with blessing, making us a source of fresh water and fruit for a hungry and thirsty world.

Prayer: **Father, in humility I seek your wisdom today that through it I may always bless and bring blessing to others. Amen.**

Saturday, September 13   Read Mark 8:27-33.

Have in mind the things of God

To those who knew Jesus while he was here on earth, he was a wise teacher, perhaps even the promised Messiah. Who was he? Peter had the answer, "You are the Christ" (NIV). The parallel passage in Matthew 16 records Jesus as saying that Peter's statement was true, but that such knowledge came by divine revelation—not by human wisdom. Later in today's reading, we see that Peter lapsed into human wisdom in rebuking Jesus concerning the prediction of his coming death. Jesus responded to Peter, "You do not have in mind the things of God." Peter is relying on earthly wisdom.

Peter's two responses convey an important truth. Though Peter was a loyal follower of Jesus, he was still prone to rely on his own experience rather than on God's wisdom. Peter might be excused, in one sense. The fact that the sinless Son of Man would come to earth not to set up a kingdom at that time but to lay down his life for sinful humanity might, humanly speaking, be called the most irrational fact of the universe. Yet Jesus' revelation that he was going to lay down his life and be raised again was true. By revelation on the day of Pentecost, the disciples understood fully the meaning of Christ's death and resurrection.

We often make the greatest mistakes in our Christian walk when we set aside God's wisdom—the truth revealed in the scriptures—and begin to trust in our own understanding.

Prayer: **Father, make me one who relies solely on your wisdom from above. Amen.**

Sunday, September 14   Read Mark 8:34-38.

Saying no to the body and yes to the soul

For people in Jesus' day, everything about the world suggested to them that hard work, keeping the law, helping the poor—being a good person—would work to their benefit, ensure long life, fruitful vines, and good harvests. Do good, and they would prosper in body and soul. The heart of that motive seemed to be self-preservation—looking out for number one.

Jesus' words must have shocked them. It was not by trying to preserve one's life but by laying it down, saying "no" to the body that spiritual blessing and eternal life might come to the soul. Surely the disciples understood part of this; following Jesus had already cost them a lot. Yet only later would they understand the magnitude of Jesus' words. History tells us that many of them were martyred for their decision to follow Christ.

Understanding the principle of life that Jesus was teaching became wisdom from God. As God's wisdom usually appears to be, it contradicted all of human wisdom, which was to hang on to world and earthly life at all costs. Jesus said that the cost might be very dear indeed: "What good is it for [one] to gain the whole world, yet forfeit his [or her] soul?" (NIV).

Following Jesus takes God-given wisdom, but it is costly. Christianity costs us something—time, money, or personal sacrifice—for Jesus said, "If any want to become my followers, let them deny themselves and take up their cross and follow me."

Prayer: **Father, help me today to make the wise decision to follow Jesus, whatever the cost. Amen.**

MODELS OF GOODNESS

September 15–21, 1997   **Raymond K. DeHainaut✤**
Monday, September 15   Read Proverbs 31:10-22.

This week's scriptures offer us various models of true piety.

What a coincidence! Today's verses from Proverbs, which celebrate the good wife, are the text I used at the funeral of a dear friend and coworker. Clara was my administrative assistant at the University of South Florida campus ministry for twelve years back in the '70s and '80s. She was an efficient and friendly worker. Many generations of students loved her and considered her their on-campus mom and confidant. Both her husband and a son with health problems relied heavily on her salary and her cheerful and proficient way of managing her household despite her own deteriorating health.

These verses describe a capable woman with a good heart. She uses her time wisely and expresses concern for all within her household as well as the poor and needy. The author of Proverbs tells us that women like Clara are "far more precious than jewels." Their value rests in their true piety, a piety that reflects a close relationship to God and a love that enables them to give themselves in unselfish service to others. At times our encounters with false religiosity may disillusion us, but as we look back we know that authentic people do come along to influence our lives tremendously. The witness of these saints challenges us to improve the ways our own lives touch others.

Prayer: **Thank you, Lord, for these "precious" servants you have sent my way. Grant me the grace to follow their example. Amen.**

✤Teacher of international studies at the University of South Florida; retired from forty-two years of service as campus minister as well as a United Methodist missionary in Latin America.

Tuesday, September 16   Read Proverbs 31:23-31.

Just a few days after Clara's funeral, I invited a young professor who had attended the Fourth World Conference on Women in Beijing to share her experience with my international studies class. She was very outspoken on behalf of women's rights and shared her concern about the many reports she heard regarding the exploitation of women in Latin America and Asia.

I imagine that if I had asked her or some of my students to comment on these verses about the good wife, they would have considered them a patriarchal justification for traditional gender roles. The good wife "rises while it is still night and provides food for her household" (31:15). "Her lamp does not go out at night" (31:18). In contrast, "her husband is known in the city gates, taking his seat among the elders of the land" (31:23). He could brag that his wife was not one of those "contentious" women condemned in 21:9; 25:24; and 27:15. Some of my students would probably wonder if his daily prayers included the ancient thanksgiving that he had "not been born a woman."

Some will argue that it is unfair to look back and criticize gender roles in ancient times or even contemporary non-Western cultures from a feminist perspective. But in a sense, Paul looked back and around him and proclaimed a revolution when he said that "There is no longer Jew or Greek, there is no longer slave or free, there is no longer male or female; for all of you are one in Christ Jesus" (Gal. 3:28). We must not be too hard on the good wife's husband for reflecting the values of his day, but we can be thankful that we have received a gospel of equality and unity in Christ.

Suggestion for meditation: **How can I witness more effectively and lovingly in the area of human rights and gender roles?**

Wednesday, September 17   Read Psalm 1.

Some Christian interpreters who maintain a strong distinction between *law* and *gospel* have called the psalter "the handbook of the pious Jew." And it is true that many psalms glorify the law. "Oh, how I love your law!" (Psalm 119:97). Our text also announces the felicity of those whose "delight is in the law of the LORD." They are the good and fruitful people, unlike the wicked who "are like chaff that the wind drives away."

This psalm is troublesome to those who believe that we are incapable of keeping the law no matter how much we love it or meditate on it. And many interpreters of Paul's doctrine of justification by faith (Rom. 3:28) insist that the law can only be seen as the occasion for sin. John Wesley, who believed in the possibility of faithful Christians living a holy life, writes in his journal regarding Luther: "How blasphemously does he speak of good works and of the Law of God; constantly coupling the Law with sin, death, hell, or the devil." Wesley taught his followers a doctrine of holiness that was centered in grace; a grace that empowered them to do what God's law commanded.

Those who delight in the law and attempt to live by it must be "like trees planted by streams of water" (1:3). This means that the good life is possible if our spiritual roots are drawing upon this fountain of grace. Its first condition is that we are connected with the Spirit which empowers us to live the fruitful lives we were created to live.

Prayer: **O Lord, who can aspire to live up to the lofty requirements of your law of purity, love, and compassion? Draw me nearer to yourself that I may reflect your image and be what you would have me to be. Amen.**

Thursday, September 18   Read James 3:13–4:3.

Some scholars have criticized the Letter of James for containing what they consider to be a great deal of pre-Christian Jewish material that emphasizes the good life and good works. In "The Principles of a Methodist," John Wesley agreed wholeheartedly with Luther that "St. Paul requires nothing on the part of [humanity], but only a true and living faith." Then he qualifies this by observing: "Yet this faith does not shut out repentance, hope, and love, which are joined with faith in every [one] that is justified."

Most of us would agree that we are saved by God's grace and not by our own works. For the writer of James, our works indicate the source of our wisdom—our spiritual grounding translates into particular modes of behavior and emotions. The writer encourages those acting out of a wisdom from above to "show by your good life that your works are done with gentleness born of wisdom."

Rather than accuse the writer of heresy, we might express our gratitude for the writer's lifting up the characteristics of genuineness and exposing our tendency to live a life of pretense. The season of Pentecost is a good time to take an honest spiritual inventory. How does my spiritual walk look in terms of James's description of the fruitful "good life." Am I able to show with my life that I am really in touch with the wisdom from above? In what ways do I reflect my spiritual growth in the way I relate to and serve others and carry out my responsibilities?

Prayer: **O Lord, I admit that my life does not measure up to the faith that I profess. Forgive me and enable me to improve my daily walk with you. Amen.**

Friday, September 19   Read James 4:7-8*a*.

From the very beginning of his letter, the writer of James contends that true happiness comes to the believers who maintain "endurance" when their faith is tested (1:3). James leaves no doubt that these tests will come, but God will give us the necessary wisdom to endure if we pray earnestly and without being "double-minded." He was aware that many of our failures in prayer are due to the fact that they are halfhearted, betraying our continued "friendship with the world" (4:4). Augustine confessed that he once prayed, "Give me chastity and continence, but not yet."

"Submit yourselves. . . . Draw near to God, and he will draw near to you." When we read the entire fourth chapter, it is clear that he is now addressing those who have allowed themselves to slip into the worst kind of double-mindedness by involvement in constant conflicts and obsession with carnal cravings and murderous ideas. Even worse, they have become proud.

Your double-mindedness or mine may not fit the above description, but we need to be honest about the present health of our spirit and our relationship to God. Our pride and lack of humility is certainly something we need to acknowledge. "Submit yourselves." A Muslim student recently reminded me that the word *Islam* in Arabic means "total submission" to Allah, or God. We as Christians can certainly do no less than offer ourselves to God in total submission. If we draw near to God in total surrender, God will certainly draw near to us.

Prayer: **O Lord and Creator of all humankind, I confess that I am often prone to forget my nature as a creature made in your own image. At times in my life I have allowed myself to drift away from you. Help me to be sincere in my desire to draw closer to you and so open myself up to your presence that my joy may be full and my witness genuine. Amen.**

Saturday, September 20   Read Mark 9:30-32.

Most of us consider ourselves good disciples of Christ and intend to live our lives according to his will. But we, like his original disciples, have difficulty letting go of our preconceived notions about God—the way God works and the nature of the kingdom. We often act as though we have God in our pocket. We ignore God's warning through the prophet Isaiah that "as the heavens are higher than the earth, so are my ways higher than your ways and my thoughts than your thoughts" (55:9).

Our reading today indicates that after Jesus told his disciples that the Son of Man would have to be killed and then would be raised after three days, they "did not understand what he was saying" (9:32). A few days prior to this, Peter had rebuked Jesus for making this same announcement. Later on—at the arrest, trial, and crucifixion—the disciples were all equally confused. Their minds had been programmed with one very definite concept of the Messiah and the Messiah's accomplishments.

True discipleship comes after a conversion to a new mind-set, an openness to God's perspective revealed in Jesus Christ that can shatter old prejudices, radicalize our faith, and lead us beyond a shallow religiosity. We tend to limit God to neat little denominational packages.

How can we question or limit the God who created our universe, the vastness of which we are just beginning to realize through recent breakthroughs in astronomy. We can only marvel before the mystery that the Creator of such vast reaches could care for you and me. We are disciples, knowing through Jesus Christ that we can trust God and remain open to the many surprises along the way.

Suggestion for meditation: **Contemplate your relationship to God and God's majesty.**

Sunday, September 21   Read Mark 9:33-37.

After sensing the disciples' concern about status and prestige, Jesus calls them together and sits them down to hear a new radical teaching: "Whoever wants to be first must be last of all and servant of all." Here Jesus is revealing the revolutionary nature of his teaching, and he is calling his disciples to turn history and its values upside down.

Living the good life and achieving greatness are in not in contradiction. Jesus' teachings actually encourage the achievement of greatness—but greatness understood in a radically different way. Jesus himself gave the supreme example of true greatness. He was born in a stable during the reign of the great Roman Emperor Augustus (Luke 2:1), Julius Caesar's adopted heir who tracked down Caesar's assassins, eliminated all of his rivals, unified the empire, and is said to have "found Rome brick and left it marble." He was considered the greatest man of his day. But he pales in significance when compared to the humble carpenter who has become the Lord of history.

Those of us who dare to follow Jesus' revolutionary example are called to find ways to be his agents in history, actively working and struggling to help him establish his kingdom. We may seem insignificant when compared to the Augustus-like figures of today, those acclaimed for their political power or international fame. However, if we take Jesus' revolutionary model seriously, we can find ways to work with and on behalf of the poor, the victims of exploitation and discrimination. We will also promote the welfare of others as peacemakers. There is nothing wrong with our achieving greatness on Jesus' terms.

Prayer: **O Lord, free me from my preoccupation with my own self-centered interests to the extent that I can give myself in service to others. Amen.**

TOOLS OF THE TRADE

September 22–28, 1997   **Susan Ives Spieth✤**
Monday, September 22   Read James 5:13-18.

Prayer

God has empowered us with certain "tools of the trade" to do the work of ministry. The greatest of these tools is, of course, the Holy Spirit. Yet we have even more resources at our disposal. Each passage this week focuses on a different tool that enables us to carry out our mission as followers of Christ.

James speaks of the second greatest "tool of the trade"—prayer. Often we give prayer more lip service than real effort. Do our schedules include regular time alone with the Lord? Does our order (or pattern) of worship leave room for the spontaneous prayers of the people? In our Bible study groups, do we allow time for silences within spoken prayer? Are we committed to praying daily for the needs of others?

Our prayers are vital for helping expand the sphere of God's kingdom. "The prayer of the righteous is powerful and effective." Genuine and persistent prayer enables us to remain faithful to our ministry and to perform it with integrity, love, and joy.

Prayer: Gracious God, lead me again in prayer, away from all distraction and into a quiet time of renewal in your presence. Amen.

✤Associate pastor of Hillcrest United Methodist Church, Nashville, Tennessee.

Tuesday, September 23   Read James 5:19-20.

Accountability and faithful living

"Whoever brings back a sinner from wandering will save the sinner's soul." James is not addressing those outside the church when he speaks of sinners. Those words are meant for us who are saved in Jesus Christ. We have a tendency to wander from the truth, and that wandering can desensitize us to what it means to live as faithful disciples. But other believers can be a third tool available to us, for they can help us by lovingly holding us accountable as Christians seeking to live faithfully.

Persons who do this most effectively do not even realize it. The believer does not say, "Aha! John here is wandering from the truth. I am going to bring him back in line." Rather, the most compelling argument for wanderers is simply the lives of those who walk with God. These folks turn sinners back from wandering, and they do it by going about their lives in faithfulness to God.

Sometimes those who do the greatest work for God are those who are least aware of themselves. Their focus and concern is how their words and actions can further God's kingdom on earth. As they do their kingdom work, they show all of us how to live faithfully. Praise God for those faithful servants who quietly minister to all the "wanderers."

Prayer: Loving God, may I live in such a way as to be an example to others. And may I seek out those who keep me strong in the faith and say thank-you. Amen.

Wednesday, September 24   Read Mark 9:38-41.

Good People

Our family was headed to the airport in a rental car when we ran out of gas on Interstate 75, just outside Philadelphia. We were ill-prepared for this sort of thing—no gas cans, no car phone, no relatives nearby—so I made a paper sign that said, "Please call for help."

In a short time, a policeman arrived and asked us to put away our sign because so many people were calling in about us. We were even more amazed by the kindness of the young woman who drove me to the nearest gas station to fill *her* gas cans (the station didn't have any either) and returned me to my husband, children, and rented car.

As workers for the kingdom, we find a few surprise resources in our "toolbox." One of these surprises is those good people who may be outside the body of Christ. "Whoever is not against us is for us." The young woman who rescued my family may not have believed in Jesus Christ. She may not have been to church in a long time. She may never have read the Bible or attended prayer meetings. But she showed up when we desperately needed her, and she graced us with her presence and her provisions. For that I lift her in prayer, and I know that she will "by no means lose the reward."

Prayer: **Eternal God, thank you for those around me who are made in your image and whom you died to save. May I never cease being grateful that the world is filled with good people who serve you and minister to me. Amen.**

Thursday, September 25   Read Mark 9:42-50.

Action

Possibly the worst enemy in the kingdom of God is ourselves. Jesus tangled most often with the scribes and Pharisees—the very ones responsible for teaching the word of God. Because of their own hypocrisy and their misinterpretation of scripture, Jesus directed his harshest words toward them (see Matthew 23).

In today's reading, Jesus warns us of the danger of causing ourselves and others to stumble. In fact, Jesus feels so strongly about this point that his words are hard to hear: "If your hand causes you to stumble, cut it off. . . . And if your foot causes you to stumble, cut it off. . . . And if your eye causes you to stumble, tear it out." I believe that Jesus is not speaking literally, yet his point is most serious. Jesus expects us to live by the highest standards. We hold a sacred responsibility for helping others; if any attitude of ours, any word of ours, any action of ours distorts Jesus' message, then we must work to change ourselves and to correct our distortion of the good news.

Here is the fifth "tool" for ministry—action. We can, we should, and we must be proactive, deliberate, and purposeful in certain matters. The kingdom of God requires that we act—especially to cease from doing anything that might cause someone to stumble. Our willingness to do so is a test of our commitment to Christ. Are we willing to cut ourselves off from attitudes, words, relationships, or actions that may have become comfortable for us but in fact distort Christ's message of good news?

***Prayer:* Precious Lord, may all that I say and do reflect the light of your love. If anything I do or say distorts that message, give me the strength and courage to separate myself from it so that my life may glorify you. Amen.**

Friday, September 26   Read Esther 7:1-6, 9-10.

God with us

Have you ever been talking to someone only to have that person walk into another room or start reading the paper or begin chatting with someone else? When this happens, we know the other person is not really listening to us. Yet at times we need a person's undivided attention.

Queen Esther needed King Ahasuerus's undivided attention. She had something extremely important to tell him, and she wanted to be sure he would really hear her. The king assured Esther twice that he would grant her petition. Yet only after two requests and a third inquiry by the king did Esther finally reveal her purpose. Undoubtedly, she had his full attention after such elaborate efforts!

Today's scripture reminds us that we never have to wait for God to hear us. God is the Great Listener who is always "on call" for us. At first glance, this may not seem like a tool for ministry, but I cannot count the number of times I have needed to rush in a request to the "King," as did Esther. Sometimes we are in need of urgent graces, immediate relief, and quick answers. At these times we cannot wait to make an appointment, get on the calendar, or get a call in the morning. We need God's attention, and we need it now. What a wonderful tool we have in knowing that God is never too busy or too tired or too distracted to hear from us.

Prayer: **Almighty God, thank you for being the "Great Listener" who hears the thoughts on my heart even before they are uttered on my lips. May I be a better listener for others, and may my voice echo the words from your heart. Amen.**

Saturday, September 27   Read Esther 9:20-22.

Celebration and praise

"Their sorrow was turned into joy and their mourning into a day of celebration." This statement summarizes the whole story of the Bible. Those age-old enemies of sorrow and mourning never have the final word—not while we have breath to praise and celebrate God. The Creator God, the Sustainer God, and the Redeemer God has spoken, has broken through the barrier of death, and has made a way for us to overcome even that great enemy. We are victorious in God!

The Hebrew Scriptures are filled with examples of God's calling the chosen people to celebrate: the Feast of Unleavened Bread, the Feast of the Harvest, and the Feast of the Ingathering (Exod. 23:14-16), to name a few. God commanded these celebrations as reminders of divine goodness and grace.

Celebration and praise are another "tool" that strengthens us. It comes as no surprise that God's people would set aside a time for rejoicing and celebrating. Acts of praise nourish the human soul.

Have you ever noticed that it is practically impossible to stay downhearted when you praise God? Celebrating the glory of God gives your mental attitude a lift. Try it sometime.

Prayer: **Sustainer God, when I am feeling overwhelmed or beaten down, help me focus on your glorious grace, mercy, and love. Then may my soul rise up and sing praises to your holy name. Amen.**

Sunday, September 28   Read Psalm 124.

God's help

Psalm 124 is a song of thanksgiving to God for protection and deliverance through a long and perilous journey. The writer reflects on all the dangers that could have broken their bodies or crushed their spirits had God not been Israel's helper. The psalmist writes as if looking back over a period of time when danger was imminent from either the enemy's anger or the raging waters. In vivid detail, the author recalls the feelings of becoming undone—of being swallowed alive or swept away.

But "Blessed be the LORD. . . . We have escaped like a bird." God's help in time of trouble brings freedom and peace. God's help is the final tool of the trade. Not only is God with us as the Great Listener to our needs—God is also ready and willing to help us. God is not merely a spectator in our lives. God is an active participant, seeking us out—especially in hard times—to be our strength and our helper. This tool is truly the most amazing and humbling—that the God of the universe would care so deeply for you and for me.

***Prayer:* Helper God, I stand in awe of your love for me. Thank you for loving me and helping me through life's journey. Amen.**

LIVING WITH INTEGRITY

September 29–October 5, 1997   **Sister Barbara Jean, SHN✤**
Monday, September 29   Read Job 1:1; 2:1-10.

"Then his wife said to him, 'Do you still hold fast to your integrity? Curse God and die!'" (NKJV).

In questioning her husband in such a way, Job's wife was not a demon in disguise. She did not want Job to curse God out of some blasphemous rebellion; rather, she wanted to help bring his pain and suffering to a swift end. She knew that no one who dared curse God could live. She was looking for the quickest way to end his torment. Job's wife loved her husband and was suffering herself from the agony of watching him suffer.

The obvious theme in this week's readings concerns integrity—integrity in living in relationship with God. In our present culture—and sadly enough, even in the church—this quality seems to be in short supply. The church's emphasis is often on conversion, the giving of one's life to Jesus. Proclaiming the gospel of salvation is certainly a priority, but teaching must follow the proclamation; teaching the redeemed to live out their salvation with integrity.

It was not enough for Job to be considered a "good Hebrew." His devotion called him to act out of his understanding of himself as a created being. *Integrity* comes from the root word *integer,* which means "whole or complete." For a person to have integrity like Job's, one must accept the truth of humanity in all its dimensions and limitations. Our integrity as human beings puts us in proper relation with others, with the universe, and ultimately with God.

Prayer: **Heavenly Father, you have made me by your love. Teach me what it means to be truly human and to live with integrity. Amen.**

✤A sister of the Holy Nativity—a religious order of the Episcopal Church, currently based in Santa Barbara, California.

Tuesday, September 30   Read Job 1:1; 2:1-10.

"Shall we indeed accept good from God, and shall we not accept adversity?" (NKJV)

Many people lack this understanding of what it means to be human; therefore, all their relationships are out of balance. Spouses abuse each other; parents and children find uneasy rest; business colleagues undermine one another's work; friends betray one another; human beings pollute, destroy, and kill—all for their own gain. To be truly human, to follow the example of Christ, who showed us the perfection of humanity, we must come to an acceptance of ourselves as creatures of a divine creation. This includes an acceptance of our potentialities as well as our limitations.

As we adopt a truly comprehensive approach to what being human means and to what our personal humanity means, we begin to grow into that understanding. We will also begin to grow into integrity. Integrity puts an end to a false sense of self, the lie we have perpetuated by our continued victimization by an ungodly world. As we begin to grasp the truth that we are created in the image and likeness of God, we can begin to change our behaviors and attitudes toward the life we have been given as gift.

Far from a naive fatalism of accepting both the good and the bad circumstances of life as coming to us from God who loves us; through a broken world, we begin to experience the peace that passes understanding.

Prayer: **Lord, help me to understand and accept that all things work together for good to those who love you. Help me trust that in all that happens to me you will always be with me. Amen.**

Wednesday, October 1   Read Psalm 26.

"Vindicate me, O LORD, for I have walked in my integrity. I have also trusted in the LORD; I shall not slip" (NKJV).

The great medieval monk Bernard of Clairvaux understood that his merits depended upon God's mercies. Like the psalmist, he understood God to be his ultimate judge. In this psalm, the writer opens himself to scrutiny by the All-knowing One. If he has been accused justly or unjustly by others, it does not matter. God knows the truth; God knows whether the psalmist possesses or lacks integrity.

Many Christians walk about with a burden of guilt resting heavily upon their shoulders. Often this sense of guilt is a parasite that comes from a false sense of responsibility or a misunderstanding of human frailty. How often do we accept responsibility that is not ours, and how often do we shirk responsibility that is truly ours? We spend tremendous amounts of energy by carrying perceived guilt, when the real thing is heavy enough to bear.

If we trust in the Lord's assurance, "My yoke is easy, and my burden is light" (Matt. 11:30), then we will be able to stand up under the scrutiny of God's examination. Integrity helps us assume responsibility for our true guilt and reject any false guilt. We will be able to move more freely in God's guidance.

Suggestion for meditation: **Consider all the burdens you are carrying. Which ones are really yours and which ones that you have accepted really belong to another? Picture yourself standing before the merciful gaze of God.**

Thursday, October 2   Read Hebrews 1:1-4; 2:5-12.

"But we see Jesus, who was made a little lower than the angels, for the suffering of death crowned with glory and honor, that He, by the grace of God, might taste death for everyone" (NKJV).

The recovery of humanity's lost destiny came through the humility of God in Christ Jesus, who was made a little lower than the angels. In him, our integrity as human beings is restored. Only in him do we discover what God truly intended us to be; and as we live into the integrity of our Christian commitment, we will move closer to the original intent of God for our destiny.

Jesus, in his great humility, never ceased to possess divinity, never denied his understanding of himself as Son of Man and Son of God even though he became vulnerable to the world. He never compromised his integrity when faced with questions by the religious leaders who were intent on trapping him. Jesus always centered his answers to those questions in the truth; as such, they enlightened, informed, and convicted those whom he addressed.

The Son of God did not come to earth simply to teach humanity a better way. He came; he lived; he taught. He died and was raised from the dead to help humanity become what it was meant to be. God's desire is to restore us to the perfection we lost through rebellion and sin. Yet we must learn to cooperate with the grace God offers through the humility of Christ.

Suggestion for meditation: **Consider your daily life as an experiment in honesty. Do you really live as though your destiny has been restored by the sacrifice of Christ on the cross? What could be different if you lived more honestly?**

Friday, October 3   Read Mark 10:2-16.

"And Jesus answered and said to them, 'Because of the hardness of your heart [Moses] wrote you this precept'" (NKJV).

Integrity opposes legalism. Jesus met this challenge from the Pharisees by questioning the need for the law. Instead of trying to find a loophole in the law so a person could legally get out of a commitment or contractual agreement, Jesus pressed the Pharisees to consider the implications of their question. He offered no argument about the various categories, the various violations that make divorce possible. Instead, he offered a restatement of the true intention of marriage.

Too often we are looking for excuses that will aid us in disguising our true intentions and desires. A person of integrity works hard, often against tough odds, to fulfill the responsibility and commitment once freely made.

Moses gave his people a loophole because their hearts were hard and their ears were deaf to the deeper truths. They lacked integrity. He knew that divorce was not God's desire or intention for humanity. Over and over in scripture we hear the plea to not harden your hearts. Yet for many this has become second nature. And just what is hardness of heart? It is wanting what *I* want, when *I* want it, regardless of others and the will of God.

Prayer: **Lord Jesus, soften my heart that I may seek only what accords with your will. Give me the courage and strength to live up to my responsibilities and to meet all my commitments. Amen.**

Saturday, October 4   Read Mark 10:2-16.

"Assuredly, I say to you, whoever does not receive the kingdom of God as a little child will by no means enter it" (NKJV).

The qualities of humility, peace, and joy do not earn children a place in the kingdom. It is not their purity or their innocence but rather their powerlessness—their vulnerability, their need for help—that makes them fit for entrance into that kingdom. Children have neither social influence nor personal strength upon which to rely. All they can do is trust the parent or guardian. Part of integrity is the acknowledgment that ultimately we are not in charge of our life, not in control of our destiny.

Children usually have a keen sense of integrity. They are honest sometimes to the embarrassment of many adults. As they grow, as they begin more and more to mimic the adults and older children around them; they often lose their sense of integrity. For many, life becomes topsy-turvy and right and wrong no longer have clear and distinguishable boundaries.

Children are drawn to truth naturally, even when clothed in the fantasy of story. Adults who have lost their childlike neart become blind to the truth when it lies beneath the surface. We cease to look past the obvious, to go deeper into the heart of the matter. Children look into our eyes to find truth because instinctively they know that through the eyes one can read the heart, the dwelling place of integrity.

Prayer: **Heavenly Father, let me look into your eyes and find there my protection, my comfort, and my true identity as your beloved child. Amen.**

Sunday, October 5   Read Psalm 26.

"But as for me, I will walk in my integrity; Redeem me and be merciful to me" (NKJV).

To walk in integrity is our personal choice. It is the choice of being fully human, of becoming what God intends us to be. We make this choice daily, sometimes moment by moment. The psalmist's prayer for redemption was a cry for help in making the right choices, in having his heart turned toward God and toward righteousness. Yet he knew he was weak, unable to accomplish all that God required, so we hear him plead his case and then ask for mercy.

God sets high standards for creation, yet we see God's love in the mercy with which God judges those who fail to live up to divine standards. God redeems the wayward, saves the broken, and urges on those who continue to call upon God. One of the biggest differences between God's standards and human standards is that our standards lack mercy. God continues to love, encourage, support, and grace God's children even when they fall. Mercy tempers God's chastisement; God's creatures continue to live in the assurance of love, while we are yet sinners. Human standards—often even a parent's standards—have strings attached. Those who fail to meet the standards of society live in fear of rejection and abandonment. To be truly Christian standards, we must temper our standards with mercy.

Suggestion for meditation: **Think about the ways you have showed mercy to those who have failed to meet your standards. Think about the times you yourself have failed. Did you experience only judgment or was judgment tempered by mercy?**

WHEN GOD SEEMS FAR AWAY

October 6–12, 1997   **Richard Bowyer**✤
Monday, October 6   Read Job 23:1-9.

When you cannot sense God's nearness

For many who lead worship or study groups at church, Monday is often a day when God seems far away. Pastors, teachers, and musicians give their all on Sunday. Monday is a time of emptiness and loneliness.

Others live with emptiness and loneliness over extended periods. Tragedy, death, disappointment, disillusionment, and other experiences create barriers between the believer and God. Job was every person. He experienced every conceivable loss: broken and strained relationships; alienation; loss of status, health, and material possessions.

Job expresses feelings often stated to pastors and counselors or uttered to a spouse or intimate friend: "If I knew where to find God, I would go there"(CEV). Job was a role model for us in such times. The completion of verse 3 and the rest of our text is an affirmation of faith: "If I knew where to find God, I would go there and argue my case." Job has not lost faith; he has lost touch with God. Only deep faith can propose to find God, stand in God's presence, and assert one's innocence. It is the act of one who knows that "God is always at work, though I never see him" (CEV).

Perhaps it was familiarity with this passage that led a Moravian pastor to advise John Wesley to preach faith until he had it.

Prayer: **God, wherever you are, I plead my case and trust your justice and mercy. Amen.**

✤Campus minister for The Wesley Foundation at Fairmont State College, Fairmont, West Virginia.

Tuesday, October 7   Read Job 23:1-9; 16-17.

When you want to complain and there's no one to listen

Life offers much about which to complain. The pressures of living often cause frustration. For those whose ministry or vocation involves dealing with others, such pressure and frustration can prove difficult to bear.

For those living alone it can be overwhelming when there is no one to hear or to listen. The complexities for those who do not live alone may also prevent needed sharing. When two people have burdens, problems, frustrations, or complaints to be heard, who is there to listen?

We have been conditioned to pray in structured ways: prayers of petition, thanksgiving, intercession, or confession. For those for whom praying is part of the "job," prayer can be difficult in private and personal times of need.

When life seems to be falling apart, when stress begins to tear away at the very fabric of our lives, when our efforts go unnoticed or unappreciated, or when we are misunderstood or mistrusted, God often seems to be on a leave of absence. At times you need to complain, and even God is not there to hear.

So much of Job's experience is like our own. His frustration and distress are common to all who walk this journey of life. Job's tenacity was awesome.

Job held on because he knew—as surely as we do—that "God is always at work, though I never see him" (CEV). Job's relationship with God was such that he could honestly reveal his feelings, express his concerns, issue his demands, and utter his complaints. Job knew that God knew his pain, even when God's presence was not apparent. In other words, God is there for us even when it seems that God is not here with us.

Prayer: **Thank you, God, for the freedom to share my complaints with you. Amen.**

293

Wednesday, October 8   Read Psalm 22:1-10.

When it seems God has deserted you

Although Jesus quoted this scripture from the cross, it reflects a sentiment we may feel today. Many times we have uttered or heard a parishioner, close friend, or associate exclaim, "God, . . . why are you so far away? . . . I cry out day and night, but you don't answer" (CEV).

It is not merely the cry of the disillusioned or of those confronted with tragic news of someone's death or diagnosis of a terminal illness. It is not reserved for those who have lost a job or a mate or who may have been hurt by some bureaucratic action of a committee. It is the cry of burnout. God seems far away. We feel deserted. Prayer goes unanswered. Our cries fall on deaf ears.

In such times this psalm can guide us. Like Job, the psalmist is a person of faith. That faith in the God of our ancestors will bring us through. Verses 3-5 recall that the "holy God, . . . praised by Israel" rescued our ancestors, saved them when they cried for help, and did not let them down. Verses 9 and 10 recall that it was God who brought the psalmist safely through birth and infancy to the present moment.

It is the recalling of faith and trust that brings light to the darkness. The powerful resonance of the holy God is present even in God's absence, and that brings us through.

Prayer: **God, even when it seems you have left me to die, and you do not answer my cries; yet I will join with Israel to praise the holy God. Amen.**

Thursday, October 9   Read Psalms 22:14-15;
                                           Hebrews 4:12-16.

When your strength has dried up

Often scripture can help us interpret scripture. The lectionary readings provide such a tool. When we read the anguish of Psalm 22:14-15 alongside Hebrews 4:12-16, we gain a new insight on the psalm.

Often the pressures of ministry leave us convinced that our strength "has dried up" (CEV), our "bones are out of joint," and our heart "is like melted wax" (CEV). But the power of these texts rests in their response to the very anguish they describe. How often in those times of near despair, utter frustration, and virtual emptiness does the word of God cut through our joints and marrow?

One of the tragedies or travesties of much popular religion is its superficiality. We do not allow our relationship with God to cut to our deepest feelings. Like beauty, much of our religion is only skin-deep. Spiritual giants we have known have experienced the depths described by the psalmist. And in those depths, they have discovered the two-edged sword of God as the very force that touched the marrow of their bones and refreshed their dryness with living water.

The good news is that God cuts through our spirits and souls, our joints and marrow, until God discovers the desires and thoughts of our hearts. Denial often is the greatest obstacle to vital and active faith, to freedom and joy. But the cutting edge of God's word leaves nothing hidden. God "sees through everything, and we will have to tell [God] the truth" (Heb. 4:13, CEV). Perhaps that is the truth that sets us free.

Prayer: **The truth, O God, is that my soul is parched and my strength dried up without you. Amen.**

Friday, October 10   Read Psalm 22:11-13;
Hebrews 4:12-16.

When you feel surrounded

At times we feel just like the psalmist. It seems as if enemies or, at the very least, problems and demands are all around. They seem to be charging like wild bulls and roaring lions.

My favorite scene in the play and movie *Jesus Christ Superstar* is that moment when Jesus screams. He screams because at every turn all he can see and hear are people reaching, grasping, and pleading. They all want his attention and blessing. Anyone involved in ministry has been there. It must be like that for the mother trapped at home with several crying and pleading children. I like that scene in the play because it affirms my sense that Jesus knows exactly how I feel sometimes.

Our text from Hebrews offers that same assurance. God's word cuts through everything "until it discovers the desires and thoughts of our hearts" (CEV). At such demanding times, that desire may simply be, "Help!"

The psalmist's prayer is instructive. He does not make great demands on God. He does not plead for removal from the situation. The psalmist prays a prayer that can only come from the deep faith: "Don't stay far off when I am in trouble with no one to help me" (CEV). What more could one ask for in times of trouble than to have God near?

Unfortunately our prayers of petition are usually more complex. We demand a way out of the situation. Often our prayers are for God to turn those raging bulls into puppy dogs and those roaring lions into purring kittens.

Prayer: **Lord, in every time of trouble remind me that you are never far away. Amen.**

296

Saturday, October 11   Read Mark 10:17-31.

When you are tempted to go away gloomy and sad

Several years ago a revival preacher in a conservative country church proclaimed to his shocked hearers: "The problem with you is you are too liberal!" He quickly added, "Yes, you're so liberal you take everything I say and apply it to other people."

We are too liberal in our application of the story of the rich man. The cartoon character Pogo said of the enemy, "he is us." Our possessions, properties, and pensions often become our prisons. We lose the freedom to risk for the sake of others.

So easily and often our faithfulness becomes perfunctory. We may keep the commandments, but it is more of a safekeeping approach. We protect, defend, and preserve them far more than we practice them.

Often when genuine opportunities for ministry arise, we too go "away gloomy and sad" (CEV). Perhaps the rise of burnout and lack of joy in ministry is due to the fact that, by whatever standards, we are very rich.

The other poignant message of Jesus in this passage is often overlooked. We are so tempted to hear only what we want to hear or that which sounds good. His promise in verses 29-30 sounds so good: "You can be sure that anyone who gives up . . . [everything] for me and for the good news will be rewarded" (CEV). The promise is for a hundredfold blessings of material good and "in the world to come, they will have eternal life." But hidden in those words of promise is a very powerful phrase: "though they will also be mistreated!" We can realize the glorious riches of God, both in this world and the next, only through suffering. The cross precedes resurrection.

Prayer: Lord, free me from the material things that possess me, that I may know the joy of serving others. Amen.

Sunday, October 12   Read Mark 10:17-31.

When we acknowledge our riches

Riches of any sort may be an obstacle to salvation. Whether money, land, or inordinate clinging to family, possessions may possess us. The history of ancient Israel parallels the personal journeys of many who find general prosperity to be a distraction to service to others and to trust in God.

But that need not be so. Churches continue to create opportunities to put one's material gains to the immediate and long-range benefit of others. Stories abound of persons of moderate means who invested well and left substantial gifts to the mission and ministry of local churches and to others.

Following the Civil War, many former slaves founded benevolent societies as they prospered with hard work, wise investments, and sound business. African Americans not only helped one another but contributed to the economic well-being of their larger communities.[*]

The exciting stories of church-based community economic development projects through Shalom Zones, cooperative ministries, and other organizations offer ways to fulfill Jesus' promise of a hundredfold increase. While riches often are a needle's eye passage to God's kingdom; when used in God's service, they may be a gateway to blessings for oneself and others.

Suggestion for meditation: **Pause and reflect on your possessions and investments. How might they be better used through wise stewardship to God's glory? What possibilities exist through your church and community to enhance economic development for the poor? Who do you know that can be approached after prayerful consideration to use their wealth and influence in such ways?**

----

[*]James A. Joseph, *Remaking America* (Jossey-Bass, San Francisco: 1995).

DEPENDENCE, OBEDIENCE, AND FREEDOM

October 13–19, 1997   **Larry R. Kalajainen**✤
Monday, October 13   Read Job 38:1-7.

The story of Job is, at the very least, great literature. For centuries, it has spoken eloquently to one of humankind's most enduring questions: Why do bad things happen to good people? Job, the innocent and righteous man, loses all he has—his property, his family, and even his health. His wife counsels angry defiance in the face of God's injustice; his friends and comforters recommend ruthless self-examination and penitent confession of secret sin, which must be incurring God's wrath. Throughout, however, Job refuses to confess that he is a secret sinner or to charge God with being a capricious and cruel deity. He does demand an explanation from God; and in today's lesson God begins to answer.

The Lord answers Job out of a whirlwind, a common biblical symbol for the mystery that hides God from human gaze. It is not for Job to question God; it is for God to question Job. Job's sufferings, like the sufferings all of us undergo in life, always have the character of an interrogation. The pains, the disappointments, the losses we experience demand a response from us. We frequently get it backwards. When bad things happen, we demand a reason. We want to know why. But the why is cloaked in mystery; we can no more understand why than we can understand how God laid the cornerstones of the universe. What we can and must do is respond to our sufferings, either in self-pity or anger; or like Job, with trust in the face of mystery.

Suggestion for meditation: **Am I willing to acknowledge the mystery of suffering and trust God to care for me in the midst of life's trials?**

✤Senior pastor of The American Church in Paris; ordained United Methodist minister; author of several books on spirituality published by The Upper Room.

Tuesday, October 14   Read Job 38:34-41.

God's interrogation of Job forces Job to take a longer view of his situation. It forces Job to look beyond his own personal misery and suffering to consider the orderliness and design observable in the universe. If Job can enlarge his angle of view, perhaps he will see that his suffering, though beyond comprehension, is no more so than the orderly workings of the physical world, which he takes for granted. God's appeal in this rehearsal of the wonders of creation is for Job to trust God's sovereignty and wisdom in his own personal situation just as Job trusts God's creative order of the seasons, the weather, and God's providential care for the wild animals. If the orderliness of the physical universe bears witness to a competent Creator, can Job not trust the Creator's competence in regard to his own life?

While this line of reasoning might not appeal to someone who is a thoroughgoing materialist, it does have a certain logic for people of faith. One of the insidious effects of any kind of suffering, is that it tends to reduce the world to the size of one's own misery. Pain, bereavement, or trauma has the power to wonderfully concentrate our attention. Our own predicament looms so large that we can see nothing else around. The sufferer is always in danger of becoming wholly self-centered.

What we may need at such times is the ability to see our own situation in a larger frame of reference. This frame of reference will not answer the questions Why? or Why me?, but it may help call forth a response other than despair. It may permit us to trust in the love and sovereignty of God as Job did.

Suggestion for meditation: **Am I willing to trust in God's care for me, even when my situation casts doubt upon that care?**

Wednesday, October 15   Read Hebrews 4:14–5:10.

The writer of Hebrews, taking his point of departure from the Hebrew Scriptures' descriptions of the role of the high priest in Israel's worship, describes Jesus as our high priest. The task of the priest, he says, is to represent the people before God in all their human frailty and sinfulness. A good priest undertakes this awesome task with humility and gentleness, because he knows that he too is mortal; he too is a sinner. Moreover, the high priest does not choose this office; he is chosen and called to it by God.

Jesus fulfills all the qualifications of the ideal high priest, with one very important addition: He did not yield to sin when brought to the ultimate test. He is able to identify with us in our human frailty, because in every respect he has been tested as we are. No temptation, no trial, no adversity, nothing that touches any human being can ever be alien to God. Jesus has experienced it all.

This is the marvelous meaning of the Incarnation. Because of Jesus our representative, God knows intimately what it means to be human, to be mortal, to be subject to weakness and temptation. Just as the high priest, in a sense, bears the people in himself as he stands before God, so Jesus as our representative takes our humanity up into God. The third-century bishop Athanasius said, "He became what we are that he might make us what he is." Incarnation is not so much a lowering of the divine as it is a raising up of the human. Dust we may be, but because of the work of our high priest, we are glorious dust.

Suggestion for meditation: **If salvation means a raising of my humanity to the divine, what concrete form will this salvation take in my life?**

Thursday, October 16   Read Hebrews 4:14–5:10.

It is probably accurate to say that the primal fear of all human beings is the fear of death. Death represents our unmaking. Death is Not-Being. The writer of Hebrews implies that Jesus not only shared our human nature fully but shared this deepest fear as well. Yet it was not simply Jesus' fearful cry to God to save him from death that gained God's approval; rather, the writer says, it was because of his reverent submission . . . he learned obedience through what he suffered.

This submission, this obedience, was not a passive surrender to death; it was an active surrender to God. It was not the defeated surrender of a beaten enemy to a powerful conqueror but the willing surrender of a Beloved to the Lover. Jesus could give himself over to death's power to destroy, because he first gave himself up to God's loving will and purpose. He trusted himself into the hands of the only One who can create life. Jesus did not save himself, nor did he rise from the dead by his own power. Jesus' resurrection is nothing less than a new act of creation by God. It is God alone who is the Source and Author of life; by Jesus' submission to God, by his obedience to God's will, even in the face of his own unmaking, he did what God wants every person to do—to trust God for his or her very life. Because of his obedient trust, Jesus is the source of eternal salvation for all who obey him. To place ourselves wholly in God's hands by active surrender is to follow Jesus into Life.

Suggestion for meditation: **On what am I staking my very existence? In whom am I placing my ultimate trust? What will it mean for me to be obedient?**

Friday, October 17   Read Mark 10:35-45.

The role of the disciples in Mark's Gospel is often to be foils for, or negative examples of, the point Mark is making. Mark deliberately sets the ambitious request of James and John immediately after Jesus has announced his coming passion for the third time. James and John are speaking of position and power and precedence. Like the other disciples most of the time in this Gospel, they just don't get it. To use a contemporary expression, they are clueless.

Jesus sets them straight with a rather blunt reply, "You do not know what you are asking." The fact that they are ambitious is not, in itself, a bad thing. Ambition can be a powerful spur to action. When channeled and disciplined in service to a larger purpose than one's own aggrandizement or self-interest, ambition often can mean the difference between success and failure in an enterprise. But ambition is always dangerous because it is so easily deflected toward self-promotion. The good of the enterprise becomes indistinguishable from the good of the ambitious person.

Jesus was ambitious for the doing of God's will, for the flowering of God's rule in human life. He did not shrink from that ambition, even though it cost him his life. His stark question to James and John, "Are you able to drink the cup that I drink?" should, at the least, give us pause before we reach for our hymnals to sing a rousing chorus of "Lord, we are able." If we are not to answer that question as glibly as James and John, we first need to examine the roots and the goals of our ambition.

Suggestion for meditation: **To what is my ambition directed: God's will or my own success?**

Saturday, October 18   Read Mark 10:35-45.

The misdirected ambition of James and John leads to strife within the community of disciples. Jesus' response points the way to peaceful relationships and personal freedom. Strife is the natural by-product of self-centered ambition. When one is working primarily to further one's own interests, even when that interest is camouflaged behind religious piety or pragmatic rationalizations, others are viewed as means to further one's own ends. They become objects to be manipulated rather than persons to be loved. Small wonder that persons become angry when devalued.

The ambition to be great is a legitimate ambition, as Jesus makes very clear, so long as we understand that greatness from Jesus' perspective. The person who achieves greatness is not the one who lords it over others but the one who lifts others up by serving them. This is obviously not the way the world understands greatness. The world seeks greatness through coercive power; the disciple knows to find it in loving service. The model for this redefinition of greatness is Jesus. Verse 45 is the climactic statement of the entire Gospel of Mark: "For the Son of Man came not to be served but to serve, and to give his life a ransom for many."

The paradox of discipleship is that loving, sacrificial service to others is not only the way to become truly great, but it is the road to personal freedom as well. Only those who can give themselves away are truly free. When we serve only our own interests, we become imprisoned within the confining walls of that demanding self; we are isolated and alone. When we serve the needs of others, we breach those walls and discover love; and love is never lonely.

Suggestion for meditation: **What changes must there be in my life in order to become great?**

Sunday, October 19   Read Psalm 104:1-9, 24, 35.

We began this week with God's interrogation of long-suffering Job. God demands to know why Job feels justified in calling God to account for his sufferings when Job is incapable of understanding the mysteries of creation. We end the week with a calm and beautiful hymn that celebrates God's power and wisdom as revealed in the created world. The psalm exudes a quiet, yet awe-filled confidence in God. It celebrates not only the wonders of creation; it celebrates the God of creation. "O Lord my God, you are very great. . . . You stretch out the heavens . . . you make the clouds your chariot . . . you make the winds your messengers. . . . you set the earth on its foundations" . . . *you . . . you . . . you.*

This is the voice of one who has learned full well his own creatureliness and is content. The speaker knows that human power can never create nor human wisdom fathom all the mysteries and wonders of weather and wind and tides. Therefore, the speaker is content to play his own role in that order, that of the human subject, whose duty and glory it is to contemplate what God has done and respond with praise and blessing. There is no note of compulsion, no dissonant chords of fear or anxiety; there is only a melody of praise interwoven with the harmony of a soul who has learned that submission to God leads not to slavery but to freedom, not to subjection but to the dignity for which humans were created. When the psalmist exclaims, "O LORD how manifold are your works! In wisdom you have made them all; the earth is full of your creatures," he includes himself among them and is at peace.

Suggestion for meditation: **Am I content to be God's creature? Can I trust the God whose wisdom is revealed in creation?**

305

October 20–26, 1997
Monday, October 20

Arturio Mariscal✤
Read Job 42:1-6.

"My ears had heard of you but now my eyes have seen you" (NIV). Every time I read or hear this scripture, I think of my father-in-law. He went through a lot of suffering while growing up in Mexico. He was very poor. He had only his mother and many brothers and sisters.

When his mother brought all of her family to Texas, they still had to struggle to survive. Even as a young married man, times were hard for him. What made a big difference in his life was the experience he had with his Lord. Something wonderful happened when the family came to the USA; they found the Lord. Through their experience with the church, many things changed.

My father-in-law was still poor, but he was happy. One day while at his work in a lumberyard, he felt the call to be a minister. He immediately stopped his work and went to tell his boss: "I am leaving; today is my last day. I am going to be a minster." Many times I remember his preaching or witnessing. "My ears had heard of you but now my eyes have seen." That was his experience with the Lord, and he lived it.

Prayer: **Lord, even though I go through a lot of struggles, you have something special in mind for me. Amen.**

✤United Methodist clergy member, Río Grande Conference; pastor, Kelsey Memorial United Methodist Church, Corpus Christi, Texas.

Tuesday, October 21   Read Job 42:10-1

Let us recall that one reason Job was suffering was because God allowed it. Job was a good man who was "blameless and upright; he feared God" (Job 1:1, NIV). To understand Job's suffering, it is important that we see the whole picture of Job's life.

Despite all that happened to him, Job was faithful to the end. Even then, he surrendered completely to God's will. Job's repentance opened the door for other blessings. Job was able to pray for his three friends, and God blessed Job twice as much as before.

What should be of greatest importance to us is how we live our lives and how we face the end of our lives. Job lived an abundant life with his family, his friends, and his Lord (see verse 17).

When I came to serve as pastor of my current church, I felt blessed because I was going to have an associate pastor. But as it turned out, he fell ill and soon afterward passed away. His living witness, his ministry, and his wonderful relationship with his family made an impact on the lives of many, as well as my own life. During his ministry he would pass out small aluminum crosses. That was his "trademark." During the funeral his family distributed crosses to representatives of the various congregations where he had served. As the crosses were given, the statement was made, "Take this cross and pass it on, for he will no longer have need of it."

How true! He like Job had lived a full life. At the end of his journey it could be said of him too: "And he died, old and full of years" (NIV).

Prayer: **Lord, your mercies will carry me through the hardest trials, pains, and suffering. Amen.**

Wednesday, October 22   Read Psalm 34:1-4.

Have you ever had a prayer meeting of just praise and thanksgiving? Try it; you will find it to be a wonderful experience.

If we were to analyze our prayers, I think we would discover that by habit we spend more time *asking* than *thanking* our Lord for God's blessings. In counting our blessings, it may surprise us to realize that the Lord gives us blessing after blessing.

Most of the psalms are songs or prayers. Psalm 34 is, without a doubt, a song. The writer invites everyone to praise the Lord: those who are afflicted, those who are sick, those who have problems, those who are suffering. The psalmist invites all to praise God, along with those, who by the mercies of God, are fulfilled. In such joyful praise, we can experience the joy and peace of the Lord.

I am sure having a prayer meeting of praise and thanksgiving is not an original idea. Persons of faith have been doing this since before the time of the psalms. But for me and my wife this form of prayer and worship was a new discovery.

At first my concern centered around finishing too quickly—having too few items to list. What a surprise! Our prayer of thanksgiving lasted longer than our regular mixed prayer of petition and praise. It is so wonderful to know that God's loving mercies continue to manifest themselves in our lives. Much more would happen if we would only let God guide us in all we do and think and say.

Prayer: **Thank you, Lord, for new opportunities I receive to experience your loving mercies. Amen.**

Thursday, October 23   Read Psalm 34:5-8.

If we read the history of David we realize that his life was full of struggle, persecution, and anxiety. No wonder he depended so much on the Lord for balance in his life. David depended on the Lord, knowing that anyone who trusted in the Lord would find shelter in times of trouble.

By simply reading Psalm 34:5-8, we find such words as *anxiety*, *trouble*, *desperation*, *assurance*, and *security*. These verses also depict our security in the Lord. If we learn to trust in the Lord, we find rest and peace. Our faith grows when we experience the Lord's response to our requests. These verses affirm that we can experience God's goodness in a very special way.

Isn't it true that often the testimony and experience of others invite us to trust in the Lord? The psalm is an open invitation to call upon the Lord—to know that God is close to us forever. Despite our troubles and anxieties, our looking to the Lord can bring comfort and peace. Our faces will be radiant because God's presence is real in our lives.

Prayer: **Lord, give me the faith I need to live each day as it comes. Amen.**

Friday, October 24   Read Hebrews 7:23-28.

Just as the priests in the Hebrew Scriptures were limited in their priesthood, so are we limited because of our humanity and our mortality. Jesus, on the other hand, is our eternal priest. He lives and reigns forever. He is our new covenant. We are no longer under the law of Moses but under the loving care of our Lord Jesus Christ. Jesus Christ, our priest, has the power to save us. We only have to come to him penitently. He can save us from our troubles, our pains, and our anxieties. Most of all, he can save us from our sins and give us eternal life.

If we were to ask the bank for a loan, first we would need to make an application. Then we would need to offer something we own as collateral or someone to guarantee the note. The bank wants to be sure to get its money. Jesus as our eternal priest guarantees before God that through his loving grace we are secure. Jesus Christ has paid our debt. We do not have to offer any more sacrifices because he offered himself once and for all.

By accepting Jesus as our priest, we take in his holiness. When we allow him into our lives, we are saying that he is our loving sacrifice. By affirming him as our priest, we become clean and there is nothing inside of us but God's lovingkindness.

The blessedness of our Lord is real—at home, at church, at work, at play—wherever faithful persons have reached out to Christ and said to him, "You are my priest."

Prayer: **Lord, today I accept you as my priest. Amen.**

Saturday, October 25   Read Mark 10:46-48.

In this week's scriptures, we find a common thread—the mercy of our Lord. We see it in the Book of Job, in Psalm 34, in Hebrews, and now in Mark.

Here we see Bartimaeus—a blind beggar with a big need, surrounded by a great, noisy crowd. Did someone go and tell Jesus, "There is a beggar back there who wants to see you"? No, Bartimaeus's own *persistence* and shouting caught the kind and compassionate ear of Jesus. "Son of David, have mercy on me!"

Jesus and the crowd were almost outside the city of Jericho. The blind man was being left behind; his hope was fading. Those who passed by and heard him were demanding that he be quiet, but his determination would not let him. He did not intend to allow this opportunity (perhaps his last and best hope for sight) to pass. So he persisted in shouting at the top of his voice, "Jesus, Son of David, have mercy on me!"

Although Bartimaeus could not see, he could hear. Probably he knew about Jesus and had heard about the miracles Jesus had performed. If so, he *knew* that Jesus was the person he had to confront with his trouble. In desperation, Bartimaeus kept on; his faith told him that he was going to be heard.

Wouldn't it be wonderful if the church was as desperate, as determined, as persistent in its seeking of the Lord? How many more miracles would be taking place in our lives if we would hold fast to the kernel of hope placed within our hearts by our faith? How many more miracles would we experience, would we see in others, if we allowed the Lord Jesus to act in our lives?

We can be blind in our pews as we pretend to follow ritual in hollow worship. We cannot rightly lift up a creed, a prayer, or a song to the Lord until we feel that same deep need and desire to meet Jesus as did Bartimaeus.

Prayer: **"Son of David, have mercy on me." Amen.**

Sunday, October 26   Read Mark 10:49-52.

No rebuke, no crowd, or anything else is going to stop you from reaching out to the only one that has the answer to your need. So, like Bartimaeus, you persist until you know by the silence of the crowd that things have changed.

Suddenly you hear Jesus' voice say, "Call him." Your persistence has prevailed. There is an invitation—"Cheer up! On your feet! He is calling you." What will you do with God's calling? Bartimaeus went into action. He got up, put his cloak aside, and moved. Everything happened so quickly; before he realized it, he was before the Master.

If your need is great, and you are desperate like Bartimaeus, you will do the same. You will jump and move quickly to stand before the Lord. Now for the big question (be ready to answer): "What do you want me to do?" Yes, Jesus is asking. What is your response? Bartimaeus did not take long to respond; he already knew what he wanted: "Rabbi, I want to see."

Whatever your need or your problem, be assured that the Lord will stop to listen to you, and he will ask, "What is it that you need?" And you will respond according to your need. Be assured that you will hear the voice of God saying, "Your faith has healed you. It is your faith that has given you what you need."

This is not the end of Bartimaeus's story. "Immediately he received his sight and followed Jesus." Bartimaeus was a person of gratitude. He did not go his own way; he followed Jesus. He showed his faithfulness, for his need had been met. That is the least we also can do and that is what God expects of us—gratitude and faithfulness. What a way to be a disciple!

Prayer: **For your mercies, Lord, we are thankful. Amen.**

THE SAINTS—PAST, PRESENT, AND FUTURE

October 27–November 2, 1997 **Betsy Schwarzentraub✣**
Monday, October 27 Read Psalm 146.

Praise for a lifetime

This week leads up to All Saints' Day and All Souls' Day, November 1 and 2, respectively, when we thank God for people who live as models of faith, whether in past, present, or future generations.

Who are the saints? They are the "holy ones," those called faithful and righteous who are driven to live for God's justice in both attitude and action. Revelation pictures them gathered around Christ's throne, praising God at the end of time.

The last five psalms serve as the final doxology of praise. Praise is the hallmark of Psalm 146, which is the first of the final hallelujah psalms. "Happy are those whose help is the God of Jacob, . . . who made heaven and earth, . . . who keeps faith forever; who executes justice for the oppressed."

The saints are not perfect people. They simply depend upon God and trust God with their lives. They rely upon the guiding God of human history, the faithful God of all creation, the compassionate God of justice.

Praise is the mark of holy living not because life is easy but because the work of love is so great. The saints have enough praise for a lifetime and are willing to live it out.

"I will praise the LORD as long as I live; I will sing praises to my God all my life long."

Suggestion for meditation: Who have been models for my faith journey so far? Have I thanked those who are still around me for how they have modeled trust in God?

✣Church consultant; clergy member of the California-Nevada Conference of The United Methodist Church; David, California.

Tuesday, October 28   Read Ruth 1:1-18.

A lifelong commitment

At first blush, Ruth the Moabite seems an unlikely saint and her bond with her mother-in-law a strange kind of fidelity. She reminds us that we do not have to limit family to those born into the same household. A family can also be people who choose to care for one another.

When Ruth's husband and father-in-law dies, the grieving Naomi proposes that Ruth return to her homeland to fend for herself. In their societies, without husbands, sons, or uncles, women ceased to be persons. They were left without a man to act as clan connection, closest of kin, and advocate for justice. Ruth and Naomi had no identity, no rights, no future, no way to make a living, and no people among whom to live.

When Naomi decides to return to her homeland of Judah, she encourages Ruth to return to her mother's home. Ruth refuses to leave her, saying, "Where you go, I will go; where you lodge, I will lodge." Ruth vowed, "Your people shall be my people, and your God my God."

Ruth goes to Judah with Naomi and marries a kind provider. All the pieces fall into place. Naomi becomes a grandmother, blessed and connected with her people. The story of Ruth affirms that there are no outsiders in God's family—no matter where people come from or what their background. Through their bold action, saints like Ruth and Naomi make a lifelong commitment, revealing the God who chooses to travel with us and to claim us as God's people.

Prayer: Dear God, you are my redeemer, closest of kin, and the one who saves me. I cling to you and will follow you, no matter where you would have me go. Amen.

Wednesday, October 29   Read Isaiah 25:6-9.

A living reunion

First Isaiah spoke to a forlorn people living in a corrupted land. Those who clung to their faith hungered for justice for the working poor: those whose livelihood was pouring into the pockets of the rich. Their society was parched for compassion. Their focus was on wealth no matter what the cost. So God gave the people hope even in the midst of needed judgment—the vision of a day when their hunger and thirst would be satisfied.

First would come the judgment. Soon an army would overthrow their leaders and ruin their homeland. The people would become prisoners of war, enduring a full generation of exile in a foreign land. Only after that would a chastened remnant be allowed to return.

But alongside that stunning judgment, Isaiah promised fulfillment. He vowed they would feast on God's living presence, God's character of holiness made real in human lives. For the Israelites, like ourselves, this personal presence overshadows everything else, even the loss of loved ones and home. God's presence swallows up death forever, so it no longer has final say over our lives.

When we are in exile or isolation, the reality is that God is with us, Emmanuel. This is a taste of the feast that nourishes us and gives us inner resilience to make it through the times of exile and isolation. Beyond all the exiles of this life, the full banquet awaits us.

The saints are those who look forward to that final feast in God's presence. Their way of living offers a foretaste of God's justice and compassion here and now.

Suggestion for meditation: **Where do I see people in need? Where is God's presence in my midst? How can my life reflect God's heavenly banquet right where I am now?**

Thursday, October 30   Read Mark 12:28-34.

Living praises

After the people returned from Exile, their sacred writings reflected two essential strands of holiness: a way of being that was continual worship, and a way of acting that was ethical toward others.

Jesus also voiced this inseparable combination when a rabbi asked him to name the greatest commandment in the Torah. Jesus answered that we are to love God with all that we are and love our neighbor as ourself. Together these form one commandment, which is the greatest of all.

Here is a way of being. It means loving God with our "heart"— the way in which our life leans, our lifestyle, the direction of our life. It means loving God with our "soul"—our life breath (the Hebrew translation), our existence. It means loving God with our "mind"—including our intellect, reason, and imagination. It means loving God with our "strength"—our physical self.

But loving God is also action. We cannot separate who we are from how we live. Throughout the Hebrew Scriptures and New Testament, the scriptures declare that God cares equally for all people, showing "no partiality" (Acts 10:34) and that we are to act the same way, not distorting justice (Deut. 16:19).

Jesus made the radical connection that the only way we can show our love of God is by loving and caring for our neighbor. Jesus called us to care for neighbor by acting on behalf of "the least of these"—our human brothers and sisters (Matt. 25:40, 45). Holiness is worshipful being and everyday action.

Suggestion for meditation: **How could I embody praise of God as part of a community of "holy ones"? How could I work with others, turning worship into deed for people in need?**

Friday, October 31   Read John 11:32-44.

Life renewed

"Lazarus, come out!" Jesus shouted to the four-day-old corpse of his friend.

The mourners gasped as the dead man emerged. Lazarus inched his way forward into the light, brought back to life but still bound within the bandages that had sealed him neatly away from the living. Jesus turned to the crowd of astonished mourners and said, "Unbind him, and let him go."

At least two miracles took place that day. One was Jesus' doing—restoring life and personality to a human body that already had begun to decay. But the other wonder perhaps was even greater. It was the work of the community as people edged their way to the upright body of their neighbor. It was a moment both of terror and joy as they stood face-to-face with his utter vulnerability, not knowing what lay beneath the bandages that covered him from head to toe. Then one person dared to begin unwrapping his bonds.

Through Jesus' direct action, people die to their old lives and arrive at a new beginning, a brand new life, a new birth (see Romans 6:4; John 3:3-5). But without human help in a worshiping, serving community, they remain bound up in death, not knowing how to live the new life that Christ has given them.

"Unbind him, and let him go," Jesus said. This is the work of the church; the work of everyday, extraordinary saints.

Prayer: **Thank you, God, for those persons who were willing to unwrap the bandages that bound me to my old, dead life and who trusted in your work of renewal within me. Please give me the courage to step forward in faith and help unbind others as they seek to live for you. This I pray by your grace shown supremely in Jesus. Amen.**

Saturday, November 1   Read Revelation 21:1-6.

Life with God

Holiness is not only the innermost character of God but also the quality of life we choose in response to God's presence. Those who seek to become saints—holy persons—weave together focused worship and ethical action so that God can make a home in human lives once more.

The Hebrew people spoke of the God who travels with us. Our God always has been on the move. The God of Abraham and Sarah went with the people wherever they traveled—incarnate in human lives.

God was distinctively present in Jesus but that is not the end of the incarnation. God continues to make a home in successive generations of Jesus' disciples. Individually and together, members of the community of faith are "God's temple" (1 Cor. 3:17) and "a dwelling place for God" (Eph. 2:21).

"See, the home of God is among mortals" says Revelation, declaring fulfillment of God's promises from humanity's beginning. In language that reminds us of God's promise to Abraham, Revelation declares that God will dwell with humans as their God and will be with them personally. In the end time, God promises "a new heaven and a new earth."

"See, I am making all things new," God says—not about some far-off future but about the present moment, wherever we are. For some crazy reason, God keeps deciding to dwell in the midst of human lives. God's holiness is on the move, and we can choose to be part of it.

Prayer: **God of compassion, please make a home in my life, transforming all that I do according to your will. I pray this in Jesus' name. Amen.**

Sunday, November 2   Read Psalm 24.

All life is holy

"The earth is the LORD'S and all that is in it, the world and those who live in it," declared the psalmist. This psalm is an ancient congregational litany, which was sung back and forth between two groups of worshipers at the entrance to the Jerusalem temple.

Imagine pilgrims pausing at the foot of the hill that rose up to Jerusalem. "Who shall ascend the hill of the LORD?" asked the priest. "Who shall stand in his holy place?" The people answered as one, "Those who have clean hands and pure hearts, who do not lift up their souls to what is false, and do not swear deceitfully." This answer describes someone whose integrity or inner focus matches his or her worship and moral actions.

The pilgrims continued up Jerusalem's hill, at last reaching the Temple gates. "Lift up your heads, O gates!" they cried. "That the King of glory may come in."

"Who is the King of glory?" asked those inside, who then received a description of a God who is vital and alive, strong and present with God's people.

So we come full circle in this week's readings, returning to the saints. These "holy ones" are faithful, reflecting God's righteousness. They worship and work as living praises, freeing others for new life. They hunger for justice and await an eternal feast with God. They love God with all that they are by caring for their neighbors. They claim God as their Redeemer and live as advocates for all God's people.

Prayer: **Holy God, I thank you for the saints of past, present, and future. Please give me your grace to live as a holy one for others in Jesus' name. Amen.**

GIVE TO REALLY LIVE

November 3–9, 1997   **Charles B. Simmons**❖
Monday, November 3   Read Hebrews 9:24.

Picture a place where what should be, already is—indeed, always was and shall forever be. Modern minds find it fanciful, but the ancient who wrote the Letter to the Hebrews is confident such a world exists. Influenced by Platonic thinking, he believes this idealistic yet invisible realm is, in fact, the only real world. Everything else is—like the sanctuary in the Jerusalem temple—"a mere copy of the true one." Thus, life on earth derives its "rightness" based on the degree to which it resembles the heavenly.

We need not subscribe to the author's dualism to benefit from his argument. The epistle's central thesis is that Christ gave himself as a sacrifice for us. This self-giving action is what is most real. It is therefore *the* pattern that people on earth are to emulate. Giving makes life genuine, meaningful, and worth living.

This theme underlies and unites our scripture passages this week. All affirm that to be authentic, the faithful must be self-giving. For followers of Jesus, that means to live like our Lord.

As we begin these meditations, ask yourself: "Do I want to be a *real* Christian—a giver? Where in life now am I only a *replica*?

Prayer: **Lord, my life seems but a shadow of what you created me to be. Shine through the darkness and illuminate my witness. Amen.**

❖Senior minister, Broadmoor United Methodist Church, Baton Rouge, Louisiana.

Tuesday, November 4   Read Ruth 3:1-5.

This mother-in-law surprises us. Naomi acts more like a "nineties woman" than a widow in ancient times. She goes after what she wants. Here she spells out her bold plan for securing Ruth's future by awakening Boaz to his responsibility as her kinsman.

After the barley is winnowed in the evening, the workers party merrily before sleeping on the threshing floor. Naomi instructs Ruth to make herself beautiful, then to make her move once Boaz has eaten and drunk enough to be receptive. Despite precedent in Hebrew history (Gen. 38:13), the request is radical.

Ruth's response is the real surprise. To the unseemly suggestion that she obtain her security by seduction, she offers no protest. "All that you tell me I will do," she replies obediently. She trusts that her mother-in-law has her best interests at heart. Thus Ruth gives over control of the situation, of her life, to Naomi.

To whom would you give control of your life? Past disappointments make it hard to trust others enough to place our well-being in their hands. Given human sinfulness and the need for personal responsibility, Ruth's situation calls for caution. But Ruth's willingness to let go of the reins and allow another to lead her illustrates the risks required of those who live lovingly.

Perhaps leaders are rare today because so few people have the courage to follow. Well-placed trust and careful submission are not options for a Christian, however. To know abundant life, deny yourself and follow me, Jesus said. *To really live, we must learn to give . . . over control.*

Prayer: God, when I hesitate to trust anyone other than myself to know what is best, let me turn over control to you. Amen.

321

Wednesday, November 5   Read Ruth 4:13-17.

If yesterday's reading teaches about the risks that come with selfless living, our text today reveals the rewards. Ruth's faithful response to Naomi's counsel sets in motion a series of events that reap amazing results. All the characters in the story end up with everything they wanted, and more.

Ruth gets a husband, who represents her security, and becomes a mother. Boaz gains respect both by fulfilling his duty as her kinsman and by producing a son. And Naomi receives blessings beyond her dreams. She becomes a caregiver for her new grandson, and the women of the neighborhood claim he will be for her "a restorer of life and a nourisher of your old age." They lovingly refer to the boy as the "son . . born to Naomi"!

Prior to lavishing praise upon Naomi, these women raise their voices in thanksgiving, saying, "Blessed be the LORD." The matrons have no doubt as to whom the real credit for these gifts is due. Despite Ruth's obedience, Boaz's attention to duty, and Naomi's responsible action in pursuing worthy goals, the good now evident in their lives is *ultimately* not their doing. God has blessed them. In return, they are to *offer gratitude*.

After taking similar risks and working equally hard to accomplish something in life, are you as clear about who deserves the credit? Or do you see God's hand only in those times when your role in determining the outcome is less than obvious?

Before puffing up with a pride that can rob your life of reality and joy, learn from those neighborhood women to say, "Blessed be the LORD!" Ruth never expected her faithfulness to lead to a marriage that includes as a descendant the great King David and an even greater descendant Jesus. Bless the Lord, indeed!

Prayer: **Gracious God, give me a grateful heart this day! Amen.**

Thursday, November 6   Read Psalm 127.

Earlier we introduced the need for our recognition of the source of all good things in life. Today's psalm illustrates both the extent of these blessings and the manner of praise for God's generous provision. Sung by pilgrims en route to Jerusalem, it affirms that we are wholly dependent on God in every area of life.

Consisting of five wisdom sayings, the psalm has two parts. Verses 1-2 protest the worried, frantic toil that epitomizes a worker who is unaware of a constant cooperation with God. Unless the Lord's purpose is served and human labor corresponds to heaven's work, any project is doomed. Verses 3-5 testify to the value of children and what they add to family life. Sons represented security in ancient cultures, assets that translate into strength when contending with enemies, and thus are to be cherished as "a heritage from the LORD."

What unites these sections is a common theme: *Trust in God is the key to abundant living*. No aspect of daily life is beyond the divine's activity. Even the base elements of ordinary existence— work and family—are blessings we receive. Fruitful labor and "the fruit of the womb" are not certainties guaranteed by endeavor but mysteries of grace. For human beings to anxiously or arrogantly believe that everything depends upon us is a senseless and sinful attitude. *To really live, we must give up.*

Which attitude best characterizes your daily actions: independence or dependence? Are you fretful or faithful at work? At home or elsewhere, are children you encounter taken for granted or treated as blessings, which God has entrusted into your care?

Prayer: **Lord, liberate me from the illusion that I alone am in charge of and responsible for today; teach me trust. Amen.**

Friday, November 7   Read Mark 12:38-40.

Here is Jesus' unambiguous warning to the crowd: "Beware of the scribes." These religious leaders are hypocrites to be exposed, not holy men to be emulated. He points out that scribal piety is pretentious and based upon outward appearance rather than inward purity. While they win human approval by means of "long robes," being "greeted with respect," and "places of honor," they gain God's contempt. Even worse than such egotism cloaked in religiosity is the misconduct of these legal experts in dealing with the vulnerable. Saying "long prayers" after shameless profiteering at the expense of widows only deepens their damnation.

Many debate whether such a sweeping assessment is fair to the scribal office, but few question these sayings as being utterances of Jesus. The warning mirrors his teachings about the self-giving—not self-serving—lifestyle demanded of disciples. The contrast merely illustrates the irony: Often the ones who look authentic and authoritative are actually conceited counterfeiters and condemned; whereas, those who forego earthly prestige to follow Christ's example of selfless love find life made abundant. *To really live, we must possess humility.*

From fine vestments to slick press releases, modern parallels to the vestiges of pretense and pride among religious people, particularly leaders, are easy to find. Harder is the personal discernment of the differences between one's own ways in public and in private, when no one sees. Lest you become another of Christ's targets, dare to ask him (friends too!) for an honest appraisal of the airs characterizing your witness today.

Prayer: **May you, who humbled yourself, keep me humble today. Amen.**

Saturday, November 8   Read Mark 12:41-44.

The verses preceding today's text paint a portrait of scribes who pursue personal power and prestige. Not unlike disciples, past and present, who dream of honor and places of privilege, the scribal authorities regarded religion as the art of self-advancement. Implacably egotistical, they exploited widows under the pretense of piety. Now a widow's generosity forms the ideal opposite to the scribal establishment.

Jesus calls the disciples' attention to her offering because she gives "her whole living" (RSV). The two copper coins (*leptons*, the smallest denomination of Greek-Syrian money) equal only a penny, the smallest Roman coin. Their cash value pales when compared to the "large sums" the rich proudly put into the containers outside the Temple. By contrast, the Master teaches that God cares nothing for money but measures a gift by what it represents to the giver—a percentage of abundance of one's all.

Although Jesus offers no evidence, he implies that all the other contributors that day limited their giving—retaining a portion of money for their own use. The widow stands alone as the imprudent one who turned over to God's use all she had. Those two tiny coins represented her only hope and hedge against the threat of starvation. Hence, over against the self-serving demeanor and false piety of the scribes, Jesus holds up the widow's self-giving as an example of genuine piety. Ultimately disciples trust heaven alone. *To really live, we must give away substitute security.*

Suggestion for meditation: **Can I name a real sacrifice I am making for Christ? Whether time, talent, or treasure, are the gifts I give to carry out God's work in the world costing me enough?**

Sunday, November 9   Read Hebrews 9:25-28.

Two-world thinking frames the arguments in this letter. There is an earthly realm, which is visible but only a shadow of the real; and the heavenly, which is the "really real," unseen yet eternal. The writer of Hebrews interprets Jesus' death as reason for putting the Jewish rites and institutions in the first category, those of Christianity in the second.

The author points out that Christ did not offer himself annually as was the custom on the Jewish Day of Atonement but "once for all . . . to remove sin." As the incarnate Son through whom God created the world (1:2-3), his self-sacrifice is a matchless historical and eschatological happening. Repeatable events are unreal. Christ is no copy but the definitive disclosure of the "really real."

However, the inability of the disciples to duplicate Christ's offering does not do away with the need for disciples to follow in his footsteps. Patterning one's life after Jesus' self-giving is the road to authenticity and abundance. It is the way to really live.

Otherwise we run the risk of filling ourselves with need for control or credit or independence or security so that we have no room left for God's gifts. One must have capacity, emptiness to fill. Often that requires relinquishing something to make room for something better. It means *giving to receive*, which is how the kingdom of God comes.

As we close this week, what room do you have left in you and your life for God to fill? If none, *give to really live*. In so doing, you will be rich even after having let go of your last penny.

Prayer: **Lead me to follow your way, Lord, giving into receiving. Amen.**

In Covenant with God

November 10–16, 1997   **Hugo Luciano López**✤
Monday, November 10   Read Hebrews 10:15-18.

"This is the covenant"

Two characteristics of biblical covenant set it apart from any other kind of agreement: 1) One of the participants is God; the other is either an individual or a group. 2) The genesis of the covenant and the power to fulfill it always come from God; humankind accepts the covenant and tries to obey it. Because of God's participation, the Judeo-Christian tradition reserves the use of *covenant* only for this kind of divine-human pact.

The writer of Hebrews reminds us of the new covenant prophesied by Jeremiah (31:31-34), later to be mediated by Christ in our hearts. The human setting for this ultimate covenant is neither the garden nor the ark, the mountain nor the national situation. It is the heart. In the cultural tradition reflected in both Testaments, *heart* was the term used to refer to all aspects of the individual (for example, see Mark 2:6, 8; 3:5; Luke 24:32). Thus, a good way to translate this concept into our modern language is "person."

The ultimate covenant in Christ assures full and final expiation of sin. This covenant is offered to all people "in *their* hearts" and "written on *their* minds."

Prayer: **O God, give me humility to receive your covenant in my heart, love to join my sisters and brothers in Christ, and guidance to do your will. In Jesus' name. Amen.**

✤Retired member of Central Illinois Conference of The United Methodist Church; teacher and writer in both English and Spanish languages; Wilmington, North Carolina.

Tuesday, November 11   Read Hebrews 10:11-14.

Why this covenant?

In the Bible *testament* refers to the written form of a covenant. The "Old Testament" is basically the story of God's often unrequited love for Israel. Again and again God offers love-inspired covenants to the people of people; each time those covenants are first accepted and later broken. The priests are unable to achieve justice with their sacrifices; the people are unable to live up to their commitment to the Lord. In the "New Testament" God offers the new covenant, the utmost and the ultimate, in Christ.

The writer of Hebrews wants to make a basic principle clear: Justice must be done by the expiation of sin through an atoning sacrifice. He points out the contrast between the frequent repetition by the priests of "sacrifices that can never take away sins" and the once-for-all sacrifice offered by God in Christ. His death on the cross makes any other sacrifice unnecessary. This having been accomplished, Christ waits in heaven for the total defeat and the final overthrow of his enemies.

Jesus' sacrifice expiates the people's sin so completely that their sin is remembered no more; they are sanctified and perfected as God's creation. Free from slavery to sin, they are ready and willing to actualize their God-given potential by doing God's will. To their amazement, satisfaction, and gratitude, they discover that by doing God's will they find genuine abundant life in Christ.

Prayer: Forgive me, O God, if I have taken your love and Jesus' sacrifice for granted. Aware now of the implications of my decision, I choose Life. I accept your covenant in Christ. In his name. Amen.

Wednesday, November 12   Read Hebrews 10:19-25.

The way to the new covenant in Christ

Foremost in the writer's thinking is God's action in Christ who acts as priest and as atoning sacrifice for our sin. The setting for the people's worship and for God's expected action was the Temple. The Temple contained a curtain [veil] that separated "the holy place" from "the most holy" or "holiest" (Exod. 26:33) or "the first tent [tabernacle]" from "the second" (Heb. 9:6-7). In the holy place the people, led by the priest, expressed their relationship with God through ritualistic use of praise, scriptures, and prayer. But in the holiest, God expressed God's relationship with the people, represented by the priest, "and he but once a year" (Heb. 9:7). When Christ died on the cross, one of the phenomena that occurred was that "the curtain [veil] of the temple was torn in two" (Matt. 27:51; Luke 23:45). This is powerful symbolism!

This revelation of God (*revelation* = "*re*moval of the *veil*") should make us aware that the sacrifice of Christ on the cross was motivated by love, accomplished for justice, and intended for opening the way for our return to God. After Christ's removal of the veil, we go "through the curtain" into "the holiest." We leave behind the setting of the earthly sanctuary of the first (or old) covenant (Heb. 9:1-2). Now—in the setting of the new covenant—with no separation between God and us, we draw near with faith, we hold fast to God's word with hope, and we stir up one another to love and good works.

Prayer: **O God, this is the highest and ultimate covenant. Christ has made it possible for me. I seek the guidance of the Holy Spirit to remain faithful to it. Amen.**

Thursday, November 13   Read 1 Samuel 1:3-11.

Longing becomes covenant

Profound, powerful longings of the human heart struggle to become the focus of our souls and the goal of our lives. We realize in our innermost being that our life would be inane at best and a failure at worst, if our longing of the heart remains unfulfilled. Along with that realization, a powerful conviction grows in us that this is not just our human longing but also an important part of God's purpose for our life in the world.

Hannah was already beyond this stage in the process. Her whole being was clearly focused on her deep desire to have a son. Peninnah's smug and boisterous maternal satisfaction only made Hannah's childless condition more unbearable. Hannah longed to join other women in the honored tradition of motherhood. Her last resource was to pray to God for a son. To strengthen her case she vowed that she would give him to the Lord: "I will set him before you as a Nazirite [one consecrated] until the day of his death."

As we read this story, it may seem to us that this covenant between Hannah and God had its origin in Hannah. However, we need to realize that it was God who put within her this deep and powerful longing to have a son.

God has endowed us with great potential and a growing awareness of it. What is your particular longing in life? How would its fulfillment fit into God's plan for creation? With these questions in mind, ponder Ephesians 1:9-10.

Prayer: O Lord, show me your purpose for my life and give me the courage to make it my personal longing. Amen.

Friday, November 14   Read 1 Samuel 1:12-20.

Keeping our end of the covenant

"The word of the LORD was rare in those days; visions were not widespread" (1 Sam. 3:1). Furthermore, Eli was not a very perceptive priest in the care of his congregation. However, even in that low period of her people's faith, Hannah managed to keep alive her part of the covenant with God. Her answer to Eli's accusation brought a needed lesson to the priest's life and earned Eli's support and blessing for her.

This story brings a much-needed lesson to us as well. When evaluating most people's relationship with God, we could easily apply the words quoted above to our times. In our daily activities, we act and react; we are exposed to various kinds of pressures and opportunities in different settings and connections. We need to stop frequently to open ourselves to God's will for us. Maybe we use the busyness in our lives to rationalize not fulfilling our covenant with God. We need to determine our priorities in prayer. Then we need to be faithful to that first priority: our covenant with God.

"In due time Hannah conceived and bore a son." This is our second lesson for the day. With great economy of words, we learn that God keeps the covenant. However, the Hebrew Scriptures record many covenants established by God that were broken by "the junior partner." We Christians are the recipients of God's ultimate covenant in Christ. God is willing. Are we? God keeps promises. Do we?

Prayer: **O God, keep me ever mindful that I am Christ's disciple and, through Christ, a participant in your covenant. Amen.**

Saturday, November 15   Read 1 Samuel 2:1-10.

Joyful thanksgiving

Today's passage presents Hannah's joyful thanksgiving to God for granting her petition for a son. Her thanksgiving is joyful despite the fact that she has just given to God her long-desired son, according to her vow.

Most of our praying is a personal covenant with God, but our prayers do not end with the last amen. We need to remain alert, expecting God's answer. The Holy Spirit moves us to thank God and to rejoice in our faith even before receiving God's answer. When God's answer comes, we begin to realize that God is not content simply with responding to our prayer. God's action goes well beyond meeting our need; it brings to our lives the freedom we need to serve God better. The Spirit helps us understand that God's answer to our prayer is at the same time part of a greater plan.

In today's passage, God was not only granting a son to a childless woman but was also sending a leader to the chosen people at a time when they were in great need of one. The spiritual condition of the people was low. Samuel would bring the necessary leadership. He has been considered the last of the judges (Acts 13:20) and the first of the prophets (Acts 3:24).

This is an invitation to perceive God's action beyond the satisfaction of our immediate needs. God can use even "personal" covenants for the fulfillment of astounding, earth- and heaven-shaking mystery. Ephesians 1:9-10 helps us anticipate that fulfillment: "to gather up all things in him."

Prayer: O God, guide me to seek your kingdom and your righteousness, that I may have a part in fulfilling your will for the world. Amen.

Sunday, November 16   Read Mark 13:1-8.

Signs of the end

We turn our attention now to Jesus' words of condemnation for the impressive buildings of the Temple in Jerusalem. We have been discussing covenants. The most important item in the early tabernacle was the ark of the covenant, containing the two tablets of the Ten Commandments. The ark was placed in the holy of holies, mentioned in our Wednesday meditation. The ark of the covenant and its setting symbolized the presence of God, guiding the lives of the people with the commandments.

However, by Jesus' time that symbolic means had become a materialistic end in itself. Neither portable nor simple any more, the Temple was stationary, elaborate, and costly (see 1 Kings 5-6). Jesus had strong words of condemnation for such a change, for the perversion of the divine teachings it represented, and for the unethical dealings that took place in it.

Therefore, Jesus announces the end of that perverted symbol. All kinds of terrible things will happen, including the coming of false messiahs. What are we supposed to do? If we remain idle and frightened about our own safety, we are lost. We need to remain faithful to God's covenant in Christ. Jesus summarized all the commandments of the old covenant in two great commandments and gave them a positive form: the love of God and the love of neighbor (see Exod. 20:1-17; Deut. 5:1-22; Matt. 22:34-40; Luke 10:25-28).

May our commitment to their practice keep us busy and hopeful!

Prayer: O God, I make the closing words of the Bible my final prayer for this week: "The one who testifies to these things says, 'Surely I am coming soon.' Amen. Come, Lord Jesus! The grace of the Lord Jesus be with all the saints. Amen" (Rev. 22:20-21).

BEING GOD'S KINGDOM

November 17–23, 1997   Charles A. Waugaman✤
Monday, November 17   Read Psalm 132:1-12.

That's some oath, David. I can just see you sitting on the porch and not closing your eyes until you find a dwelling place for God. It's gonna be a long wait, David—we know Solomon got that privilege. Better be careful what you swear and to whom you vow. God hears.

What does this impossible vow say to me?

That the psalmist who quoted it was silly? (If the psalmist was historian enough to know David's vow, he surely knew who built the Temple.)

That God clutters God's word with meaningless matter? (Hardly. God says David was a man after God's own heart. Thus David's actions and way of being becomes my goal.)

That I do not understand what David means by "a dwelling"? (What dwelling did he find for the Almighty?)

Advent is just around the corner—a time of preparation and expectation, a time of assessment and repositioning. Just as David brought the ark to its new home in Jerusalem, consider what in your life needs a new "dwelling," a new spot center stage. With the birth of the Almighty, what dwelling do you offer? Is your inn already booked? Is your heart ready for what's ahead?

Prayer: **Jesus, you have been listening in on my vows. Is there still time to clarify them? clean them up? widen the vision? Help me! Amen.**

✤Pastor, High Street Community Church, Conneaut Lake, Pennsylvania.

Tuesday, November 18   Read Revelation 1:4-8.

Inn. Stable. Heart.

My first thought is always to live in the past. To be content with personal experience. To crave comfort . . . control. Even when success means tight walls and narrowed horizons.

Then you push me into *revelation*. The very sound of the word calls to mind spaciousness. You make of me—with my dumpy stable mentality—a kingdom, a home for the ruler of all the kings of the earth. You make it the prize of freedom, freedom from sin.

Two wonders spring upon me with the thought. The first is that despite the constraints of sin, you envision possibilities beyond my confines—long-awaited vistas and galaxies of potential. The second wonder is that sin can be so restrictive in its vision that I become competitive and envious of the cobwebs and strictures of human success.

No wonder the cross was necessary. It must become a triumphal arch through which we drag ourselves, self-prisoners.

Prayer: **Dear God, forgiveness was easy to accept—it reinstated me. But grace and peace demand that I grow. The husk of this seed is so comfortable. Water me in love. Amen.**

Wednesday, November 19   Read 2 Samuel 23:1-7.

"Is not my house right with God?" (NIV).

What can David mean by such a bold and all-inclusive affirmation? Does he refer to his residence? his household? his genealogical family? Does he speak with knowledge or hope?

Did David worry about his children? Am I unique that I worry about my children? I feel more akin to Job than David. I would gladly sacrifice my time and my very being to their parties, their weekends with friends, and their escapades if I could fill any emptiness in their worship of or commitment to God.

What can David mean, "Is not my house right with God?" What of Bathsheba? What of Ammon? Tamar? *Oh my son Absalom!*

I often weep for my children—biological, adopted, spiritual, church, nieces, nephews, cousins. For all my personal faith, can I affirm that my house is right with God?

Perhaps the clue is that final phrase *with God*? Can I be at peace leaving my house "with God"? Can I leave them "with God" without their consent or cooperation?

Prayer: **Jesus, you bought me that freedom. Help me permit you to be king. Amen.**

Thursday, November 20   Read John 18:33-37.

The ancient creed affirms that Jesus was "true God from true God. . . . He came down from heaven . . . and became truly human." Many kings and emperors have claimed godhead as well as royal rights. None has ever proved the claim. Death snatched them all, quickly separating the divine and human; quickly leaving their kingdoms of "this world" to new leaders.

Jesus makes no claims for this world—not yet. His kingdom exists elsewhere. His model prayer, however, taught us hope. "Thy kingdom come . . . in earth" (Matt. 6:10, KJV) is to be our daily petition. And there is only one true way we can work toward making that happen.

"Thy kingdom come . . ." in me! What is this kingdom like? What must I embrace in life and thought and action that can verify my petition?

One way, of course, is truth. Jesus tells Pilate his kingdom is one of truth. That truth was resident in Jesus, and if he is resident in us, we must live truth. Our tendency is to hedge. This passage shows how Jesus lived truth when hedging might have been advantageous.

Prayer: **Jesus, being spirit as well as earth, I can hold your kingdom now. I hunger for truth . . . for you. Come, reign in me. Amen.**

Friday, November 21   Read Psalm 132:6-12.

"We have heard it in Ephrathah . . . Let us go to his dwelling place."

Is it only because I am writing these devotions in January and the sharp, dry decorations are not all down that Christmas echoes in these passages?

Expectation hovers over such passages like angels perched above the throne or star-splashed skies over Judean shepherds. Pluck a chord in scripture, and all the Bible reverberates. Christmas brushes Calvary; rapture rubs remorse.

How can we go to Bethlehem and find a kingdom that is "not of this world"? How can we "go to his dwelling place" (Luke 17:21, KJV) that is within us?

Our problem is with words. *Kingdom* continues to speak to our human ear with connotations of geographic location, rise and fall, expansion and contraction, sensual and selfish monarchs, and tyranny.

Yet Emmanuel is as much promise as possession. He comes as the Word to our bewildering vocabulary, for Emmanuel is neither geographic nor static. He "is, and . . . was, and . . . is to come"— personal.

"We have heard. . . . Let us go."

Prayer: **"Joy to the world! the Lord is come: Let earth [us] receive her [our] King."** *

---

*Isaac Watts (1674–1748), adapted from Psalm 98.

Saturday, November 22   Read Psalm 132:13-18.

David's family expected to be the dwelling place for God's Messiah by descent and by inheritance. But that was on the human, physical side. It was only thus that David's house and kingdom hoped to endure "for ever and ever."

Christians become God's family and dwelling place through faith—through belief in his only begotten son as Savior. We enter by adoption. Are we therefore only of God's family, or do we enter David's lineage also? Is DNA the only identifying element? Can one join God and not join all continuity? Surely eternal life does not progress in only one direction.

And if we are God's dwelling place (Ps. 90:1; 1 Cor. 3:9) are we also Zion? (Ps. 123:13). Surely our complacency denies the possibility.

What does it mean to contain the energy of Love, the vibrancy of Light, the endless creativity that God is? Surely a kingdom is more than a life, a mountain, a location.

Yet it is within us. And he is in us. And in him "we live and move and have our being" (Acts 17:28).

Prayer: **Dear God, all the old examples fail. It is not sufficient to be clay; I need to be expanded as well as shaped. O, "may your kingdom come . . . in me!" Amen.**

Sunday, November 23 Read John 18:36-37;
Revelation 1:4-6.

"To him who loves us and has freed us from our sins . . ."

Only freedom from sin allows us to enter the kingdom of which Jesus speaks. Surely this is cause for celebration. And the key is "by his blood."

Celebrations are part and parcel of life. Births, anniversaries, marriages, and deaths all ignite celebration. And the scarlet cord of God's love weaves through them all.

Why do we imbue the Lord's Supper with such solemnity? Funerals are most solemn. Yet the dinner following (in my experience so often held in a church) almost always ends in reminiscence, joy, and laughter.

If, as Christians, we have eternal life; if, as Christians, the kingdom is within us; if, as Christians, we are family in the truest sense, should not every Communion be a preview of heaven's ultimate "marriage of the Lamb" (Rev. 19:7)?

"Everyone who belongs to the truth listens to my voice." Come, let us worship; let us feast; let us rejoice in the presence of the King.

Prayer: **Dear Jesus, teach me kingdom living. Teach me celebration. Teach me truth. Amen. Amen.**

STAYING ON THE PATH

November 24–30, 1997   **Yolanda Pupo-Ortíz**✢
Monday, November 24   Read Jeremiah 33:14-16.

A real promise for a hurting people

The words of the prophet must have sounded like music to the people of Judah. In the midst of their suffering, Jeremiah is proclaiming physical and spiritual restoration. The words come at a time of utter hopelessness. With certainty Jeremiah proclaims not only the fulfillment of the promise but its immediacy. God's promise, Jeremiah says, is not confined to the end of time. It is for the "now." By God's power and mercy, justice and righteousness are returning to the land.

It is appropriate that as we begin the Advent season we reflect on this passage. Our condition, like that of the people of Judah, needs restoration. There is brokenness and violence in our streets and in our homes. The hatred of war is devastating several countries. There is much affliction in God's global family today.

We need the fulfillment of God's promise as much today as ever. Like the people of Judah, we can lift up our hearts in anticipation of the restoration that the Lord is bringing to the world.

Prayer: Your promise, O God, is like the reminder of the daylight in the middle of a painful night. Thank you for the spirit of hope that you put in me through Jesus Christ. Amen.

✢United Methodist clergy member of the Baltimore-Washington Conference; Associate General Secretary of the General Conference on Religion and Race.

Tuesday, November 25   Read Jeremiah 33:14-16.

Justice and righteousness for our lives

For the people of Judah the fulfillment of the promise meant physical and spiritual restoration for their nation and for their own personal lives.

Sometime ago a woman came to me for counseling, totally broken. Her older daughter (fifteen years old) had left home to join a gang. Her husband had asked for a divorce, and she had just found out that her second daughter was expelled from school because of drugs. "Where did we go wrong?" she asked. "We tried to give our children the best!"

This woman was right. She and her husband had worked hard to be good providers and good parents. Yet something had gone wrong. It seemed to her that there was absolutely no hope for her or her family.

What could I say to this woman? We prayed together and then we summarized this passage from Jeremiah in our own words: "Justice and righteousness are at hand. That is the promise of the Lord, and the Lord's promises are never unfulfilled." I asked her, "Do you believe that the promise is for you too?" Silently, tearfully, she nodded her head yes. We cried together and prayed some more. "Then," I said, "Let's show it right now. Anticipating the promise is to begin living it."

She looked at me, and I will never forget the look in her eyes. I knew that she had found hope and that restoration for her and her family was at hand. The promise in them was fulfilled!

Prayer: O God, how wonderful to hear your words spoken to me again. Justice and righteousness can be a reality in my home, my community, my church, my own life. Thank you for the gift of hope. Amen.

Wednesday, November 26   Read Psalm 25:1-10.

Always waiting for the Lord

The psalm is a prayer that many people know well, pronouncing these words as their own on many occasions, feeling them deeply in their hearts! One phrase especially caught my attention: "For you I wait all day long."

My Aunt Nina, whom I loved very much, moved away from my hometown when I was ten. After that, she came to visit for two months every year. As the time for her visit drew nearer, my excitement grew and I began counting the days. In addition, I did my homework punctually, my grades improved, and I helped my mother more intentionally with the housecleaning. I was happier. The anticipation of Aunt Nina's visit affected both my spirit and my behavior.

What a wonderful day is the day of the person who waits for the Lord. Have you tried it? When I have tried it, I have discovered that I am more patient with others, more cheerful, and more tolerant. I acquire a special sense of what is really important in my life and what is not.

It is too bad that in spite of my discovery, I allow work, pressures, and the rush of daily life to take me away from this spirit of anticipation. Only when I lift up my eyes to wait for the Lord all the day long are things right again.

Prayer: To wait for you, O God, is to center myself, to put everything into its proper place. To wait for you is to witness your love, to live in you. Help me, God, to always wait for you all day long. Amen.

Thursday, November 27   Read Psalm 25:1-10.

A prayer for obedience

When we carefully read this psalm, we hear the main plea of the prayer: "Make me to know your ways, . . . teach me your paths." The psalmist has many worries and concerns, and he reflects many of them in his petitions. But the heart of the prayer is the recognition that above everything else, what is needed is to be obedient, to live in God's paths.

The psalm is a prayer for obedience. To be in God's paths is to see with different eyes, to feel with a different heart, and to hear with different ears. When we live in God's paths, we will still encounter problems and difficulties; those never go away. The difference is our approach to them, and this difference is the major distinction of our faith.

Do you need to say this prayer today? I do! There are so many issues around me that are confusing! There are so many new situations for the church to address. I ask myself, *How can I know that my decisions are the right ones? How can I know that the positions I take are on God's side? How can I confront evil and injustice and still have the compassion needed to minister and to lead?*

Sometimes it is difficult to discern God's will. It is scary too. At those times I find myself crying to the Lord with the psalmist, "Teach me your paths." Through this prayer I dare to respond and initiate. I take risks in the hope that every step is within the paths of our God.

Prayer: **This is my prayer, God, my fervent desire. This is the cry of my heart: "Teach me your paths. Lead me in your truth . . . you are the God of my salvation; for you I wait all day long." Amen.**

344

Friday, November 28   Read 1 Thessalonians 3:9-13.

Preparing our hearts in holiness

Paul is anticipating a visit to his congregation in Thessalonica. The possibility of meeting with the members again fills his heart with joy. After he prays that God and Jesus direct his way to them, he reminds the church of a greater anticipation: the larger reunion with God at the coming of Jesus with all his saints. Paul tells the members of the congregation that they need to prepare, to strengthen their hearts in holiness for that reunion.

Sometimes we hesitate to think of ourselves as holy because we feel unworthy. However, holiness begins with love. There is no holiness where there is no love. There was joy in the reunion of Paul and his congregation because there was much love. There will be joy in the reunion with the Lord because there is an even greater love in that communion. We are holy when the love of God overflows our hearts and enables us to love back. We are holy when we live in the Lord. The best preparation for us to strengthen our hearts in holiness is to abound in love.

Prayer: **To meet with you, O Lord, is my prayer—to meet you in those who cry and hurt, in those who are happy and playful, in those whom I love, and in those whom I am trying to love in spite of myself. I seek to meet you, not only at the end of the times, but every day in the holiness of this journey and in the holiness of my heart. Amen.**

Saturday, November 29   Read Luke 21:25-36.

The hope in the triumph of God's reign

The school had sent the little boy to me for counseling. He seemed fine; but as we began to talk, I realized he was a terrified child. He was sure that the world was about to end, and this knowledge interfered with his entire life.

"Why do you believe this?" I asked.

"It is in the Bible. We read it at church all the time," he answered, somewhat surprised. Surely, as a pastor, I should know this.

I replied, "Some of the passages you have read sound frightening, but what they are really saying is not a reason to be afraid. On the contrary, these passages give us a reason to celebrate."

"To celebrate?"

"Yes. What the Bible says is that God is the one with the last word."

"You mean, God is the hero?"

I smiled. "Yes, God is the hero who makes things right." The boy then began to relax. He even smiled.

To have faith in God is to live in the now and in the still to come. The eschatological message of Jesus is a reassurance of the unquestionable power of God. At times it seems that evil is stronger than goodness. We often wonder about the future of our world. It is then that we need to be reminded that the reign of God is already here, that we are part of it, and that nothing can interfere with its fulfillment.

Prayer: **When I cry in the face of selfishness and exploitation; when I despair because nothing is right, I pray to you, O Lord. In your presence, I am strengthened again because yours is the power, the reign, and the glory—today and forever. Amen.**

Sunday, November 30   Read Luke 21:25-36.

Staying alert in the journey

Jesus ends his sermon with a plea for his people to be alert so that they can stand before the Son of God when the time comes.

The season of Advent reminds us of the end of time. The anticipated coming of the Lord is also the anticipated ultimate fulfillment of God's will. The Word was made flesh to bring salvation to God's entire creation.

To anticipate the coming of Jesus is to embark on a different journey or path. Only last Thursday we prayed that we would be able to remain faithful in God's paths.

Last winter I was driving down a hilly road at night. An animal caught my attention. I looked at it for only a moment, but that was enough to lose control of my car and go off the road.

Jesus knew that it was not going to be easy for us to stay in his path. He knew that the journey was going to be hard and misleading at times. That is why he gave us not only the advice but the "how to" for staying alert: prayer.

Only in the spirit of prayer are we able to have the strength to denounce evil, to confront the powers of the world, and to be instruments of change. Only in the spirit of prayer are we able to examine ourselves for continued growth.

Prayer: Help me be alert, God—examine my ways, my attitudes, and my spiritual growth. Help me uncover my hidden feelings. Help me be alert—to stay in the journey, to walk with no other guidance but yours. That is my prayer, O God. Amen.

FORERUNNERS OF GOD'S REIGN

December 1–7, 1997   John D. Copenhaver, Jr.✤
Monday, December 1   Read Malachi 3:1-4.

After our cozy and often indulgent celebrations of Thanksgiving, the themes of early Advent come as a shock. The Lord is coming; purify yourselves and be vigilant! What a rude awakening as we emerge from the haze of holiday meals. Advent is the sobering cold shower that stands between our celebrations of Thanksgiving and Christmas. For culturally accommodated Christians, these themes may seem like an intrusion on the holiday mood; but for those who hunger and thirst after righteousness, they come as a welcome invitation to prepare the way for God's coming.

Malachi recalled the covenant God made with Israel, a covenant of life and well-being (2:5); but Israel had despised the covenant. Rather than calling the people back to God, the priests had corrupted the covenant. Malachi knows that God will correct and heal them. He prophesies that God will send a messenger to prepare the way for God's coming. The people had better heed the messenger, for God will come suddenly and cleanse the temple. The wicked will be consumed, but for those who revere God "the sun of righteousness shall rise, with healing in its wings" and they "shall go out leaping like calves from the stall" (4:2). What a robust image of vitality! Let us renew our covenant with God so that we may joyfully engage in preparing the way for God.

Suggestion for meditation: **Imagine the healing wings of God covering you and refreshing you for service. Amen.**

✤Chair of the Shenandoah University Department of Religion and Philosophy; cofounder of the Shenandoah Institute for Christian Spiritual Formation, Shenandoah, Virginia.

Tuesday, December 2   Read Luke 1:69-79.

In yesterday's reading, Malachi prophesied that God would send a messenger who would come and prepare the way for the "messenger of the covenant" (3:1). Later in Malachi's prophecy, he identifies the initial messenger as Elijah (4:5). In the Gospels of Matthew, Mark, and Luke, Jesus discloses that John the Baptist is this messenger. As we read through the scriptures, it is fascinating to see how God is always preparing the way through chosen people.

Before John could prepare the way, God had to prepare an extraordinary couple to raise him. Surprisingly, Luke tells us more about John's parents than about the parents of Jesus. Zechariah is a priest, and Elizabeth is a descendant of the priestly family of Aaron. Both are deemed "righteous before God, living blamelessly" (Luke 1:6). Like Abraham and Sarah, their faith had been tested by infertility. Like Abraham and Sarah, Zechariah had a hard time accepting the angelic promise of a son. The sign and penance given him for his doubt was muteness during the months of Elizabeth's pregnancy. Zechariah's muteness must have been a fruitful spiritual discipline, for when at last he was able to speak, he uttered some of the most beautiful poetry in the New Testament.

The pregnancies of Elizabeth and Mary and Zechariah's muteness all suggest the holy anticipation that marks the Advent season. If we hope to welcome Jesus' birth with the profound praise we see reflected in Zechariah's poem, we might well imitate his muteness during portions of the Advent season. Though time is scarce in this busy season, we would be wise to carve out times for quiet reflection and contemplation.

Suggestion for meditation: **Reflect on your holiday calendar and try to make time for pregnant silence and mute contemplation. Amen.**

Wednesday, December 3   Read Luke 1:69-79.

I identify with the struggles of Zechariah and Abraham. Though not as old as they were, my wife and I had endured five discouraging years of infertility. I was nearing forty before our first child was born. The birth of our child was probably the most blessed experience of my life. I wanted to tell everyone.

For weeks after Thomas's birth, I gave chocolates to everyone I met. I cannot imagine being silent. But Zechariah had been mute for nine months and remained mute through the birth of his firstborn child. What a trial that must have been! Only on the eighth day, at the circumcision and naming, did Zechariah recover his speech.

In giving the child the name told him by the angel, Zechariah fulfilled the promised sign. Then it was as if a dam broke! A torrent of exalted praise sprang from Zechariah's lips, and the people were filled with wonder.

Zechariah prophesied that John would go before the Lord and give the knowledge of salvation to the people by the forgiveness of their sins. We learn that the knowledge of salvation is not some intellectual breakthrough but *education of the heart*, the experience of grace. We learn that we come to know salvation by humbly receiving the love and forgiveness that ceaselessly flows from the heart of God.

Prayer: **Gracious Lord, expand my heart to receive the love and grace you shower upon me. Forgive me for neglecting the means of grace, as if I were spiritually self-sufficient. Help me recognize my poverty of spirit and turn to you, who bestows grace so richly. Then send me forth as a beacon of your love, in Christ's name. Amen.**

Thursday, December 4   Read Philippians 1:3-11.

Paul enjoyed a close and warm relationship with the church at Philippi. This letter reflects his deep affection and respect. Compare this happy association with his often painful relationship with the church in Corinth. During the difficult days of his imprisonment, Paul takes great comfort in remembering the steadfast faith and loving support of the Philippian church.

The Philippian church had experienced strong opposition since its inception. Paul and Silas had been severely flogged and locked in stocks because they had spoiled the lucrative fortune-telling business of some men in Philippi. The persecution of the Philippian church continued long after Paul and Silas had left. Paul writes in order to encourage and comfort the members in the face of opposition from without and division from within.

Though the persecution is strong, Paul knows that they will not falter. God, who has begun a good work in them, will bring it to completion at the return of Christ. They will endure to the end because God is their helper; God is their strength; God is their joy. They have been granted the great privilege of not only believing the gospel but of suffering for it (v. 29). But suffering and affliction are not the last word, for grace accompanies them: the grace to endure and, finally, to triumph.

Prayer: **God of grace, give me the holy boldness of Paul so that I may witness to Christ in the face of opposition of indifference. Continue your holy work in me until I know with Paul and the Philippians the grace that comes from suffering for the gospel. Amen.**

Friday, December 5   Read Philippians 1:3-11.

Paul's happy memories of his friends in Philippi are a great comfort to him during his imprisonment. Paul writes that he always remembers them as he prays constantly. Too often I think we dismiss Paul's claims to unceasing prayer as a forgivable exaggeration. But is it so hard to imagine that Paul's heart and mind are always turned to God? His long labors in the gospel, his undying love for the Christian communities he has founded, and his fellowship in Christ's sufferings have disposed him to unbroken fellowship with God. In that constant communion with God, he remembers with joy his children in the faith, the fruit of his gospel labors in Philippi.

Just like a parent separated from beloved children, Paul longs to see them. But Paul's love and compassion for them is rooted in Christ's love for his church. The heart of Christ has taken over the affections of Paul's heart, and he would undoubtedly lay down his life for them.

Paul then gives us a glimpse into his prayer for them. He prays for them as a community of faith, not as loosely connected individual believers. He desires that they will grow in knowledge and discernment, grounded in love, so that they can fulfill God's will. If they do this, they will produce a harvest of righteousness and will be kept blameless until Christ's return.

Prayer: **O compassionate Christ, fill my heart with your love for your redeemed people. Give me, I pray, the wisdom, discernment, and love I need to know and do your will. I pray in your name. Amen.**

Saturday, December 6   Read Luke 3:1-6.

So much had been prepared! Prophets had proclaimed both the coming Messiah and the new covenant written on the heart. Malachi had prophesied that Elijah would come to prepare the way. Zechariah, stunned into silence for nine months, saw his son as the sign that these prophecies had been fulfilled and that the first wave of God's reign was breaking on the shores of this corrupt and violent age. And yet the reign of God requires even more preparation. John's ministry is indispensable!

Think of John as a pioneer who has just landed on the shores of a new land. From the shores of God's eternal purpose, he must build a road into an impenetrable wilderness of human heart. He is thrust forward by consecrated parents, by the prophecies of Israel's great seers, and by his own call. But what a difficult and lonely path it is!

John is called to be a road builder for the Messiah. If he fails, the Messiah may never reach the homeland of human heart that needs healing so desperately. John must hack away at the dense undergrowth that obstructs the passage of God's grace. The dense undergrowth is the accumulated customs and laws that had become so burdensome for the ordinary Israelite. Though intended to foster righteousness, the ruling religious class had obscured God's essentially gracious nature. John cuts through all of that to reveal God's desire to forgive and save the people. Hard hearts are made tender; the undergrowth is cleared. Come Lord, save your people!

Prayer: **O Lord, how much preparation is needed for your grace to reach and heal the human heart! Make me, like John, a road builder who clears the way for your saving grace in Christ our Lord. Amen.**

Sunday, December 7   Read Luke 3:1-6.

On the second Sunday of Advent, what should be our attitude? This Gospel makes it clear: repentance. Repentance was the sharp blade with which John cleared away the undergrowth that obstructed the pathway of God's grace. The customs and laws that guided Israelites in the ways of justice and obedience to God were good and holy, but the people often missed the forest for the trees. The fundamental attitude that lies behind all holy living is the turning of the heart to God. John was a turner!

The root meaning of *repentance* is turning away from sin and selfishness and turning toward God. John's urgent and imperative call to repentance cut through the smothering overlay of customs and offered people a clear choice: wholehearted turning to God or willful hardening of the heart. No wonder Jesus was so disturbed by those religious leaders who ignored John's call.

John, and those who heeded his call, prepared the way and built the road for the first coming of God's messiah. Let us not imagine that the Messiah's second coming will occur without preparation. While we cannot bring God's reign, we are called to anticipate it by living today as citizens under God's rule. Though the world may have accepted racism, injustice, and violence as the order of the day, Christians must actively resist them and be forerunners of the just and peaceable reign of Christ. May our lives and churches embody the future God is bringing.

Prayer: **Dear God, may I so embrace your reign that all my worship and work express my fervent desire that your will be done on earth as it is in heaven. Amen.**

AWAKEN TO GOD'S PRESENCE WITH JOY

December 8–14, 1997 **Judith Freeman Clark✤**
Monday, December 8 Read Zephaniah 3:17-20.

Advent's message can be confusing. Although Zephaniah says the Lord is in our midst, we know that Advent is a season of preparation. We anticipate Christ's birth, but we know also that he is present to us now. Christians cherish the knowledge that Christ's love embraces all people at all times in all places. How, then, do we make sense of Advent's special significance as the time *before* his birth? How do we acknowledge God's presence *and* await his coming?

Each morning we open our eyes and thank God for watching over us through the night. We are aware simply of being alive. Gradually we prepare for the day and think about what might lie ahead. We do not know what will come—but we are certain of being in the midst of it, so we consider the ways in which we need to be ready.

During Advent our awareness of God is like our early-morning experience: first, we are merely awake; then we anticipate the day. The immediacy of God's love is always apparent. But we know God's love will be manifest in the future as well. Just as we awaken daily to God's mercy, we anticipate God's unrevealed blessings.

Suggestion for meditation: **When you awaken, think about God's constant love. Recall God's gifts and thank God frequently throughout the day. Try to reflect on God's love in your actions. Amen.**

✤Episcopalian laywoman; seminary student; Trinity Episcopal Church, Claremont, New Hampshire.

Tuesday, December 9   Read Isaiah 12:2-4;
                                          Philippians 4:4-5.

When Jesus lived among us, we came to know the glory of God's love. In Advent, the knowledge that his appearance is imminent in our lives assures us that we can fully, and without anxiety, put aside any fear about the future. We can prepare to celebrate his birth with gladness. This is why, in its focus on God's coming again, the prophet Isaiah's message resonates with such joy: "I will trust, and will not be afraid; for the LORD GOD is my strength and my song, and he has become my salvation" (RSV).

Isaiah's prophecy is more than just a hopeful comment—it is a battle cry of affirmation. During Advent, these strong words stir us up and encourage in us an excitement about what is to happen shortly. Advent's place in the secular year is a time when we may feel tired, indifferent, or disinterested. As December comes, we find we may have grown weary of what we as Christians are called to accomplish.

This tendency among faithful people to grow slack, lazy, or disengaged is not new. Paul's letter to the church at Philippi recognizes this phenomenon, and his message aims at rousing his listeners: "Rejoice in the Lord always, again I will say, Rejoice" (RSV). Paul's message to us, across the centuries, is the same. Just as he did for the early Christians, Paul calls on us to be joyful—and reminds us of the reason for celebration: "The Lord is at hand" (RSV).

Prayer: **Dear God, affirm in me a knowledge of your strength. Create in me an open heart in which to receive you with rejoicing, and send me forth with love. Amen.**

Wednesday, December 10   Read Zephaniah 3:17-20.

Today's reading is as uplifting as a small child's laughter or a thankful glance from a homeless man entering a shelter on a winter evening. It is not difficult to sense the jubilant feeling that the prophet Zephaniah had as he wrote that God "will rejoice over you with gladness" (RSV).

We cannot ignore this message. We cannot run from it or hide in the hope that it will go away. It is impossible to be a Christian and remain indifferent to joy. We cannot insulate ourselves from the love of—and for—others and still call ourselves followers of Christ. We are a people chosen by God for greatness and for gladness. It is our sacred obligation to extend that love through our lives to others.

Zephaniah tells us that the Lord is in the middle of what we do. Let the prophet's words, written to celebrate deliverance from the hands of an enemy, rouse us from our Advent apathy. This penitential season traditionally challenges us to incorporate fasting, prayer, and other disciplines into our routines. But God challenges us to take up our tasks "with loud singing as on a day of festival" (RSV). The third week in Advent is special because we not only reflect on Christ's coming, but we also celebrate this first season in the Christian year—the season of the miracle that will occur: God's dwelling among us.

Prayer: **Dear God, keep me awake to the love with which you sent your only Son to live among us. Kindle joy in me, and offer me daily opportunities to put that joyful spirit to work to the glory of your holy name. Amen.**

Thursday, December 11   Read Isaiah 12:4-6.

As we move through Advent, awaiting God's arrival, we need to be on the lookout for ways to "make known his deeds among the nations" (RSV). Everything around us attests to God's presence, indicates God's desire to dwell among us, invites us to enter the kingdom. When we encounter these signs, we need to be ready to respond and to call them to others' attention.

We are a people called by God, even though some of God's signs are difficult to understand. Some signs are risky because they involve change. Some signs are hidden, quiet, or obscure. Some are unmistakable and hard to miss. Each is God's way of inviting us to awaken, to prepare the way for the great One in our midst—"the Holy One of Israel" (RSV).

Through Christ's birth we come to know God's love as he lived among us; through his coming again, our world will be made new. Isaiah says that the Lord has done glorious things. We are to go out and tell everyone about it. This is a powerful charge, but Advent is a time when we need powerful images to provoke us. We may be partially blind to the signs of God's coming, signs that mark our paths each day. Therefore, we need this time to unsettle us. We need an interval during which we can wake up, so that we may then prepare for God's coming in our lives.

Suggestion for meditation: **As you move through your day, repeat the phrase *Awaken me, Lord* frequently. Seek signs of God's love as you find ways to serve others.**

Friday, December 12   Read Philippians 4:6-7.

As a child, I lived on my grandparents' small farm where they raised chickens. When I grew old enough to feed the hens and gather the eggs, I felt proud to take part in these chores. My grandparents offered me a safe home and taught me many lessons about love and security. Paul's message concerning anxiety and fear reflects these lessons.

What I disliked about my grandparents' farm was the rooster. I was afraid of him—he pecked at me if I got too close. And, as roosters do, he was terribly noisy in the morning. As the night sky faded to dawn, the rooster crowed his loudest—signaling a new day. Although I burrowed under my blankets, trying to ignore him, the rooster's message rang clear: "Wake up! It's daytime! Get ready!" And, of course, I got up. I may have been afraid of the rooster, but he *did* help me prepare for my day.

Advent is like that rooster—its role is to remind us to wake up and get going. It is a time both to celebrate Jesus' birth *and* prepare for Christ's arrival. We have no way of knowing when he will come. We do not know when he will ask us to let him in. Christmas helps us recall Jesus' birth; Easter recalls his death and resurrection. Advent reminds us that we must be prayerfully ready for God's coming at any time.

Prayer: **Dear God, in your love you give me many reminders of your presence and your coming again. Give me wisdom to hear the many roosters of Advent—and the courage to respond to their messages without fear. Amen.**

Saturday, December 13   Read Luke 3:7-14.

John the Baptist issues a stern warning as we move through Advent. Unlike Paul's gentle reminder to the Philippians, John the Baptist takes aim at our too-human tendency to make excuses. In calling us to prepare for God's coming, the Baptist hits us squarely in the middle of our lives and requires that we abandon pretense, confront our weaknesses, change our ways, ask forgiveness.

To admit our frailties is never easy. And in the days preceding the celebration of Jesus' birth, it can be especially difficult to find the strength to do so. "Share!" we are instructed. "Take only what is your due," the Baptist thunders. And as a final admonition, he warns, "Be content!" We would do so willingly—if only it were easy. But we know from past failures that it is not.

During simple times it takes determination to live according to Christ's example. As the festive season approaches, to live simply—in all humility and with care only for others' needs—seems an impossible task. In reverent anticipation of God's coming we *ought* to have no trouble being responsive to the needs of those around us. Instead, Advent seems to provoke a struggle. What does God really want? Why is it so hard to discern God's call and live up to it? How can we more joyfully embrace our responsibilities toward others?

Prayer: **Lord God, during Advent draw me near to you as I ask "What shall I do?" Remind me that in your infinite love you have equipped me to discern the answer—if only I will turn to you for guidance. Amen.**

Sunday, December 14   Read Luke 3:15-18.

It is a humble but confident John the Baptist who explains to the people his role as a servant of God. As we review his teachings, we see that he outlines the path we must follow today as servants of Christ. During the weeks leading up to the nativity, the Baptist counsels us to reflect on our shortcomings and our faults. Indeed, the scripture readings throughout Advent emphasize the importance of preparing ourselves for the One who, in John the Baptist's words, "will baptize [us] with the Holy Spirit" (RSV).

During Advent, we wait and we watch. But for Advent's meaning to resonate fully in our lives, we must understand that the task of the season is more complex than one of mere waiting. The charge is that we repent—that we *actively* seek a better way; that we make ready our heart, body, and spirit so that we might receive Christ *completely* when he comes.

This is a season of reflection—but it is also a time to resolve any conflict we may have about the life to which God calls us. It is an interval set aside for us to make ourselves ready to serve God in all ways. It is a time to quietly rejoice that we are named by God as chosen ones—and that shortly we are to receive the good news that John the Baptist foretold.

Prayer: **Dear God, as I anticipate the birth of your Son, keep me mindful of how great is my need to prepare fully to serve others, to put my own needs behind me, and thereby to glorify your holy name. Amen.**

EXPECTING THE UNEXPECTED

December 15–21, 1997   **M. Robert Mulholland**✤
Monday, December 15   Read Luke 1:46-55.

Openness to the unexpected

There is a story about a golf hacker who challenged the club pro. The club pro was skeptical, seeing no point in playing with a person who had no chance of winning. When she expressed her concern, the hacker's response was, "That's OK. Just give me two 'gotchas.' " When asked what a "gotcha" was, the hacker replied, "You'll see." Intrigued by this, the pro agreed to play.

Things went as expected, and the pro was leading easily after two holes. As she prepared to hit her second shot on the third hole, the hacker slipped up behind her, jabbed her in the ribs, and shouted, "Gotcha!" The pro, completely unnerved, sliced the shot into the woods and ended up losing the hole. For the rest of the round, the hacker would slip behind the pro for each shot or putt but never used the second "gotcha." Totally distracted with the expectation of the unexpected, the pro played the worst game of her life and lost to the hacker by several strokes.

Expecting the unexpected disrupts our control of life.

Prayer: O God, I so often think of you as the God of "gotchas," always lurking in the background, turning my well-ordered and completely controlled life upside down. Help me release my attempts at total control and be open to your unexpected advents that you may have space to enter into my life with transforming touches. Amen.

✤Vice President and Provost of Asbury Theological Seminary; Elder in the Baltimore-Washington Conference of The United Methodist Church; adjunct faculty of The Upper Room Academy for Spiritual Formation.

Tuesday, December 16   Read Micah 5:2.

Unexpected reversals

Western culture is largely shaped by the belief that bigger is better; more is always desirable; and success is related to magnitude of possessions, programs, or performances. This perspective usually carries the presumption that God operates on the same basic principles. The rise of the "prosperity gospel" is symptomatic of a culture that presumes abundance as the norm of the good life.

To such a perspective, Micah's word is a disturbing and disruptive reminder that our definitions of success and prosperity do not fit well with God's ways. Bethlehem was a minor, insignificant village of Judea in Micah's day. Surely God would not look to such an insignificant settlement for the future leader of Israel, not with the might and glory of Jerusalem and Samaria.

The attitudes of the people were much like today. Thus God says to them, "Hear this, you rulers of the house of Jacob and chiefs of the house of Israel, who abhor justice and pervert all equity, who build Zion with blood and Jerusalem with wrong! Its rulers give judgment for a bribe, its priests teach for a price, its prophets give oracles for money; yet they lean upon the LORD and say, 'Surely the LORD is with us! No harm shall come upon us!'" (3:9-11).

Perhaps it is this tendency of God to work through the little, weak, and insignificant things that Paul expressed: "Power is made perfect in weakness" (2 Cor. 12:9)—truly an unexpected perspective for our culture.

Prayer: **You, whose way moves against the grain of my expectations, help me hold my perceptions and expectations lightly enough for you to work in unexpected ways in my life. Amen.**

Wednesday, December 17   Read Micah 5:3.

Unexpected timing

If you do not believe we live in an instant gratification world, sit near a vending machine and watch what happens when someone does not get the expected product. We expect instant returns on our investments of time, energy, or resources. We think that if only we can take the right pill, learn the proper methods, or develop the necessary technology, we can overcome any problem or difficulty at once.

How often do we expect God to respond instantly to our prayers? How often do we begin to question the faith of either the one praying or the one prayed for if results are not evident? The "name it and claim it" form of prayer, like the "prosperity gospel" from which it comes, is another symptom of our instant gratification world.

However, God works on a different schedule. The faithful people of Micah's day could easily have expected God to rectify the intolerable situation of corruption and apostasy at once and restore them as a righteous and obedient people. The word of God through Micah, however, was that there would be a gestation period before God brought forth restoration.

An essential part of expecting God's unexpected interventions is the willingness to abandon one's self to God's schedule. If we trust God only to work on our schedule, we make God our servant. If we allow God to work on God's schedule, we become God's servants.

Prayer: **O God, who often hastens when I prefer delay and delays when I demand immediate response, may I be so yielded to you that when you hasten I am ready and when you delay I am content. I pray in the name of the One who came in the fullness of your time. Amen.**

Thursday, December 18   Read Luke 1:39-41.

Unexpected encounters

In a sense, every Christian is called to be a Mary. We are called to offer ourselves to God in such radical abandonment and availability that the Christ of God can be brought forth through our lives into the world. Paul articulated the goal: "It is no longer I who live, but it is Christ who lives in me" (Gal. 2:20).

Many desire this and actively offer to God disciplines of loving obedience through which Christ can be formed in them. Many also think, however, that until God has pretty well completed the process there is not much they can do to bring forth Christ into their world.

Mary serves as an illustration to the contrary. According to Luke's account, Mary visited Elizabeth shortly after conceiving (vv. 26, 56-57). The Christ had hardly begun to be formed in her, to say nothing of being fully brought forth into the world. Yet when she met Elizabeth, the work of God within Mary touched the work of God within Elizabeth, and Elizabeth was filled with God's spirit. Probably neither expected the presence of God in that encounter. Each undoubtedly thought that until their children had been born and grown to maturity, nothing much would happen.

We need to remember that the Christ that is coming to birth in us can bring about unexpected touches of grace in our encounters with others.

Suggestion for meditation: **The secret of being an agent of God's grace to others seems to lie not so much in the depth of my growth to maturity in Christ but in the depth of my abandonment and availability to God. Amen.**

Friday, December 19   Read Hebrews 10:5-7.

Unexpected redemption

Hebrews was written to Jewish Christians who apparently had accepted Jesus as Messiah—but within the old sacrificial system. Since they had always maintained right relationship with God through the sacrifices offered at the Temple, they presumed this was still the means of maintaining such a relationship.

We are tempted to think we would never be so foolish. However, whenever we establish a particular set of behaviors as the "norm" of right relationship with God, we are substituting our system of redemption for God's. Whenever a particular form of worship becomes the "only" way to worship God, whenever a particular style of devotional life becomes the "only" way to "do devotions," we have created our own system of "sacrifices and offerings" to maintain our relationship with God.

Hebrews says, "Sacrifices and offerings you have not desired, but a body you have prepared for me." While the immediate reference is to Jesus' death as the event that consummates the whole sacrificial system, at another level it speaks to those who follow Christ. Our redemption is not maintained by activities we do to please God. Our redemption is actualized by the daily offering of our very being to God. This is what Paul points us toward when he says, "I appeal to you therefore, brothers and sisters, by the mercies of God, to present your bodies as a living sacrifice, holy and acceptable to God, which is your spiritual worship" (Rom. 12:1).

Prayer: O God, I so easily substitute a variety of "offerings and sacrifices" to you rather than offering myself to you. Help me, in this season when you offer yourself to me, to offer myself to you as a living sacrifice. Amen.

Saturday, December 20   Read Psalm 80:1-7.

Unexpected "abandonment"

"Restore us, O God; Let your face shine, that we may be saved."

Israel found itself "abandoned" by God. The Israelites were exiled from their promised land. Their temple, God's dwelling place, had been destroyed. The kingdom of David had been overthrown. All that gave their life meaning, value, identity, and purpose was gone. Never had they expected that their covenant God would abandon them in such a manner as this. Oh, how their hearts ached for the "good old days."

Their first cry was for God to restore them as before, to bring them back—back to the promised land, back to the Temple with its sacrifices, back to the kingdom with the house of David upon the throne, back to things as they had been. Whenever we find ourselves "abandoned" by God, isn't this the first cry of our hearts? Don't we also long for the restoration of what once was?

Then the psalmist seemingly realizes that restoring the past is not the solution to the problem. Restoring the past would only recreate the conditions that led to the "abandonment." And so the psalmist moves from a desire for the return of the old to an openness to a new future in God's grace: "Let your face shine, that we may be saved." This is a cry of unconditional yielding to God that opens us to God's future. One of the problems with expectations is that they always seem to wear the clothing of what has been. God's response to our expectations is always unexpected because God opens us to a new and different future.

Prayer: O God, help me abandon my compulsive grip on the past that you may lead me into your unexpected future. In the name of the expected One who is always so unexpected in coming. Amen.

Sunday, December 21   Read Hebrews 10:10.

Unexpected sanctification

One of the common expectations related to God's coming into human life is that everything will be set straight. How often do we use or hear the phrase, "Why doesn't God do something about this?" or its variant, "Why did God let this happen?" Micah saw that God would overthrow the corrupt and apostate and restore the faithful. Mary sang that God would put down those who had exalted themselves and would exalt the marginalized. The psalmist prayed for God not simply to restore the past but to bring a new future.

However, all too often we expect God to change circumstances, alter situations, resolve matters in the external affairs of our lives. We expect God to deal with the symptoms of human brokenness. We give little thought to having God deal with the cause of those symptoms—the deep and pervasive brokenness at the heart of human existence.

The writer of Hebrews realized that in Christ God opened the way for new relationship with God as well as to experience sanctification—being restored to wholeness in the image of Christ. Perhaps this is the most unexpected aspect of God's coming in Christ. God comes not merely to forgive but to liberate us from the deep inner brokenness of being that causes those dehumanizing and destructive behaviors that alienate us from God, from one another, and from ourselves.

In the expectancy of Advent, God will always come in unexpected ways.

Prayer: O God, no matter how deep my expectation of your coming, you always exceed my expectations. Help me, in this Advent, to let you surprise me and take me beyond my expectations into the fullness of your sanctifying purpose for my life. Amen.

WEARING THE CLOTHES OF CHRIST

December 22–28, 1997   **Phyllis Tyler-Wayman**✤
Monday, December 22   Read Psalm 148.

During Advent we have been getting ready for God to become flesh and blood. We have been waiting for truth and beauty to come into our lives; waiting to make sense of daily routines, to make sense of our tragedy and our laughter.

God may come in an ocean wave of insight, in the wind of change, or in a direct hit of a particular incident. Whatever way God chooses to enter our lives, we can prepare by reading and digesting Psalm 148.

This psalm is not descriptive or pensive. This psalm is imperative. To praise, to thank God, is the command, the directive. Praise the Breath of Life, all you stars and moon and sun. Praise the Energy that keeps the power coming, all you sea monsters and stormy wind and snow. Praise the Teasing Delight, all you kings and presidents and CEOs. Praise the Discomforter and Gentleness-Giver, all you people of Chicago, Miami, Seattle, and Nashville. Prepare yourself to receive God in flesh and blood. People who seek, praise and thank you without ceasing. God is getting ready to come to us in flesh and blood, in a body like ours with skin and hair and toenails.

Suggestion for meditation: **Sing or pray the hymn "God of the Sparrow, God of the Whale" (The United Methodist Hymnal, No. 122).**

✤Pastor of College United Methodist Church, Ventura, California; poet, seeker, friend of all living things; co-member of the Sisters of Loretto.

Tuesday, December 23   Read 1 Samuel 2:18-22, 26.

What attitudes, what stories, what skills, and what influences can I offer to my child or the children I teach to prepare them for whatever lies ahead?

One day when my son was three years old, he and I were listening to a song by Sammy Davis, Jr. The song was "I Want to Be Free." My son looked puzzled when the song ended. He blurted out his disbelief, "I'm three. I want to be four. Why does he want to be three?"

Our children may hear the world differently than we do. How can we be wise ones for those who look to us for guidance in their lives?

The parents of Samuel and of Jesus may have been uneasy about their readiness to parent. In First Samuel we read that Samuel's mother made clothes for him each year and took him to visit Eli.

With what do we clothe our children and with whom do we have them visit?

Prayer: **Prepare my ears to listen, my heart and my soul to connect with the longings of those who search for the living, caring God. Amen.**

Wednesday, December 24   Read Luke 2:41-51.

Mary and Joseph were frustrated parents of a twelve year old who had taken off on his own and stayed in Jerusalem without telling them what he was doing. Does this scenario sound familiar to those of you who are responsible for children ages twelve to eighteen?

This is Christmas Eve day. We are preparing to remember the birth of a child who will grow into a teenager. Why do you suppose that Jesus at age twelve followed his own agenda to stay in Jerusalem when his parents' agenda was to return to Nazareth?

Perhaps Jesus was preparing his parents to release their control of him. Perhaps by following his own agenda at age twelve, Jesus was preparing them for his later leaving of his home of origin. Perhaps he was preparing them for when he got in trouble with the officials of the synagogue and of Rome. Perhaps he was preparing them for his final leaving on the cross.

After age twelve a person moves decidedly away from parental control and begins to make her or his own decisions. Are we ready to let go of our children so they can dance their own dance in the world?

Prayer: **Ever-present God, on this Christmas Eve prepare me to let go of my responsibilities and to clothe myself in your presence. Amen.**

Christmas Day
Thursday, December 25   Read Luke 2:1-20.

A Christmas Poem: The Ring of a Circus

We are searching
    those of us creatures with a soul and a heart
    and wings you cannot see.
When flesh and blood
    marries the divine in a union of perfection
    we know our circus ring of searching is completed.
We know on this birth-day, this Christmas Day,
    we no longer need to thirst and hunger for life
    because we have been found by the One who called us
    by name—Child of God.
We have been found by the One who seeks us,
    who is clothed with flesh and blood like ours
    and who laughs when tickled and screams when
    stabbed.
Today we come to know the meaning of promise
    as Moses offered it to those who searched, who went
    about in the wilderness.
The ring of the circus is complete, and we need not wander
    about aimlessly in the desert.

Suggestion for meditation: **Listen and watch and feel and smell all around you. Then name for yourself the ways the God of flesh and blood is being revealed to you where you live.**

Friday, December 26   Read Colossians 3:12-17.

The gang members of Los Angeles declare their status and membership by their clothing. We readily identify police officers and the Amish because of their clothes.

What are you wearing this first day after Christmas? What are you wearing beneath your exterior presentation? In Paul's letter to the church people at Colossae he told them to clothe themselves with compassion, with kindness, with humility, with meekness, and with patience. He said, "Clothe yourselves with love, which binds everything together in perfect harmony."

If we clothe ourselves this Christmas season with the threads that Paul suggests, we may need to clear our closet of any old prejudices, ill-fitting pride, strangling intolerance, mismatched idolatry, and stained apathy. We may need to make new selections, choosing those items that more clearly align with our interior values. The color of a bird's feathers often identifies a bird. In what ways does our "plumage" identify us?

How do you and I clothe ourselves? What do we desire to wear? Do people recognize us as Jesus Christ's people because we are clothed in compassion for those who suffer disease, injustice, and loneliness? As Christ's people we bring fabric woven with the threads of love that will not fall away with age and wear.

Prayer: **Ever-weaving God, create for me a cloth of compassion that I may wear your garments before all who seek you. Amen.**

Saturday, December 27   Read Luke 2:52.

During this time of the year in most parts of the United States there are few flower gardens. But here in southern California there are flowers of various kinds all year long.

Gardeners can teach us the importance of watchfulness and continuous care in growing a garden of flowers. The soil must be rich in nutrients for the flowers to grow well. The sun and water must be regular ingredients. The rabbits and snails have to be persuaded to dine elsewhere. Weeds and vines must be eliminated from the garden of flowers. And the garden is best designed by using a complement of flowers that grow well together. The gardener needs to possess the gift of patience, a watchful eye to remove the enemies of the flowers, and true appreciation for the flowers that grow.

As Mary and Joseph raised Jesus to be a man, they were not unlike the gardener of a flower garden. And each step along the way, they wanted to offer the food to help Jesus grow in wisdom and years and in favor with others and with God.

Whatever we grow—be it flowers, children, a class of learners, or friendships—we can learn much from the gardeners of flowers who have learned the art of being cocreators of beauty.

Prayer: **God of all life, grow within me a spirit of the gardener that I might enable all that I touch to grow to beauty and fullness. Amen.**

Sunday, December 28   Read Psalm 148.

The most remarkable part to me of Jesus' sacrifice was that on the night that he was betrayed he took bread and wine and gave thanks to God. To thank and praise God in the good times is logical. However, to thank and praise God in times of betrayal, cancer, loss of job, broken relationships, imprisonment, or unexpected death is the foolishness of living with Jesus Christ.

Psalm 148 is a psalm of praise from beginning to end; the psalmist invites all creation to join in praise of God. I wonder if the writer was in the good time or the betrayal time of life. How much easier it is to praise God when all is well than when suffering looms heavy. How much easier it is to love friends than it is to love enemies. How much easier it is to praise God at Christmas than during Holy Week.

The Jesus Christ whose birth we celebrate this season praised God during betrayal and loved those who crucified him by asking God to forgive them.

Prayer: **God who never gives up, mold and shape and gently create my heart to praise you without ceasing and to be so filled with love that I bless even my enemies with your blessing and not a curse of destruction. Amen.**

December 29–31, 1997 **Cindy Schnasa Jacobsen**✤
David Schnasa Jacobsen✤✤

Monday, December 29 Read Jeremiah 31:7-9.

The right word at the right time

It is never enough simply to speak the right word. Just saying the *right thing* does not suffice. Timing is everything. We need to speak the right word *at the right time*.

Sometimes we so blithely mouth our terms of endearment that they drop to the floor like so much costume jewelry off a cheap string. Yet consider what a pearl of beauty an "I love you" is in the middle of a harried day. Or, for that matter, consider how a parent's well-timed "I'm so proud of you" can move even a cantankerous child to value himself or herself as a precious gift. With words, timing matters.

The prophet Jeremiah seems to understand the value of the right word at the right time. Nestled among oracle upon oracle is Jeremiah 30–31. Scholars call these two little chapters "The Book of Consolation." By their very position in Jeremiah's prophetic ministry, they open up the possibility of joy for his hearers—even amidst the doom and gloom of a hopeless future. Perhaps as the darkness of winter closes in around *our* post-Christmas churches, a timely word like Jeremiah's could make all the difference in the world.

Prayer: **Gracious God, time and time again you speak the right word at the right moment. In the midst of winter drear, open our hearts once again to joy. Amen.**

✤Evangelical Lutheran Church in America clergy, pastoral counselor; Ontario, Canada.
✤✤Professor of Homiletics at Waterloo Lutheran Seminary in Ontario, Canada.

Tuesday, December 30   Read Jeremiah 31:10-14.

The abundant word of God

"Hear the word of the Lord . . . 'He who scattered Israel will gather him.'" With a word, God invites Israel home. Yet this word of the Lord is not just redemptive. It is a creative word. An abundance of grain, wine, oil, watered gardens, and even fat priests accompanies God's spoken word.

Yet should we be surprised? We know that in Jesus Christ the same God who redeems by the word also *recreates* by the word. We who are so mercifully ransomed from slavery do not receive the word of invitation to come home for old time's sake. As if redemption consisted in singing "Auld Lang Syne"—again! Rather, we receive God's inviting word of redemption to be recreated—to enjoy anew the fullness of the God who once created worldly fruitfulness with a word and, in a word, called it good.

Perhaps it is no accident that many church funerals seem to go a certain way. No matter what church hosts the funeral, after the graveside ceremony the pastor issues a word of invitation: "All are invited to join the family for a hot supper back at the church." And come they do: some family, some friends; some churchfolk, some not. They all come for a sumptuous meal. Now some *do* come to remember the deceased through tears liberally laced with laughter. Yet all come to the feast as a way to move through it together. Apparently, it is not just the dead who need life on the other side of the grave! *We* need a word of invitation to be redeemed again. *We* need to be recreated around the table. Thanks be to God, we get it in abundance!

Suggestion for meditation: How has God's abundant word redeemed and recreated *me*?

377

Wednesday, December 31   Read Psalm 147:12-20.

God's creative word

Many have marveled that the sculptor Michelangelo could make huge blocks of stone yield such symmetry and beauty. From his memorable rendition of *David* to the intricately wrought *Pietà*, so many of this Renaissance master's sculptures leave us mere mortals staring in wide-eyed wonder.

Someone once asked Michelangelo how he could create such exquisite sculptures from huge, unwieldy slabs of marble. Michelangelo responded by saying that he saw himself as freeing the image from the material. As a creator, he was just bringing out the aesthetic order already in the marble.

God's creative word in Psalm 147 seems to work in the same way. The psalmist begins by calling the people to praise God. After all, God's creative blessing is given to the elect, supplying them with security, satiety, and shalom. Yet all of this is just God's creative word at work. With a creative word God sends out the snow, frost, and hail—they fly forth as by command. With a creative word God melts them, burning them into flowing waters. With a final creative word, God *gives the law to Israel*. The point is this: God issues the creative word of blessing not just to leave us with a slab of undifferentiated fullness but to create an *ordered* fullness for our lives. The beauty of God's creative word is like the beauty of Michelangelo's sculpting: It is a blessing seeking order—a freeing from the marbled stone for the symmetry of the divine image.

Prayer: Creator God, through your Word, Jesus Christ, you not only bless me but create me anew. Mold me ever more into your gracious image. Amen.

The Revised Common Lectionary* for 1997
Year B–Advent/Christmas Year C
(*Disciplines* Edition)

January 1–5
Jeremiah 31:7-14
Psalm 147:12-20
Ephesians 1:3-14
John 1:10-18

January 6–12
BAPTISM OF THE LORD
Genesis 1:1-5
Psalm 29
Acts 19:1-7
Mark 1:4-11

EPIPHANY, January 6
Isaiah 60:1-6
Psalm 72:1-7, 10-14
Ephesians 3:1-12
Matthew 2:1-12

January 13–19
1 Samuel 3:1-10 (11-20)
Psalm 139:1-6, 13-18
1 Corinthians 6:12-20
John 1:43-51

January 20–26
Jonah 3:1-5, 10
Psalm 62:5-12
1 Corinthians 7:29-31
Mark 1:14-20

January 27–February 2
Deuteronomy 18:15-20
Psalm 111
1 Corinthians 8:1-13
Mark 1:21-28

February 3–9
TRANSFIGURATION
2 Kings 2:1-12
Psalm 50:1-6
2 Corinthians 4:3-6
Mark 9:2-9

ASH WEDNESDAY
February 12
Joel 2:1-2, 12-17
(*or* Isaiah 58:1-12)
Psalm 51:1-17
2 Corinthians
5:20*b*–6:10
Matthew 6:1-6, 16-21

February 10–16
First Sunday in Lent
Genesis 9:8-17
Psalm 25:1-10
1 Peter 3:18-22
Mark 1:9-15

February 17–23
Second Sunday in Lent
Genesis 17:1-7, 15-16
Psalm 22:23-31
Romans 4:13-25
Mark 8:31-38
(*or* Mark 9:2-9)

February 24–March 2
Third Sunday in Lent
Exodus 20:1-17
Psalm 19
1 Corinthians 1:18-25
John 2:13-22

March 3–9
Fourth Sunday in Lent
Numbers 21:4-9
Psalm 107:1-3, 17-22
Ephesians 2:1-10
John 3:14-21

*Copyright © 1992
by the Consultation on
Common Texts (CCT).
Used by permission.

March 10–16
Fifth Sunday in Lent
Jeremiah 31:31-34
Psalm 51:1-12
  (*or* Psalm 119:9-16)
Hebrews 5:5-10
John 12:20-33

March 17–23
PASSION / PALM SUNDAY

Liturgy of the Palms
Mark 11:1-11
  (*or* John 12:12-16)
Psalm 118:1-2, 19-29

Liturgy of the Passion
Isaiah 50:4-9*a*
Psalm 31:9-16
Philippians 2:5-11
Mark 14:1–15:47
  (*or* Mark 15:1-39)

Week of March 24–30
  HOLY WEEK
  (selected lections)

  Monday, March 24
  Isaiah 42:1-9
  John 12:1-11

  Tuesday, March 25
  Isaiah 49:1-7
  John 12:20-36

  Wednesday, March 26
  Isaiah 50:4-9*a*
  John 13:21-32

Maundy Thursday
Exodus 12:1-4, (5-10), 11-14
Psalm 116:1-2, 12-19
John 13:1-17, 31*b*-35

Good Friday
Isaiah 52:13–53:12
Psalm 22
Hebrews 10:16-25
John 18:1–19:42

Holy Saturday
Job 14:11-14
Psalm 31:1-4, 15-16
1 Peter 4:1-8
John 19:38-42

EASTER SUNDAY,
  March 30
Acts 10:34-43
  (*or* Isaiah 25:6-9)
Psalm 118:1-2, 14-24
1 Corinthians 15:1-11
John 20:1-18
  (*or* Mark 16:1-8)

March 31–April 6
Acts 4:32-35
Psalm 133
1 John 1:1–2:2
John 20:19-31

April 7–13
Acts 3:12-19
Psalm 4
1 John 3:1-7
Luke 24:36*b*-48

April 14–20
Acts 4:5-12
Psalm 23
1 John 3:16-24
John 10:11-18

April 21–27
Acts 8:26-40
Psalm 22:25-31
1 John 4:7-21
John 15:1-8

April 28—May 4
Acts 10:44-48
Psalm 98
1 John 5:1-6
John 15:9-17

May 5–11
Acts 1:15-17, 21-26
Psalm 1
1 John 5:9-13
John 17:6-19

ASCENSION DAY, May 8
*(These readings may
be used for Sunday,
May 11.)*
Acts 1:1-11
Psalm 47
Ephesians 1:15-23
Luke 24:44-53

May 12–18
PENTECOST
Acts 2:1-21
Psalm 104:24-34, 35*b*
Romans 8:22-27
John 15:26-27; 16:4*b*-15

May 19–25
TRINITY SUNDAY
Isaiah 6:1-8
Psalm 29
Romans 8:12-17
John 3:1-17

May 26–June 1
1 Samuel 3:1-10, (11-20)
Psalm 139:1-6, 13-18
2 Corinthians 4:5-12
Mark 2:23–3:6

June 2–8
1 Samuel 8:4-20;
   (11:14-15)
Psalm 138
2 Corinthians 4:13–5:1
Mark 3:20-35

June 9–15
1 Samuel 15:34–16:13
Psalm 20
2 Corinthians 5:6-10,
   (11-13), 14-17
Mark 4:26-34

June 16–22
1 Samuel 17:(1*a*, 4-11,
   19-23), 32-49
Psalm 9:9-20
2 Corinthians 6:1-13
Mark 4:35-41

June 23–29
2 Samuel 1:1, 17-27
Psalm 133
2 Corinthians 8:7-15
Mark 5:21-43

June 30–July 6
2 Samuel 5:1-5, 9-10
Psalm 48
2 Corinthians 12:2-10
Mark 6:1-13

July 7–13
2 Samuel 6:1-5, 12*b*-19
Psalm 24
Ephesians 1:3-14
Mark 6:14-29

July 14–20
2 Samuel 7:1-14*a*
Psalm 89:20-37
Ephesians 2:11-22
Mark 6:30-34, 53-56

July 21–27
2 Samuel 11:1-15
Psalm 14
Ephesians 3:14-21
John 6:1-21

July 28–August 3
2 Samuel 11:26–12:13*a*
Psalm 51:1-12
Ephesians 4:1-16
John 6:24-35

August 4–10
2 Samuel 18:5-9, 15,
   31-33
Psalm 130
Ephesians 4:25–5:2
John 6:35, 41-51

August 11–17
1 Kings 2:10-12; 3:3-14
Psalm 111
Ephesians 5:15-20
John 6:51-58

August 18–24
1 Kings 8:(1, 6, 10-11),
   22-30, 41-43
Psalm 84
Ephesians 6:10-20
John 6:56-69

August 25–31
Song of Solomon 2:8-13
Psalm 45:1-2, 6-9
James 1:17-27
Mark 7:1-8, 14-15, 21-23

September 1–7
Proverbs 22:1-2, 8-9,
   22-23
Psalm 125
James 2:1-10, (11-13),
   14-17
Mark 7:24-37

September 8–14
Proverbs 1:20-33
Psalm 19
James 3:1-12
Mark 8:27-38

September 15–21
Proverbs 31:10-31
Psalm 1
James 3:13–4:3, 7-8*a*
Mark 9:30-37

381

September 22–28
Esther 7:1-6, 9-10;
  9:20-22
Psalm 124
James 5:13-20
Mark 9:38-50

September 29–October 5
Job 1:1; 2:1-10
Psalm 26 (*or* Psalm 25)
Hebrews 1:1-4; 2:5-12
Mark 10:2-16

October 6–12
Job 23:1-9, 16-17
Psalm 22:1-15
Hebrews 4:12-16
Mark 10:17-31

October 13–19
Job 38:1-7, (34-41)
Psalm 104:1-9, 24, 35c
Hebrews 5:1-10
Mark 10:35-45

October 20–26
Job 42:1-6, 10-17
Psalm 34:1-8, (19-22)
Hebrews 7:23-28
Mark 10:46-52

October 27–November 2
Ruth 1:1-18
Psalm 146
Hebrews 9:11-14
Mark 12:28-34

ALL SAINTS DAY
November 1
Isaiah 25:6-9
Psalm 24
Revelation 21:1-6a
John 11:32-44

November 3–9
Ruth 3:1-5; 4:13-17
Psalm 127
Hebrews 9:24-28
Mark 12:38-44

November 10–16
1 Samuel 1:4-20
1 Samuel 2:1-10
Hebrews 10:11-14,
  (15-18), 19-25
Mark 13:1-8

November 17–23
2 Samuel 23:1-7
Psalm 132:1-12, (13-18)
Revelation 1:4b-8
John 18:33-37

Year C lections begin the First Sunday in Advent, 1997.

November 24–30
First Sunday of Advent
Jeremiah 33:14-16
Psalm 25:1-10
1 Thessalonians 3:9-13
Luke 21:25-36

THANKSGIVING DAY, USA
November 27
Joel 2:21-27
Psalm 126
1 Timothy 2:1-7
Matthew 6:25-33

December 1–7
Second Sunday of Advent
Malachi 3:1-4
Luke 1:68-79
Philippians 1:3-11
Luke 3:1-6

December 8–14
Third Sunday of Advent
Zephaniah 3:14-20
Isaiah 12:2-6
Philippians 4:4-7
Luke 3:7-18

December 15–21
Fourth Sunday of Advent
Micah 5:2-5a
Luke 1:47-55
  (*or* Psalm 80:1-7)
Hebrews 10:5-10
Luke 1:39-45, (46-55)

December 22–28
First Sunday after Christmas Day
1 Samuel 2:18-20, 26
Psalm 148
Colossians 3:12-17
Luke 2:41-52

CHRISTMAS EVE
December 24
Isaiah 9:2-7
Psalm 96
Titus 2:11-14
Luke 2:1-14, (15-20)

CHRISTMAS DAY
Isaiah 62:6-12
Psalm 97
Titus 3:4-7
Luke 2:(1-7), 8-20

December 29–January 4
Second Sunday after
  Christmas Day
Jeremiah 31:7-14
Psalm 147:12-20
Ephesians 1:3-14
John 1:(1-9), 10-18

NEW YEAR'S DAY
Ecclesiastes 3:1-13
Psalm 8
Revelation 21:1-6*a*
Matthew 25:31-46

HOLY NAME
OF JESUS
  January 1
Numbers 6:22-27
Psalm 8
Galatians 4:4-7
  (*or* Philippians 2:5-11)
Luke 2:15-21

Scripture quotations designated NKJV are from The New King James Version. Copyright © 1979, 1980, 1982, Thomas Nelson Inc., Publishers. Used by permission.

Scripture quotations designated CEV are from the Contemporary English Version. © American Bible Society 1991, 1995. Used by permission.

Scripture quotations designated JB are taken from the *Jerusalem Bible*, published and copyright © 1966, 1967, and 1968 by Darton, Longman & Todd Ltd and Doubleday & Co Inc, and are used by permission of the publishers.

Any scripture quotation designated AP is the author's paraphrase.

Meditations for the weeks of January 13–19 and March 17–23 originally appeared in *The Upper Room Disciplines 1984*, copyright © 1983 by The Upper Room.